THE PHILOSOPHY OF RELIGION

Also published in this series

The Concept of Evidence, edited by Peter Achinstein
Perceptual Knowledge, edited by Jonathan Dancy
The Philosophy of Law, edited by Ronald M. Dworkin
Theories of Ethics, edited by Philippa Foot
The Philosophy of History, edited by Patrick Gardiner
The Philosophy of Mind, edited by Jonathan Glover
Scientific Revolutions, edited by Ian Hacking
Philosophy and Economic Theory, edited by Frank Hahn and
Martin Hollis
Divine Commands and Morality, edited by Paul Helm
Hegel, edited by Michael Inwood
The Philosophy of Linguistics, edited by Jerrold J. Katz
Reference and Modality, edited by Leonard Linsky
The Concept of God, edited by Thomas V. Morris
A Priori Knowledge, edited by Paul K. Moser
The Philosophy of Education, edited by R. S. Peters
Political Philosophy, edited by Anthony Quinton
Practical Reasoning, edited by Joseph Raz
The Philosophy of Social Explanation, edited by Alan Ryan
Propositions and Attitudes, edited by Nathan Salmon and
Scott Soames
Consequentialism and its Critics, edited by Samuel Scheffler
The Philosophy of Language, edited by J. R. Searle
Semantic Syntax, edited by Pieter A. M. Seuren
Applied Ethics, edited by Peter Singer
Philosophical Logic, edited by P. F. Strawson
Locke on Human Understanding, edited by I. C. Tipton
Theories of Rights, edited by Jeremy Waldron
Free Will, edited by Gary Watson
Leibniz: Metaphysics and Philosophy of Science, edited by
R. S. Woolhouse

Other volumes are in preparation

THE PHILOSOPHY
OF RELIGION

Edited by

BASIL MITCHELL

OXFORD UNIVERSITY PRESS

Oxford University Press, Walton Street, Oxford OX2 6DP

Oxford New York Toronto
Delhi Bombay Calcutta Madras Karachi
Petaling Jaya Singapore Hong Kong Tokyo
Nairobi Dar es Salaam Cape Town
Melbourne Auckland

and associated companies in
Berlin Ibadan

Oxford is a trade mark of Oxford University Press

ISBN 0 19 875018 8

First published 1971
Reprinted 1976, 1977, 1982, 1983, 1986, 1989

Printed in Hong Kong

CONTENTS

INTRODUCTION

IT is among the fascinations of philosophy that the nature of philosophy itself is as much a controversial issue as any other that philosophers discuss. It cannot normally be assumed that any selection of philosophers will agree entirely about what they are trying to do. It can be said, however, without misrepresentation, that the philosophers whose work is reproduced here have encountered, and have to a greater or lesser extent been influenced by, the conception that the function of philosophy is essentially critical or analytic. From this point of view the philosophy of religion stands in the same relationship to religion as the philosophy of history to history, or the philosophy of science to science. In each case the philosopher is concerned to examine the arguments and clarify the concepts which are used within the discipline he is studying. He is not himself, *qua* philosopher (though, of course, he may be in another capacity), a theologian, a historian or a scientist, but he needs to have enough experience of their work and enough imaginative sympathy with it to understand what it is they are doing or trying to do.

This clear-cut distinction has not always been maintained. Indeed it is only comparatively recently that it has been thought desirable or even possible to maintain it. Nor is it even now entirely easy to maintain. Thus philosophers of history are divided as to whether historical reasoning is of the same logical type as that found in natural science or whether it has a 'logic of its own'. If a historian is offered a philosophical analysis of the way he reasons and refuses to accept it as a correct account of his procedure, how is the issue to be settled? Is the historian to be given a veto on the philosopher's analyses? Is the philosopher entitled to overrule the historian's protests? Or should they patiently go over the ground together each endeavouring to persuade the other? If they do this, can they altogether avoid discussing questions that fall within the province of history, and in that case can the philosopher maintain his neutrality?

This sort of problem arises even more acutely in the case of the philosophy of religion because all the major religions claim to be all-inclusive in a way that science and history do not. Science deals with whatever is susceptible of scientific treatment, history with what is significant in the human past, but religion has in some sense to comprehend everything. In this respect it resembles metaphysics as traditionally understood, and can even be regarded, in its theoretical aspect, as a sort of metaphysics. When, therefore, there is disagreement between critical philosopher and theologian as to the proper analysis of religious belief the issue is peculiarly acute and intractable. However genuinely the analytical philosopher may protest that he is as neutral in his attitude to religion as he is in his attitude to science or history—in each case he patiently and sympathetically elucidates the logical structure of the discipline in question—it often looks as if his presuppositions are such that, in the case of religion, he is bound to find the structure defective. So that if the final word is his, the case for religion fails. To entitle the theologian on the other hand to repudiate any philosophical analyses he dislikes is to grant him entire immunity from philosophical criticism. If, in order to avoid these alternatives, philosopher and theologian go over the ground together with a view to discovering which interpretation of religion makes the better sense, are they not both engaged in a metaphysical inquiry of a kind that is incompatible with the claim that philosophy is a purely critical activity?

The discussion on 'Theology and Falsification' (first published in 1951) illustrates some of these problems and serves as an introduction to a number of the other articles in this collection. Antony Flew puts forward a general principle to the effect that an assertion, in order to be an assertion, must rule out some conceivable state of affairs. It follows that theologians cannot be making assertions at all unless they are prepared to say what conceivable occurrences they would regard as counting against what they say. In effect he proposes a dilemma. *Either* (i) theism is meaningless because unfalsifiable *or* (ii) it is meaningful but in fact falsified. In the discussion itself two ways of dealing with the dilemma are suggested. R. M. Hare seeks to escape between the horns by suggesting that the religious believer does not, characteristically, make assertions but rather adopts what Hare calls a *blik*, a principle by which he lives and in accordance with which he interprets experience. It is more fundamental than assertions and is not capable of being refuted by evidence, because it helps to determine what shall count as evidence. In my own contribution I reject the second horn of the dilemma and argue that the theist can and does indicate the sort of thing that would tend to count against his assertions, e.g. the occurrence of evil.

In later discussion Flew's dilemma has been further examined. My own response to the 'meaningless, because unfalsifiable' charge has been developed more fully by I. M. Crombie and John Hick. Crombie argues that 'suffering that was utterly, eternally and irredeemably pointless' would count decisively against the assertion that God is merciful. Hick claims that it is in principle impossible to *falsify* theism, but that it is possible to conceive experiences after death which, if they occurred, would *verify* it. J. L. Mackie presses the 'in fact falsified' charge and argues that, as things are, the existence of evil is incompatible with the world's having been created by a benevolent and omnipotent God. Something like Hare's proposal for dealing with Flew's dilemma is developed by R. B. Braithwaite.

Crombie does a good deal to elucidate what is involved in the argument about falsifiability. The demand for falsifiability, he suggests, amounts to two requirements for the factual status of theological propositions: (i) that there should not be a *rule of language* prohibiting verification; (ii) that for the speaker to understand what he is saying he must have some idea what would serve to falsify his assertion. With respect to (i) theists do not regard demands for verification as out of place; it is just that, for statements about God, verification is hard to come by. With respect to (ii) Crombie argues that in order to understand what he means by 'God is loving' (Flew's example) the theist (*a*) needs to have some way of referring to God, i.e. of indicating what he is talking about, and (*b*) needs to be able to attach meaning to the words he uses about him. These requirements, he argues, are capable of being fulfilled so far as the nature of the case allows. The qualification is important. 'God is a mystery, and therefore you cannot expect that knowing what statements about God are about will involve anything like having a precise conception of their subject' (p. 40).

Mackie claims that theism can be refuted on the ground of inconsistency. The theist is committed to three assertions: (i) God is omnipotent; (ii) God is wholly good; (iii) evil exists. Given that 'a good thing always eliminates evil as far as it can, and that there are no limits to what an omnipotent thing can do' these three propositions cannot be true together. Throughout his article Mackie is content to leave the choice of weapons to his adversary, confident that whichever he chooses he cannot avoid defeat. Mackie regards as the most plausible defence open to the theist the contention that pain and disease ('first order evils') are necessary conditions of the existence of sympathy, courage, etc. ('second order goods'). If he adopts this defence, the theist has then to reckon with the existence of 'second order evils', which such a universe also renders possible. Mackie offers the following solution: 'First order evil (e.g. pain) may be justified as a logically necessary component to second order good (e.g. sympathy) while second order evil (e.g. cruelty) is not *justified*, but is so ascribed to human beings that God cannot be held responsible for it' (p. 100).

Mackie then poses the question, 'Why should God not have made men such that they always freely choose the good?' If he could and is benevolent, he should have done so; if he could not, he is not omnipotent. It is this issue to which Alvin Plantinga directs himself in 'The Free Will Defence'. In it he embraces the second horn of Mackie's dilemma and argues that there is no interpretation of the statement 'God creates men such that they always freely do what is right' which is both consistent and amenable to Mackie's argument. To say that God is omnipotent is to say that he can create any state of affairs S such that 'God creates S' is consistent. The question, then, is whether 'God creates men such that they always freely do what is right' is consistent. Plantinga considers two ways in which it may be taken: (i) 'God creates free men and brings it about that they always do what is right'—this is not consistent, for the men would not in that case be free; (ii) 'God creates free men and these free men always do what is right, this is consistent, but it is open to these men, being free, to do what is wrong. Therefore Mackie has not destroyed the free will defence.

Mackie has another argument which does not fall within the scope of Plantinga's chapter. Suppose it is conceded that God cannot create men so that they freely choose the good, can God subsequently control their wills? If he does, of course, they will not then be free with respect to these particular choices, but should not God, nevertheless, intervene to prevent evil actions? There would seem to be no logical impossibility in this. Therefore to say that he *cannot* do it would be to limit God's omnipotence. But if he refrains why does he do so? Mackie says that the only possible answer to this is that even in the case of a wrong free act the value of its freedom outweighs its wrongness, so that there would be an overall loss of value if God took away the wrongness and the freedom together, an answer which he believes to be inconsistent with what theists otherwise say about sin. However, it is open to question in what sense a man's good choices can be free if he is prevented from ever making bad choices. If what is meant is that God might allow men to choose wrongly, but prevent their bad choices from taking effect, it becomes problematic how the second order goods of sympathy, courage, etc., whose importance Mackie has emphasized could flourish in an environment in which choice became trivial because the evil consequences of wrong choices were regularly obviated.

In this discussion it is taken for granted that religious beliefs claim to be true. Braithwaite in 'An Empiricist's View of the Nature of Religious Belief' avoids the difficulties associated with this claim by suggesting instead that 'A religious assertion, for me, is the assertion of an intention to carry out a certain behaviour policy, subsumable under a sufficiently general principle to be a moral one, together with the implicit or explicit statement, but not the assertion, of certain stories' (p. 89). The 'stories' resemble the 'parables' in Crombie's discussion but, in Braithwaite's version, no question of truth or falsehood arises. The stories do no more than illustrate the moral policies which are fundamental to religious belief. From a purely philosophical point of view this is entirely straight-forward. But is it at all plausible as an account of what Christians mean? For instance, it looks on the face of it as if Christian morality is derived from Christian doctrine 'God loved you; *therefore* love one another', whereas for Braithwaite 'it is the intention to behave which constitutes what is known as Christian conviction' (p. 80).

Braithwaite's discussion, in its thoroughgoing empiricism, provides a particularly striking illustration of the predicament of philosophical analysis in relation to religious belief. To the complaint that his proposed analysis of religious belief distorts its structure, as commonly understood, he might well reply that, if Christianity is to make sense, this is how it must be interpreted. 'Make sense according to what criterion?'—'The criterion of falsifiability put forward by empiricist philosophers.' But if the application of this criterion in this way makes nonsense of what many thoughtful men take to be sense, the possibility has to be con-sidered that the criterion itself is inappropriate or has been wrongly applied.

It is considerations like these which lead D. Z. Phillips to claim that 'criteria of meaning in religion must be intrinsic to religion itself'. Phillips's repudiation of the critical claims of philosophers in relation to religious belief is itself based upon a philosophical position. 'Philosophy', says Wittgenstein, 'leaves everything as it is.' Hence it is a mistake to suppose that religion stands in need of justification (where this may mean either (a) in need of being shown to be intelligible or (b) in need of being shown to be true). If Phillips is right it follows: (i) that Flew, Mackie and others are mistaken in thinking that religion can be shown to be meaningless or false; (ii) that Crombie, Hick and others (including myself) are mistaken in thinking that religion is capable of or in need of being verified or falsified by reference to any kind of evidence.

The obvious objection, as Phillips recognizes, to his conception of religion as a 'language-game' having its own internal criteria of meaning is that religious belief is made to seem totally impervious to criticism and out of relation to the rest of our knowledge. Religious belief must not 'ignore or distort what we already know'. 'How otherwise', he asks, 'could there arise characteristic difficulties over religious belief?' The question, then, for Phillips is, 'What is the relation between religious beliefs and non-religious facts?'

He insists that it cannot be the relation between what is justified and its justification or a conclusion and its grounds. Phillips illustrates his point by the example of the two mothers who ask the Virgin Mary to protect their babies. One 'expects things to turn out otherwise'. This is superstition. The other 'wants the child's life to be orientated in the Virgin's virtues'. 'This', says Phillips, 'is what seeking her protection means.' In other words the latter, the truly religious, woman does not regard the truth of her belief about the Virgin's protecting her child as in any way dependent upon (to be justified by) what happens later.

It would seem that, in Phillips's view, Crombie and Hick are giving an account not of true religion, but of superstition, because they believe that what happens in the long run (though not, indeed, in this life alone) is crucially relevant to the truth and significance of religious belief. But the view which Phillips repudiates represents the central Christian tradition. What warrant, the reader may ask, has Phillips to declare that Crombie and Hick do not understand Christianity? It is tempting to conclude that Phillips's religious position, like Braithwaite's, is largely determined by what he conceives to be philosophically tenable, but this is too simple. His objection to the Crombie–Hick position is not only philosophical but moral and religious as well. To believe in God because ultimate victory is His is to make God the means to an end and to falsify the absolute character which belief in God has for many believers. In other words, Hick assumes that it is reasonable to believe in God only if in the end Christian promises are fulfilled, i.e. Christian belief 'entails certain distinctive expectations concerning the future'. It must be possible to conceive 'a situation which points unambiguously to the existence of a loving God'. By contrast Phillips argues that 'it is not the course of events which determines that God is victorious, but faith which determines what is to count as victory'. Thus the Cross counts as victory, but not as the world understands victory.

It looks at first sight as if Phillips presents us with a Christianity shorn of such central doctrines as those of the Resurrection, Providence, and Eternal Life. To such a charge he would presumably reply that he does not deny these things; he understands them properly. The Resurrection is in no sense an event additional to the Cross: it is the permanent availability of Christ's victorious spirit. God's Providence is the possibility of trust in him, no matter how things turn out; Eternal Life is the life of faith here and now.

One reason for Phillips's insistence upon making the 'criteria of meaning in religion intrinsic to religion itself' was apparently to avoid making religion answerable to 'external' philosophical tests. Yet his own analysis of religious belief seems to have been profoundly affected by the philosophy of Wittgenstein. Wittgenstein held that philosophers, generalizing illegitimately from non-religious contexts, have tended to think that 'nothing can be believed unless there is evidence or grounds for that belief'. But religious beliefs such as (to use Wittgenstein's example) belief in the Last Judgement, do not involve the weighing of evidence, or reasoning to a conclusion. What they do involve is seeing how the belief regulates a person's life. 'Believing in the picture means, for example, putting one's trust in it, sacrificing for it, letting it regulate one's life, and so on. ... Beliefs, such as belief in the Last Judgement, are not testable hypotheses but absolutes for believers' (p. 130).

The distinction between 'belief in' and 'belief that' and the relation between them is the theme of H. H. Price's article. Price concludes that some beliefs-in are reducible to beliefs-that, whereas others are not. From this he infers that there are two different senses of belief-in, on the one hand an evaluative sense, like believing in one's doctor—'something like esteeming or trusting is an essential part of belief-in in this sense'—on the other a factual sense, like belief in fairies or the belief in King Arthur. He suggests that evaluative belief-in may often be reducible to belief-that, so long as appropriate value concepts are introduced. Thus belief in one's doctor may be reduced to belief that he is good at curing one's diseases, and that that is a good thing. Furthermore, when the object of belief-in is an entity of some kind, the existence of the entity in question is presupposed. 'I cannot trust my doctor unless I at least believe that there is a person to whom the description "being my doctor" applies.'

What happens if we apply Price's finding to Wittgenstein's example of belief in the Last Judgement? Belief in the Last Judgement would seem to presuppose at least belief that there will be an event to which the description 'Last Judgement' will be appropriate (for what Price says about entities would seem to apply also to events). It will be an instance of evaluative belief-in. The believer believes that the Last Judgement will indeed be just and that it is a good thing that it should occur.

If we compare this account of the matter with Phillips's, we find that Phillips emphasizes a feature of belief-in which Price recognizes but does not stress. This is the *regulative* function of belief-in. The believer in the Last Judgement allows what Wittgenstein calls this 'picture' to regulate his life. This regulative function, in Phillips's opinion, serves to distinguish such a 'picture' from a hypothesis. It is interesting, therefore, that Price notices it in relation to belief in a theory. A theory, he says, has the power of 'reducing an apparently disconnected mass of brute facts to some sort of intelligible order'. Hence the theorist 'uses it constantly in his own investigations . . . he relies on the theory, we might even say he trusts it' (p. 147). This is compatible with his not altogether believing it in the belief-that sense. As Price suggests, something similar is true of metaphysical theories.

That religious beliefs have this regulative function does not, then, in itself rule out their being hypotheses, requiring like other hypotheses the support of evidence. A man may reasonably regulate his life according to a hypothesis which he recognizes to be open to dispute. He may, indeed, stake everything on it, in which case the belief would have for him the absolute character upon which Phillips insists, while still remaining, from a purely epistemological point of view, a hypothesis. But more is required to satisfy Phillips. Beliefs which have the 'absolute character' of religious belief not only regulate action; they also regulate thought. 'The absolute beliefs are the criteria, not the object, of assessment.' This recalls Hare's remark about *bliks*, 'without a *blik* there can be no explanation; for it is by our *bliks* that we decide what is and what is not an explanation', and to some extent also Price's reference to 'metaphysical theories of the synoptic type which claim to unify apparently disconnected facts and reconcile apparently conflicting ones'.

These remarks draw attention to a notable feature of the disagreement between believers and non-believers. Differences of opinion between them are not easily settled by straightforward appeal to evidence, because one of the points at issue is precisely how the evidence is to be taken. This problem is one of those examined by R. W. Hepburn in 'From World to God'. Hepburn argues that within traditional Christianity questions about the existence of God cannot be treated as equivalent to the question 'Does God play an intelligible role in the language-game?' because it is essential to Christianity that God be independent of the world and the world dependent on him. He concedes that philosophers who are content to accept this equivalence will not easily be persuaded that their analyses are inadequate, because they will treat *all* assertions about God, including those asserting his transcendence, as 'policy-specifying, vision-evoking bits of discourse'. Nevertheless, such analyses may be made to seem 'strained and incompatible with first-hand religious experience'. 'The cosmological argument', he maintains, 'is an indispensable part of any Christian apologetics.' Therefore an attempt must be made to make sense of the 'cosmological relation', the dependence of the world on God. That the world is *logically* dependent on God seems to be ruled out by the sort of arguments provided by Terence

Penelhum in his article on 'Divine Necessity'. If what is intended is a kind of factual dependence, expressed in language that is logically odd (cf. Crombie), how are we to tell whether there *is* any such relation? That is to say, for the notion of transcendence to be intelligible, it is not enough that one should be persuaded that, if there were such a relation, it would have to be expressed in logically anomalous ways. One needs grounds for asserting that there *is* such a relation. Hepburn considers whether grounds could be found in religious experience of the sort that Otto characterized as 'numinous', an experience as of the wholly other, a *mysterium tremendum et fascinans*. 'Could numinous experience be taken as an actual privileged awareness of the world as related to God, of God as related to the world?' (p. 173).

The trouble, as it seems to Hepburn, about this suggestion is that there is no way of telling whether the experiences in question are cognitive or non-cognitive. Considered simply as odd impressive experiences there is nothing specifically religious about them. If they are treated as evidence for the existence of God, one has to justify the inferential move from them to God and, in addition, one has somehow independently to validate the concept of God. So, Hepburn concludes, 'the situation looks ambivalent in respect of theistic or naturalistic interpretations'. In other words, one is not compelled to treat these experiences as evidence for the existence of God. The situation is not one in which there is clear agreement among all concerned as to what would constitute evidence for a particular conclusion, as there is agreement, for example, as to what would constitute evidence for the existence of a new planet. Nor is it entirely appropriate to say that there is evidence that makes it fairly probable or just possible that there is a God as there might be in the case of the planet. These expressions occur most naturally when all concerned share the same conceptual scheme, in a way that the believer and the unbeliever do not. This is, perhaps, one reason for Phillips's reluctance to discuss the justification of religious belief in terms of 'evidence' for or against it. Even to talk of the evidence as 'ambiguous' or 'ambivalent' may not be quite appropriate, as may be seen by contrasting two situations. One is that of two Roman Catholic doctors trying to decide whether a cure is miraculous. They may conclude that the evidence is ambiguous, i.e. it is impossible to determine whether the cure occurred naturally or whether there was divine intervention. In this case there is agreement as to the propriety of either explanation and as to the sort of evidence needed to establish either. The other case is that of a dispute between a Roman Catholic doctor and an atheist about a cure which the former regards as miraculous. Here the necessary agreement is lacking. The atheist is not prepared to countenance any evidence in favour of a miracle. He rejects the concept of the miraculous and the entire conceptual scheme associated with it. Something similar may occur in connection with psychical research. Events which some regard as affording evidence in this field are dismissed by others as anomalous occurrences of no theoretical interest. Even within natural science current conceptions of what is scientifically possible will tend to determine what is admissible as evidence, and these are based on the fundamental theories accepted at the time.

In the scientific case it does not follow that no question of justification arises. The fundamental theories are justified by the range and scope of their explanatory and predictive power, and where a choice has to be made between competing theories, or paradigms, that which has the greater explanatory and predictive power is to be preferred. In the case of religious experience, where, as Hepburn remarks, 'the situation looks ambivalent in respect of theistic or naturalistic interpretations', the question naturally arises whether the ambivalence could, in principle, be removed. Hick's theory of 'eschatological verification' suggests a way in which it conceivably might be. After death one might have an experience of communion with God as disclosed in Jesus Christ of such a character as to remove all rational doubt of its genuineness. It may, perhaps, be objected to Hick's proposal that it is only within a Christian's conceptual scheme that his description of this possible situation makes sense. Need a thoroughgoing atheist admit that it does? A good deal depends on the sort of atheist he is. If he is an atheist through lack of evidence, although he agrees with the theist as to what would count as evidence, then he will admit the possibility that after death conclusive evidence might be forthcoming (so long as he accepts the intelligibility of 'survival'). But it is not this sort of atheist whose difficulties Hick is chiefly trying to meet, but rather the atheist who declares himself unable to attach meaning to theistic assertions on the ground that he cannot conceive of any observations as tending to count for or against theism. Will he not complain that the language in which Hick seeks to describe the experiences which would resolve his doubts is just the language which he is unable to understand?

This suggests that talk of 'the ambiguity of our present experience' is itself ambiguous. 'Our present situation', says Hick, 'is one which in some ways seems to confirm and in other ways to contradict the truth of theism.' In *this* sort of ambiguous situation the falsifiability requirement is already satisfied; for there are *now* some experiences tending to refute and some to confirm the truth of theism. If this much is conceded, there is no need for 'eschatological verification' as a means of vindicating the meaningfulness of theistic discourse (although it might eventually serve to vindicate its truth).

If, however, our present situation is ambiguous in the more radical sense that Hepburn intends, viz. that there is no clear decision-procedure by which to determine whether 'religious experience' is what it purports to be, then the ambiguity will infect *any* alleged experience of the divine, including that which Hick imagines as occurring after death.

Hepburn concludes his article with the reflection that 'there are no short cuts in the philosophy of religion: no decisive verification test, no declaration of meaninglessness can help us'. What, we may wonder, could help us? If a clear decision-procedure is needed, nothing could be more evident than that it is not to be had. Behind the demands for a clear decision-procedure in questions of religious belief and laments for its absence there generally lies some conception of what a satisfactory decision-procedure would be like. Commonly it is based on the procedures of mathematics and natural science. The assumption that rational discourse is to be identified with and is exhausted by formal and empirical inquiry of this kind has at one time or another cast doubt upon the credentials not only of theology and metaphysics but also of such humane disciplines as history, literary criticism and political theory. It was in connection with the latter that Sir Isaiah Berlin wrote, 'Whatever may in fact causally determine our beliefs, it would be a gratuitous abdication of our powers of reasoning—based on a confusion of natural science with philosophical enquiry—not to want to know what we believe, and for what reason, what the metaphysical implications of such beliefs are, what their relation is to other types of belief, what criteria of value and truth they involve, and so what reason we have to think of them as true or valid.'[1]

Hepburn remarks that analyses of statements about God as policy-specifying, vision-evoking bits of discourse may be made to seem strained and incompatible with first-hand religious experience. In rather similar vein Crombie argues that 'One interpretation is to be preferred to another, not because the latter is thought to be refutable on paper, but because it is judged to be unconvincing in the light of familiarity with the facts. There is a partial parallel to this in historical judgement.' It looks as if it is possible to argue for or against a religion as a metaphysical position and also for or against a philosophical critique of

---

[1] 'Does Political Theory still exist?' in *Philosophy, Politics and Society*, p. 33, second series, ed. Laslett and Runeiman, (Oxford: Blackwell, 1962).

religion in ways that can be recognized as reasonable even though they do not conform to the requirements of scientific method.

If there is a single moral to be drawn from this selection of articles it is that the philosophy of religion is like the 'philosophy of' anything else in that it demands both philosophical competence and a sympathetic understanding of the subject-matter upon which it is to be exercised. It is, perhaps, unnecessary to add that in this, as in other branches of philosophy, simple and definitive solutions are rarely to be found.

I

THEOLOGY AND FALSIFICATION

A SYMPOSIUM

A. ANTONY FLEW

LET us begin with a parable. It is a parable developed from a tale told by John Wisdom in his haunting and revelatory article 'Gods'.[1] Once upon a time two explorers came upon a clearing in the jungle. In the clearing were growing many flowers and many weeds. One explorer says, 'Some gardener must tend this plot.' The other disagrees, 'There is no gardener.' So they pitch their tents and set a watch. No gardener is ever seen. 'But perhaps he is an invisible gardener.' So they set up a barbed-wire fence. They electrify it. They patrol with bloodhounds. (For they remember how H. G. Wells's 'Invisible Man' could be both smelt and touched though he could not be seen.) But no shrieks ever suggest that some intruder has received a shock. No movements of the wire ever betray an invisible climber. The bloodhounds never give cry. Yet still the Believer is not convinced. 'But there is a gardener, invisible, intangible, insensible to electric shocks, a gardener who has no scent and makes no sound, a gardener who comes secretly to look after the garden which he loves.' At last the Sceptic despairs, 'But what remains of your original assertion? Just how does what you call an invisible, intangible, eternally elusive gardener differ from an imaginary gardener or even from no gardener at all?'

In this parable we can see how what starts as an assertion, that something exists or that there is some analogy between certain complexes of phenomena, may be reduced step by step to an altogether different status, to an expression perhaps of a 'picture preference'.[2] The Sceptic says there is no gardener. The Believer says there is a gardener (but invisible,

From *New Essays in Philosophical Theology*, ed. Antony Flew and Alasdair MacIntyre (London: S.C.M., 1955), pp. 96–108. Reprinted by permission of S.C.M. Press Ltd., and The Macmillan Company.

[1] *P.A.S.*, 1944–5, reprinted as Ch. X of *Logic and Language*, Vol. 1 (Blackwell, 1951), and in his *Philosophy and Psychoanalysis* (Blackwell, 1953).

[2] Cf. J. Wisdom, 'Other Minds,' *Mind*, 1940; reprinted in his *Other Minds* (Blackwell, 1952).

etc.). One man talks about sexual behaviour. Another man prefers to talk of Aphrodite (but knows that there is not really a superhuman person additional to, and somehow responsible for, all sexual phenomena).[3] The process of qualification may be checked at any point before the original assertion is completely withdrawn and something of that first assertion will remain (tautology). Mr. Wells's invisible man could not, admittedly, be seen, but in all other respects he was a man like the rest of us. But though the process of qualification may be, and of course usually is, checked in time, it is not always judiciously so halted. Someone may dissipate his assertion completely without noticing that he has done so. A fine brash hypothesis may thus be killed by inches, the death by a thousand qualifications.

And in this, it seems to me, lies the peculiar danger, the endemic evil of theological utterance. Take such utterances as 'God has a plan', 'God created the world', 'God loves us as a father loves his children.' They look at first sight very much like assertions, vast cosmological assertions. Of course, this is no sure sign that they either are, or are intended to be, assertions. But let us confine ourselves to the cases where those who utter such sentences intend them to express assertions. (Merely remarking parenthetically that those who intend or interpret such utterances as crypto-commands, expressions of wishes, disguised ejaculations, concealed ethics, or as anything else but assertions, are unlikely to succeed in making them either properly orthodox or practically effective.)

Now to assert that such and such is the case is necessarily equivalent to denying that such and such is not the case.[4] Suppose, then that we are in doubt as to what someone who gives vent to an utterance is asserting, or suppose that, more radically, we are sceptical as to whether he is really asserting anything at all, one way of trying to understand (or perhaps it will be to expose) his utterance is to attempt to find what he would regard as counting against, or as being incompatible with, its truth. For if the utterance is indeed an assertion, it will necessarily be equivalent to a denial of the negation of that assertion. And anything which would count against the assertion, or which would induce the speaker to

[3] Cf. Lucretius, *De Rerum Natura*, II, 655–60,
   Hic siquis mare Neptunum Cereremque vocare
   Constituet fruges et Bacchi nomine abuti
   Mavolat quam laticis proprium proferre vocamen
   Concedamus ut hic terrarum dictitet orbem
   Esse deum matrem dum vera re tamen ipse
   Religione animum turpi contingere parcat.
[4] For those who prefer symbolism: $p \equiv \sim \sim p$.

withdraw it and to admit that it had been mistaken, must be part of (or the whole of) the meaning of the negation of that assertion. And to know the meaning of the negation of an assertion, is as near as makes no matter, to know the meaning of that assertion.[5] And if there is nothing which a putative assertion denies then there is nothing which it asserts either: and so it is not really an assertion. When the Sceptic in the parable asked the Believer, 'Just how does what you call an invisible, intangible, eternally elusive gardener differ from an imaginary gardener at all?' he was suggesting that the Believer's earlier statement had been so eroded by qualification that it was no longer an assertion at all.

Now it often seems to people who are not religious as if there was no conceivable event or series of events the occurrence of which would be admitted by sophisticated religious people to be a sufficient reason for conceding 'There wasn't a God after all' or 'God does not really love us then.' Someone tells us that God loves us as a father loves his children. We are reassured. But then we see a child dying of inoperable cancer of the throat. His earthly father is driven frantic in his efforts to help, but his Heavenly Father reveals no obvious sign of concern. Some qualification is made—God's love is 'not a merely human love' or it is 'an inscrutable love', perhaps—and we realize that such sufferings are quite compatible with the truth of the assertion that 'God loves us as a father (but, of course, . . .).' We are reassured again. But then perhaps we ask : what is this assurance of God's (appropriately qualified) love worth, what is this apparent guarantee really a guarantee against? Just what would have to happen not merely (morally and wrongly) to tempt but also (logically and rightly) to entitle us to say 'God does not love us' or even 'God does not exist'? I therefore put to the succeeding symposiasts the simple central questions, 'What would have to occur or to have occurred to constitute for you a disproof of the love of, or of the existence of, God?'

B.[6] R. M. HARE

I wish to make it clear that I shall not try to defend Christianity in particular, but religion in general—not because I do not believe in Christianity, but because you cannot understand what Christianity is, until you have understood what religion is.

I must begin by confessing that, on the ground marked out by Flew,

---

[5] For by simply negating $\sim p$ we get p: $\sim\sim p \equiv p$.
[6] Some references to intervening discussion have been excised.—Ed.

he seems to me to be completely victorious. I therefore shift my ground by relating another parable. A certain lunatic is convinced that all dons want to murder him. His friends introduce him to all the mildest and most respectable dons that they can find, and after each of them has retired, they say, 'You see, he doesn't really want to murder you; he spoke to you in a most cordial manner; surely you are convinced now?' But the lunatic replies, 'Yes, but that was only his diabolical cunning; he's really plotting against me the whole time, like the rest of them; I know it I tell you.' However many kindly dons are produced, the reaction is still the same.

Now we say that such a person is deluded. But what is he deluded about? About the truth or falsity of an assertion? Let us apply Flew's test to him. There is no behaviour of dons that can be enacted which he will accept as counting against his theory; and therefore his theory, on this test, asserts nothing. But it does not follow that there is no difference between what he thinks about dons and what most of us think about them—otherwise we should not call him a lunatic and ourselves sane, and dons would have no reason to feel uneasy about his presence in Oxford.

Let us call that in which we differ from this lunatic, our respective *bliks*. He has an insane *blik* about dons; we have a sane one. It is important to realize that we have a sane one, not no *blik* at all; for there must be two sides to any argument—if he has a wrong *blik,* then those who are right about dons must have a right one. Flew has shown that a *blik* does not consist in an assertion or system of them; but nevertheless it is very important to have the right *blik*.

Let us try to imagine what it would be like to have different *bliks* about other things than dons. When I am driving my car, it sometimes occurs to me to wonder whether my movements of the steering-wheel will always continue to be followed by corresponding alterations in the direction of the car. I have never had a steering failure, though I have had skids, which must be similar. Moreover, I know enough about how the steering of my car is made, to know the sort of thing that would have to go wrong for the steering to fail—steel joints would have to part, or steel rods break, or something—but how do I know that this won't happen? The truth is, I don't know; I just have a *blik* about steel and its properties, so that normally I trust the steering of my car; but I find it not at all difficult to imagine what it would be like to lose this *blik* and acquire the opposite one. People would say I was silly about steel; but there would be no mistaking the reality of the difference between our respective *bliks*—for example, I should never go in a motor-car. Yet I should hesitate to say that the difference between us was the difference between contradictory assertions. No amount of safe arrivals or bench-tests will remove my *blik* and restore the normal one; for my *blik* is compatible with any finite number of such tests.

It was Hume who taught us that our whole commerce with the world depends upon our *blik* about the world; and that differences between *bliks* about the world cannot be settled by observation of what happens in the world. That was why, having performed the interesting experiment of doubting the ordinary man's *blik* about the world, and showing that no proof could be given to make us adopt one *blik* rather than another, he turned to backgammon to take his mind off the problem. It seems, indeed, to be impossible even to formulate as an assertion the normal *blik* about the world which makes me put my confidence in the future reliability of steel joints, in the continued ability of the road to support my car, and not gape beneath it revealing nothing below; in the general non-homicidal tendencies of dons; in my own continued well-being (in some sense of that word that I may not now fully understand) if I continue to do what is right according to my lights; in the general likelihood of people like Hitler coming to a bad end. But perhaps a formulation less inadequate than most is to be found in the Psalms: 'The earth is weak and all the inhabiters thereof: I bear up the pillars of it.'

The mistake of the position which Flew selects for attack is to regard this kind of talk as some sort of *explanation*, as scientists are accustomed to use the word. As such, it would obviously be ludicrous. We no longer believe in God as an Atlas—*nous n'avons pas besoin de cette hypothèse*. But it is nevertheless true to say that, as Hume saw, without a *blik* there can be no explanation; for it is by our *bliks* that we decide what is and what is not an explanation. Suppose we believed that everything that happened, happened by pure chance. This would not of course be an assertion; for it is compatible with anything happening or not happening, and so, incidentally, is its contradictory. But if we had this belief, we should not be able to explain or predict or plan anything. Thus, although we should not be *asserting* anything different from those of a more normal belief, there would be a great difference between us; and this is the sort of difference that there is between those who really believe in God and those who really disbelieve in him.

The word 'really' is important, and may excite suspicion. I put it in, because when people have had a good Christian upbringing, as have most of those who now profess not to believe in any sort of religion, it is very hard to discover what they really believe. The reason why they find it so easy to think that they are not religious, is that they have never got into the frame of mind of one who suffers from the doubts to which religion is the answer. Not for them the terrors of the primitive jungle. Having abandoned some of the more picturesque fringes of religion, they think that they have abandoned the whole thing—whereas in fact they still have got, and could not live without, a religion of a comfortably substantial, albeit highly sophisticated, kind, which differs from that of many 'religious people' in little more than this, that 'religious people' like to sing Psalms about theirs—a very natural and proper thing to do. But nevertheless there may be a big difference lying behind—the difference between two people who, though side by side, are walking in different directions. I do not know in what direction Flew is walking; perhaps he does not know either. But we have had some examples recently of various ways in which one can walk away from Christianity, and there are any number of possibilities. After all, man has not changed biologically since primitive times; it is his religion that has changed, and it can easily change again. And if you do not think that such changes make a difference, get acquainted with some Sikhs and some Mussulmans of the same Punjabi stock; you will find them quite different sorts of people.

There is an important difference between Flew's parable and my own which we have not yet noticed. The explorers do not *mind* about their garden; they discuss it with interest, but not with concern. But my lunatic, poor fellow, minds about dons; and I mind about the steering of my car; it often has people in it that I care for. It is because I mind very much about what goes on in the garden in which I find myself, that I am unable to share the explorers' detachment.

C. BASIL MITCHELL

Flew's article is searching and perceptive, but there is, I think, something odd about his conduct of the theologian's case. The theologian surely would not deny that the fact of pain counts against the assertion that God loves men. This very incompatibility generates the most intractable of theological problems—the problem of evil. So the theologian *does* recognize the fact of pain as counting against Christian doctrine. But it is true that he will not allow it—or anything—to count decisively against it; for he is committed by his faith to trust in God. His attitude is not that of the detached observer, but of the believer.

Perhaps this can be brought out by yet another parable. In time of war in an occupied country, a member of the resistance meets one night a stranger who deeply impresses him. They spend that night together in conversation. The Stranger tells the partisan that he himself is on the side of the resistance—indeed that he is in command of it, and urges the partisan to have faith in him no matter what happens. The partisan is utterly convinced at that meeting of the Stranger's sincerity and constancy and undertakes to trust him.

They never meet in conditions of intimacy again. But sometimes the Stranger is seen helping members of the resistance, and the partisan is grateful and says to his friends, 'He is on our side.'

Sometimes he is seen in the uniform of the police handing over patriots to the occupying power. On these occasions his friends murmur against him; but the partisan still says, 'He is on our side.' He still believes that, in spite of appearances, the Stranger did not deceive him. Sometimes he asks the Stranger for help and receives it. He is then thankful. Sometimes he asks and does not receive it. Then he says, 'The Stranger knows best.' Sometimes his friends, in exasperation, say, 'Well, what *would* he have to do for you to admit that you were wrong and that he is not on our side?' But the partisan refuses to answer. He will not consent to put the Stranger to the test. And sometimes his friends complain, 'Well, if *that's* what you mean by his being on our side, the sooner he goes over to the other side the better.'

The partisan of the parable does not allow anything to count decisively against the proposition 'The Stranger is on our side.' This is because he has committed himself to trust the Stranger. But he of course recognizes that the Stranger's ambiguous behaviour *does* count against what he believes about him. It is precisely this situation which constitutes the trial of his faith.

When the partisan asks for help and doesn't get it, what can he do? He can (*a*) conclude that the stranger is not on our side; or (*b*) maintain that he is on our side, but that he has reasons for withholding help.

The first he will refuse to do. How long can he uphold the second position without its becoming just silly?

I don't think one can say in advance. It will depend on the nature of the impression created by the Stranger in the first place. It will depend, too, on the manner in which he takes the Stranger's behaviour. If he blandly dismisses it as of no consequence, as having no bearing upon his belief, it will be assumed that he is thoughtless or insane. And it quite obviously won't do for him to say easily, 'Oh, when used of the Stranger the phrase "is on our side" *means* ambiguous behaviour of this sort.' In that case he would be like the religious man who says blandly of a terrible disaster, 'It is God's will.' No, he will only be regarded as sane and reasonable in his belief, if he experiences in himself the full force of the conflict.

It is here that my parable differs from Hare's. The partisan admits that many things may and do count against his belief: whereas Hare's lunatic who has a *blik* about dons doesn't admit that anything counts against his *blik*. Nothing *can* count against *bliks*. Also the partisan has a reason for having in the first instance committed himself, viz. the character of the Stranger; whereas the lunatic has no reason for his *blik* about dons—because, of course, you can't have reasons for *bliks*.

This means that I agree with Flew that theological utterances must be assertions. The partisan is making an assertion when he says, 'The Stranger is on our side.'

Do I want to say that the partisan's belief about the Stranger is, in any sense, an explanation? I think I do. It explains and makes sense of the Stranger's behaviour: it helps to explain also the resistance movement in the context of which he appears. In each case it differs from the interpretation which the others put up on the same facts.

'God loves men' resembles 'the Stranger is on our side' (and many other significant statements, e.g. historical ones) in not being conclusively falsifiable. They can both be treated in at least three different ways: (1) as provisional hypotheses to be discarded if experience tells against them; (2) as significant articles of faith; (3) as vacuous formulae (expressing, perhaps, a desire for reassurance) to which experience makes no difference and which make no difference to life.

The Christian, once he has committed himself, is precluded by his faith from taking up the first attitude: 'Thou shalt not tempt the Lord thy God.' He is in constant danger, as Flew has observed, of slipping into the third. But he need not; and, if he does, it is a failure in faith as well as in logic.

D. ANTONY FLEW

It has been a good discussion: and I am glad to have helped to provoke it. But now—at least in *University*[7]—it must come to an end: and the Editors of *University* have asked me to make some concluding remarks. Since it is impossible to deal with all the issues raised or to comment separately upon each contribution, I will concentrate on Mitchell and Hare, as representative of two very different kinds of response to the challenge made in 'Theology and Falsification'.

[7] The journal in which this discussion first appeared, 1950–51.—Ed.

The challenge, it will be remembered, ran like this. Some theological utterances seem to, and are intended to, provide explanations or express assertions. Now an assertion, to be an assertion at all, must claim that things stand thus and thus; *and not otherwise*. Similarly an explanation, to be an explanation at all, must explain why this particular thing occurs; *and not something else*. Those last clauses are crucial. And yet sophisticated religious people—or so it seemed to me—are apt to overlook this, and tend to refuse to allow, not merely that anything actually does occur, but that anything conceivably could occur, which would count against their theological assertions and explanations. But in so far as they do this their supposed explanations are actually bogus, and their seeming assertions are really vacuous.

Mitchell's response to this challenge is admirably direct, straightforward, and understanding. He agrees 'that theological utterances must be assertions'. He agrees that if they are to be assertions, there must be something that would count against their truth. He agrees, too, that believers are in constant danger of transforming their would-be assertions into 'vacuous formulae'. But he takes me to task for an oddity in my 'conduct of the theologian's case. The theologian surely would not deny that the fact of pain counts against the assertion that God loves men. This very incompatibility generates the most intractable of theological problems, the problem of evil.' I think he is right. I should have made a distinction between two very different ways of dealing with what looks like evidence against the love of God: the way I stressed was the expedient of qualifying the original assertion; the way the theologian usually takes, at first, is to admit that it looks bad but to insist that there is—there must be—some explanation which will show that, in spite of appearances, there really is a God who loves us. His difficulty, it seems to me, is that he has given God attributes which rule out all possible saving explanations. In Mitchell's parable of the Stranger it is easy for the believer to find plausible excuses for ambiguous behaviour: for the Stranger is a man. But suppose the Stranger is God. We cannot say that he would like to help but cannot: God is omnipotent. We cannot say that he would help if he only knew: God is omniscient. We cannot say that he is not responsible for the wickedness of others: God creates those others. Indeed an omnipotent, omniscient God must be an accessory before (and during) the fact to every human misdeed! as well as being responsible for every non-moral defect in the universe. So, though I entirely concede that Mitchell was absolutely right to insist against me that the theologian's first move is to look for an *explanation*, I still think that in the end, if relentlessly pursued, he will have to resort to the avoiding action of *qualification*. And there lies the danger of that death by a thousand qualifications, which would, I agree, constitute 'a failure in faith as well as in logic'.

Hare's approach is fresh and bold. He confesses that 'on the ground marked out by Flew, he seems to me to be completely victorious'. He therefore introduces the concept of *blik*. But while I think that there is room for some such concept in philosophy, and that philosophers should be grateful to Hare for his invention, I nevertheless want to insist that any attempt to analyse Christian religious utterances as expressions or affirmations of a *blik* rather than as (at least would-be) assertions about the cosmo⌐ is fundamentally misguided. *First*, because thus interpreted, they would be entirely unorthodox. If Hare's religion really is a *blik*, involving no cosmological assertions about the nature and activities of a supposed personal creator, then surely he is not a Christian at all? *Second*, because thus interpreted, they could scarcely do the job they do. If they were not even intended as assertions then many religious activities would become fraudulent, or merely silly. If 'You ought *because* it is God's will' asserts no more than 'You ought', then the person who prefers the former phraseology is not really giving a reason, but a fraudulent substitution for one, a dialectical dud cheque. If 'My soul must be immortal *because* God loves his children, etc.' asserts no more than 'My soul must be immortal', then the man who reassures himself with theological arguments for immortality is being as silly as the man who tries to clear his overdraft by writing his bank a cheque on the same amount. (Of course neither of these utterances would be distinctively Christian: but this discussion never pretended to be so confined.) Religious utterances may indeed express false or even bogus assertions: but I simply do not believe that they are not both intended and interpreted to be or at any rate to presuppose assertions, at least in the context of religious practice; whatever shifts may be demanded, in another context, by the exigencies of theological apologetic.

One final suggestion. The philosophers of religion might well draw upon George Orwell's last appalling nightmare *1984* for the concept of *doublethink*. '*Doublethink* means the power of holding two contradictory beliefs simultaneously, and accepting both of them. The party intellectual knows that he is playing tricks with reality, but by the exercise of *doublethink* he also satisfies himself that reality is not violated' (*1984*, p. 220). Perhaps religious intellectuals too are sometimes driven to doublethink in order to retain their faith in a loving God in face of the reality of a heartless and indifferent world. But of this more another time, perhaps.

II

THE POSSIBILITY OF
THEOLOGICAL STATEMENTS

I. M. CROMBIE

1. INTRODUCTION

CHRISTIANITY, as a human activity, involves much more than simply believing certain propositions about matters of fact, such as that there is a God, that he created this world, that he is our judge. But it does involve believing these things, and this believing is, in a sense, funda-mental; not that it matters more than the other things that a Christian does, but that it is presupposed in the other things that he does, or in the manner in which he does them. This is a fact, but it is in some ways an awkward fact, and for many years some theologians have tried to sidestep it. It is an awkward fact because, for example, if one professes certain beliefs, it seems that one ought to be willing to offer some kind of grounds for them. Yet we all know that it is difficult, and some think it is impious, to offer adequate grounds for the faith. Again —a requirement which has become more prominent with recent developments in philosophy—if one professes certain beliefs it seems that one ought to be willing to map out, roughly at any rate, the extent of the claims one is making by saying what is compatible and what is incompatible with them; and that again, in the case of religious beliefs, is something which is difficult to do, for reasons which will be considered in this chapter. Therefore some theologians have tried to sidestep these problems by denying that the Christian religion involves anything that may fairly be called factual beliefs about a transcendent being. That, it is said, is metaphysics, and religion has no interest in metaphysics. A simple-minded move, that has had its devotees, consists in saying that we do not believe that there is a God; we believe in God. More sophisticated apologists have urged that credal affirmations may, without significant loss, be treated as equivalent to recommendations of the behaviour and attitudes that are agreed on all hands to be their proper corollaries.

From *Faith and Logic*, ed. Basil Mitchell (London: George Allen and Unwin, 1958), pp. 31–67. Reprinted by permission of George Allen and Unwin Ltd. Sections 5 and 6 of the original text have here been omitted.

'There is a God' thus becomes equivalent, or nearly equivalent, to something like: 'Treat all men as brothers, and revere the mystery of the universe.' Beliefs are said to be merely the expression—the somewhat misleading expression—of an attitude of worship.

But, in spite of the piety and wisdom of those who have been seduced by them, these expedients must be denounced as evasions. The distinction between *believing that* and *believing in* is, of course, valid; but it does not help us, for *believing in* is logically subsequent to *believing that*. I cannot believe in Dr. Jones if I do not first believe that there is such a person. Nor is the reduction of credal affirmations to the behaviour of worship and general charitable conduct that ought to follow from them of any avail. For Christian worship cannot be exhaustively described in terms of how the worshipper feels, of what he says and does; it retains an irreducible element of belief. Christian worship is neither a kind of poetry nor a kind of *ascesis*, neither a giving vent to feelings of awe and reverence, nor a cultivation of the soul. Fundamentally it is thought of by the Christian as an entry into relationship with a transcendent being, whom non-Christians do not believe to be there to enter into relationship with. Christian worship, therefore, is not only something which the non-Christian *does* not do, it is something which, by virtue of the difference of his beliefs, the non-Christian *cannot* do, though he can, of course, do something which, in externals, is as closely similar as you please. What the non-Christian does, whether in Church or out of it, may be better or it may be worse than what the Christian does, but it cannot be the same, because it cannot share the same credal basis.

There are then certain factual beliefs which are fundamental to Christianity, in the sense that they underlie all Christian activity, and give it its specifically Christian character. The expression of such beliefs I shall refer to as the making of *theological statements*.[1]

The problem stated

Our problem in this chapter, then, is: how are theological statements possible? For it is a fairly common philosophical position today to say that there can be no meaningful theological statements. This view may be loosely put by saying that theological statements are unverifiable, and therefore meaningless; or it may be more carefully put by attending to the rules which Christians appear to lay down for the interpretation

[1] This is, of course, a wide use of the word 'theological'. In this use theological statements are the kind of statements ('affirmations', etc., if you prefer) which all Christians make, not only theologians.

of theological statements, and contending that these rules conflict with each other in such a way that no meaningful statements could possibly be governed by such rules. For, it is said, the statements purport to be about a quasi-personal subject, and in that way to be parallel to statements about, say, Julius Caesar; and yet if we proceed to draw conclusions from them, to bring arguments against them, in general to test them as if they were parallel to statements about Julius Caesar, we are told that we have failed to grasp their function. They have, apparently, some kind of special exemption from empirical testing; and yet if one attempts, for this reason, to assimilate them to other kinds of utterances (moral judgements for example, or mathematical formulae) which enjoy similar exemption, one is at once forbidden to do so. How paradoxical this is; and how much easier it makes it to believe that the making of theological statements rests on some kind of confusion than to accept them at their face-value!

My procedure will be to ignore the loose statement of the case (the doctrine that unverifiable statements are meaningless is like the doctrine that cars are fast; not entirely false, but blanketing so many important distinctions as to be useless), and attend to the more careful one. Here I shall not dispute that theological statements have the paradoxical features attributed to them by their opponents, but I shall argue that these paradoxical features need not be regarded as demonstrating the impossibility of meaningful theological statements, but rather as contributing to a grasp of their meaning by giving a partial characterization of their subject. For, I shall argue, their paradoxical features make it clear that these statements are made about no object which falls within our normal experience, or any imaginable extension of our normal experience; and to learn this is to learn something about the nature of religion. Something, but not much. To know that God may not be identified with anything that can be indicated is only the first step in theology. I shall therefore go on to try to define the extent to which we can claim to have any positive grasp of what we are talking about when we make theological statements, and thus to elucidate the sense in which they are meaningful. Very briefly, my argument will be: the inquirer may learn from the paradoxical features of theological statements, that, if they are about anything, they are about a mystery. If he requires further specification (and he is right to ask for some, though if he is wise he will not demand that those who believe in a mystery should offer him a detailed anatomy of it) he must seek it from two sources. Firstly from the affinities and relationships which exist between theological statements and utterances of other kinds (for example moral judgements; to do the will of God is our supreme duty); and secondly by considering whether a sense of mystery seems to be the appropriate response to any part of our experience. If this enables him to see not only what theological statements are not about, but also, so to speak, in what region the mystery that they are about is located, then he may feel that he understands what it is that Christians are talking about, but not why they talk about it; for surely it is self-stultifying, both to say that something is a mystery, and also to make 'statements' about it. To this I shall reply that, if we claim to know something of the mystery, we do so because we believe ourselves to possess a revelation; that is to say a communication made in terms that we can understand; and I shall argue that if we reflect on the kind of thing such a communication would have to be, we shall see why theological statements have the characteristics that they have, and how they are to be taken. That is to say, I shall attempt to show that theological statements are meaningful by showing what they are about, and how they offer information about it. For, after all, all that is necessary for an utterance to be a meaningful statement is that it should be governed by rules which specify what it is about, and what it asserts about it. The problem about theological statements is simply that there is a sense in which we cannot know what they are about (a sense in which we cannot know God) nor what it is that they assert. The solution of the problem must consist in defining the sense in which, on the other hand, we can know enough of these things for our speech about them to have an intelligible use.

The critic's case

So much by way of preliminary sketch. Let us begin our argument by considering the case advanced by the critic, as I shall call the man who denies the meaningfulness of theological statements.

He knows, of course, that theological statements have many of the characteristics of meaningful statements, in particular that they form a system, within which inferences may be drawn, incompatibility relations obtain, and so forth; and that they command a response, both emotional and moral, in those who accept their validity. What he suspects, however, is that although they form a system, it is a system without reference to anything in the real world. The system maintains itself, not because it is seen to report the truth about certain objects, but because it is causally connected with a set of images and practices which are valued for their own sake, and in particular because it can be thought of in mythological terms. That is to say, one can think of divine judgement in terms of the pictures on medieval chancel arches; of beings with wings weighing souls in balances or driving them into a fish's mouth with pitchforks; and one may be moved, poetically and morally, by such pictorial representations. Because one is moved by the picture, one wants to believe that it is a representation of something which will really happen at the last day; because one has the picture, one is able to imagine that one is believing in something when one says that 'he shall come again with glory to judge both the quick and the dead.' Now the Christian is perfectly willing to admit that he does not expect at the last day any event having any resemblance, in any literal sense, to the events depicted in medieval dooms. Whenever a trumpet sounds he knows it is not the last trump because, whatever the last trump will be, it will not be the sound of a trumpet. But he maintains that he believes in something, of which the medieval doom is a pictorial representation. It is here that the critic dissents. He can understand why the Christian wants to believe that he believes in something underlying his mythology; but, in his judgement, there is nothing there. This judgement he bases on the peculiar elusiveness of theological statements, once they are stripped of mythological form.

In its most general terms, this elusiveness takes the following form: on the one hand the Christian claims that his statements are concerned with a particular being, God, with particular kinds of events, such as the Creation, the Last Judgement, the operation of the Holy Ghost. Yet if you try to pin him down by asking such questions as 'Which person? Where is he? What events are you talking about?' he protests that such questions display crude misunderstanding of the nature of theological language. Yet if he uses words which appear to be proper names, or which appear to refer to cosmological happenings, or to occurrences in human personalities, surely such questions are perfectly proper ones to ask. It is, of course, true that anybody who knows anything about the more abstract intellectual disciplines is familiar with many words and phrases whose use is logically much more complex, whose relationship to their subject-matter is much more devious, than that of words like 'axe' or 'butterfly'; and the critic is quite prepared to believe that the words (like 'God' and 'grace') whose use is peculiar to theological statements may be of this kind, and also that when ordinary words (such as 'loves' and 'made') are put to theological use, they are also made to work under similar conditions. But if we consider words of this kind from other spheres, such as 'electron' or 'Oedipus complex', we see that we can gather what they are about by observing how they are used, by noticing what kind of observations are held to substantiate a statement about an electron, what kind require that it be withdrawn. There are specific laboratory or clinical conditions with which these words are fairly tightly connected. But let us take a word like 'grace', and begin by observing that it appears to be used about certain happenings in human personalities. Now let us go on to try to discover which happenings these are; let us ask such questions as: 'If a man decides to go to church, is that an example of what you call "the effects of grace"?' Always we seem to get an ambiguous answer: 'It might be or it might not. It would be if it were the result of divine influence; it would not be if the decision proceeded from some other cause.' But this will not help us much; it tells us that grace is what God does to a man; but unless we know what God is and what form his action takes, we are no further forward. We tried to break our way into the system of theological statements by taking a concept—grace—which appears to refer to events in human beings in the hope that these parts of the system might be familiar to us and so enable us to understand the rest of it. But when we try to isolate the events in question, in order to discover what is being talked about, we are offered no characterization of them except that they are the results of divine influence. It would appear then that we must begin at the difficult end; if we are ever to discover what theological statements are about, we must tackle the concept of God. But if we ask what the word 'God' refers to, we are likely to be told that God is a transcendent being who cannot be known to us except in his effects.

It appears then that we are imprisoned in a circular maze. Grace is what God does, and God is the being whose action in human souls is grace. How, asks the critic, is anybody supposed to discover what this circular system of concepts is about? Is it not much easier to believe that the system is nothing but the relic of pre-scientific mythology in which God was an almost human being and grace was something concrete, like the prosperity of the law-abiding; that with growth in scientific knowledge and moral sensitivity, theological concepts have been progressively detached from the fictitious celestial being, and real, but insufficiently edifying, terrestrial events, with which they were once identified; and that the whole system has been preserved, beyond the point at which it was evacuated of all content, only for what one may brusquely call sentimental reasons?

Ambiguity of the critic's case

That, or something like it, is the case for the meaninglessness of theological statements. It is a case which I do not propose to dispute. The premises are sound enough, though the circle is not so complete as I have let it appear (it is true that the Christian will never assert positively that this or that thought or action could only have flowed from divine grace;[2] but he will claim that faith, hope and charity are supernaturally infused virtues, and he is prepared to offer, not exactly criteria for the infallible recognition of these gifts, but some account of what he takes genuine faith, hope, or charity to be). But it is indisputable that there is no region of experience which one can point to and say: 'That is what theological statements are about.' If you care to conclude from that that there is no way of discovering what theological statements are about, then that, too, is indisputable if your meaning is that one can never know what it is like to be, for example, divinely inspired, in the way in which one can know what it is like to have a cold, or even, perhaps, an Oedipus complex. What I do wish to maintain, however, is that this does not show that theological statements have no legitimate use; it is simply a partial definition of the use that they have. For the elusiveness we are considering is a consequence, indeed an expression, of the fact that all theological statements are about God, and that God is not part of the spatio-temporal world, but is in intimate relation with it.

To maintain this contention, it will be necessary to look rather more closely at this characteristic elusiveness. It derives, we must begin by insisting, not from the natural shiftiness of persons who make theological statements, but from the uses for which such statements are devised. If one is to talk about these matters, one has to do so by making use of statements governed by apparently conflicting rules. The formal properties of theological statements (that is to say, the rules determining how they are to be taken and how they are supposed to be related to statements of other kinds) have to be, at first sight, mutually contradictory if they are to do their proper work. We must turn to a more detailed consideration of these antinomies.

2. THE ANOMALIES OF THE FORMAL PROPERTIES OF THEOLOGICAL STATEMENTS

The first anomaly

Since all theological statements are, by definition, about God, then however they are worded, we may say that God is the subject of them all (statements about grace, for example, are not about a commodity which is dispensed from heaven, but about what God does to men).

[2] On this see ch. VI [of *Faith and Logic*].

Therefore we may describe the first antinomy in the following terms: theological statements are to be interpreted as if their subject was a particular individual, and yet differ in logical character from all other statements about particular individuals. Let us put it in the following way.

If I say that Tom loves Mary, you can ask me who Tom is, and it is at least logically possible for me to point him out to you. But if I say that the average man falls in love at least once between the ages of 18 and 27, you display that you do not understand the expression 'the average man' if you ask me who he is. I shall put this by saying that while 'Tom' is a *proper proper name*, statements about the average man *have to be reduced*; the first statement, I shall say is *directly* about Tom; the second is *obliquely* about people in general. Now what about the statement 'God loves mankind'? On the one hand the question 'Who is God?' is proper, and on that account the statement appears to be direct and does not have to be reduced; and yet although the question is proper, there is an important sense in which it cannot be answered. There is such an operation as introducing somebody to Tom, but there is no such operation as introducing somebody to God; or rather if there are operations which may, from the standpoint of faith, be so described, it is so only from that standpoint, and they differ vitally from ordinary introductions. If a child asks 'Who is God?' he can only be given statements (such as 'He made us') by way of answer. He can never be brought into a situation in which it is proper to say 'That is God.' The symbol 'God' might therefore be described as an *improper proper name*. It resembles a proper name like 'Tom' in that we are told that statements about God are direct statements about God and not oblique statements about something else, and yet it differs from ordinary proper names in that its use is not based fundamentally, as theirs is, on acquaintance with the being it denotes. It is not easy to see how such a symbol could have a valid use.

There are however other symbols in somewhat similar case; and it may illustrate and sharpen the point to consider some of them. Take first the expression 'point'. The rules governing the use of this expression in geometry require (1) that points be in space, but also (2) that they be not even tiny volumes. Now, one might say, I can understand that something can be sizeless; a thought, for example, has no size. But then it is also not in space. How can anything be both sizeless and also somewhere? Being somewhere is occupying space, and to occupy space one must have size. The expression 'point', therefore, like the expression 'God', seems to be governed by contradictory rules. Or take proper names for fictitious characters. 'Titania' is a proper name, and to ask 'Who is Titania?' is to ask a proper question. And yet it can only be answered by statements (such as 'She is the wife of Oberon'); there can never be a situation in which 'That is Titania' is the right thing to say, and that not because one cannot get to fairyland, but because the idea of a journey to fairyland is a logically incoherent idea. 'Titania', too, is an improper proper name.

In other words, the expression 'God' in some ways resembles words which stand for fictions. Titania is certainly a fiction, and Plato called points geometers' fictions. But the religious man will of course insist that this comparison in no way illuminates the nature of theological statements. He obviously does not want to give God the status of Titania, and it is equally fatal to give theological statements the status of geometrical statements. For geometry is about spatial relationships; and we tolerate the expression 'point', although in a sense there could not be such a thing as a point (nothing could conform to the definition), because we know clearly enough how talk about points is useful in talk about spatial relationships. If then one appeals to statements about points (admittedly respectable) in support of statements about God, one will be told that statements about points are valuable because one knows how to translate them into statements about sets of volumes; into what are statements about God to be translated? Here of course the religious man must reply that they are not to be translated, and so the point of the comparison is lost.

This comparison having failed us, we are back where we were, forced to admit that the expression 'God', being an improper proper name which is devised for non-fictional discourse, is in a logically anomalous position. On the one hand statements about God are not reducible, and in that they are like statements about Tom as opposed to statements about the average man. On the other hand, although they are not reducible, but have their own distinct subject, in the manner of 'Tom loves Mary', that subject is not an ordinary subject. And yet in saying that God is not an ordinary subject, we do not mean that he is a peculiar or extraordinary subject, like Diogenes, who lived in a tub; we mean to assert something like a logical difference, while at the same time we deny that it is any ordinary difference, like that between Tom and the average man. When we say that Tom is not the same kind of being as the average man, we mean something different from what we mean when we make the same statement about Tom and God; and yet we mean more by saying that God is not the same kind of being as Tom, than we mean by saying that my brother is not the same kind of being as my dog. The difference between God and Tom is in some ways like a logical difference, and yet it is not a logical difference. Or, to put the same point rather differently, the impossibility of going to heaven and seeing God is not a technical impossibility, like the impossibility of going to Neptune, and yet it is not a logical impossibility, like the impossibility of going to a state of perfect competition and seeing the economic man. A claim to have seen God is outrageous, without being exactly logically outrageous. The statement to a child 'You can't see God' is not like 'You can't see a virus', nor like 'You can't see the average man.' The difference between God and other subjects is neither precisely a logical nor precisely a physical difference. The religious man may claim that the difference is a metaphysical difference, that the point is that God is a transcendent being; but the critic will reply that he could only understand the meaning of these phrases—'metaphysical difference' and 'transcendent being'—in the light of an example, and that the example offered is of no use to him because he cannot understand what statements about God are supposed to be about. As far as he can see, he will say, the expression 'God' purports to stand for an individual; now some expressions ('the average man' again for example) which purport to stand for individuals do not in fact do so; they are on a different logical level from that on which they purport to be; they are used in speech about classes from a particular aspect, or something of the kind. But this kind of treatment of the expression 'God' is not permitted: 'God' is not allowed to stand collectively for human benevolent impulses or anything of the kind. But if it is claimed that it stands for an individual, what can be made of this claim, when all the normal criteria of individuality are held not to apply in this case? There are no doubt innumerable individuals (perhaps 'the oldest male on Mars' may describe one of them) of which we know nothing, but of these we do not seriously speak. Individuals about whom we do speak seriously are either known to us, or have been known to somebody (Tom, Tom's wife, or Julius Caesar), or else are uniquely characterized as satisfying some comprehensible description (the man who invented writing, the largest oak in Hampshire). God is not known to anybody, and these descriptions which are sometimes offered as uniquely characterizing him ('the first cause', 'the necessary being') are such that nobody can say what it would be like to conform to one of them (if one knew what it would be like for something to be a necessary being, then one could say that 'God' stood for whatever satisfies these conditions; but one does not), and therefore have no identifying force. How then can the reference of the expression 'God' be fixed? And if it cannot, how can this expression be treated as a proper name?

The second anomaly

This then is the first perplexity: it concerns the reference of theological statements—what they are made about. The second perplexity concerns their content—what they say about whatever it is they are about. This perplexity can be divided into two parts. We are now considering the predicates of theological statements, and, generally speaking, the predicates are or can be expressed in everyday words: '... loves us', '... made the world'. Now it is fairly obvious that these everyday words are not being used in their everyday senses. When I make a table I take some tools and some materials, but Creation is *ex nihilo*. Therefore the words which express the predicates of theological statements are presumably being used in an unusual sense, and one may want to know what that sense is. Now the second perplexity, which, as I said, can be divided into two parts, concerns the fact that nothing which happens is allowed to necessitate the withdrawal of theological statements; they are allowed to overrule all factual objections.[3] The first part of the perplexity derives from noticing this fact (and not making any difficulties about the meaning of the words in the predicate-expression), and consists in asking how, in that case, it can be claimed that theological statements can be regarded as factual statements, which can be true or false. The second part derives from noticing the irrefutability of theological statements, and asking how, in that case, we can ever learn what meaning to attach to the words in the predicate-expression, when theologically employed. The two parts are no doubt facets of the same point, but it will be convenient to consider them separately, taking the first one first.

(1) Those who believe that God loves us, or that he created the world, believe that these are factual statements. That is, they are comparable to 'Tom loves Mary' or to 'John made a model boat' and not to the large and heterogenous class of familiar utterances which are not to be regarded as factual statements. For example, 'I promise ...' does not report my promising; it is my promising: 'Shut the door' is a request: '2+2=4' is a correct arithmetical formula and not an observation about the habits of pairs. None of these can ever be false because, by virtue of being the kind of utterances they are, they are logically incapable of colliding with the facts. They are preserved from falsity not in the way in which 'John made a model boat' is preserved from falsity when

[3] As I shall argue later, this is only a half-truth.

John made a model boat, not by the existence of a fact for them to correspond to or to agree with, but by their logical incapacity to agree or disagree with any facts. Now the theist wants to say that God really does love us, that he really did make the world; and he wants to say that these are not edifying stories, or expression of pious attitudes, but statements of fact. But, says the critic, what can be meant by 'fact' in this context? When we say, of an ordinary factual statement, that it accords with the facts, we mean something like this: a statement like: 'The cat is on the mat' delimits a range. There can be very different kinds of cats, very differently disposed on very different kinds of mats. 'The cat is on the mat' therefore does not indicate just one quite specific kind of situation, but delimits a range. There are situations which cannot count as the cat's being on the mat, and situations which can; and learning to draw the line between them is learning the meaning of the sentence. When there exists a situation which falls within the range delimited by 'The cat is on the mat', then a statement to that effect will be true; when there does not, it will be false. Now, normally, to say that a statement is factual is to claim that, by virtue of its meaning, it selects in this manner between possible situations; it has a range, such that some possible situations fall outside it, and its truth is the existence of a situation which falls within its range. But, in the case of theological statements, the theist denies that there are any situations which fall outside the range of 'God loves us' or 'God created the world', and he denies this without claiming an exhaustive knowledge of all the situations which there are. 'God loves us', he says, is not an empirical hypothesis about the pious prospering; he is quite content to leave it to historians and others to find out what happens to people in the world. 'God created the world' is not meant to prejudge the deliberations of astronomers; the theist does not pretend to know how the world began; he only claims to know that, however it began, God created it. In other words, says the critic, the theist says what he says, not because he has discovered that there are in fact no situations incompatible with his assertions, but because, in his opinion, there could be none. If you ask him how God's loving us differs from the hypothetical case of God's not loving us, he denounces the second alternative as unreal, because it assumes a modification in the divine nature, whose fixity is the foundation of everything. But then, if no possible situations could fall outside the range of 'God loves us', that must surely mean that this formula is such that, by virtue of its meaning, it is incapable of choosing between situations; that is, that it is a request, performatory utterance, tautology or something of the kind, and in no sense a factual statement.

Here again, it may be worth observing in passing, fictional statements are in somewhat the same boat with theological ones. It is entirely to misunderstand 'Holmes sprang into a passing hansom' to treat it as a request, tautology or performatory utterance, and yet nothing whatever can offer the slightest ground for supposing that Holmes did not spring into a passing hansom. And yet once more the comparison is embarrassing rather than helpful to the theist; for the statement about Holmes is preserved from the possibility of a collision with the facts by belonging to a world of make-believe; and the theist does not want to take that way out. But how, in that case, are the theist's statements preserved from the possibility of collision with facts? And if they are not so preserved, how can he assert them without exhaustive knowledge of all the relevant facts? Since he makes no claim to possess this knowledge, surely he must judge it unnecessary, and surely it can only be unnecessary if his 'statements' are not intended as statements of fact, but as recommendations of attitudes, or something of the kind.

(2) So much for the first part of the second perplexity. The second part draws attention to the difficulty of learning what particular theological statements can be supposed to mean. Taking for our example the statement 'God created the world', we can put the difficulty in the form of a dilemma: either this assertion selects from among conceivable alternatives, and as such is a cosmological hypothesis subject to scientific refutation; or it does not select, and in that case it is impossible to say what it means.

For, says the critic, it is agreed that the theist is not alleging any ordinary making when he talks about creation. What he is alleging, then, remains to be discovered. How are we to discover it? Well, the statement is supposed to tell us something about the world—that it was created by God. Let us then take the propositional function 'X was created by God'. Now if we are allowed to suppose that this function delimits a range of possible situations, such that some situations fall outside this range, then the statement about any given thing that it was created by God would convey information to anybody who was apprised of the boundaries of the range. But how can we become apprised of the boundaries of the range? We need to be capable of envisaging specimen situations which fall within the range, and specimen situations which fall outside it. Since, *ex hypothesi*, there can be no actual examples of these latter in this case, the specimen situations from outside the range of 'God created the world' will have to be imaginary ones. Since I have got to be able to envisage these situations, they must consist of familiar elements rearranged. But in that case, what 'God created the world' excludes is a set of possible situations which can be fancifully constructed by taking actual objects or properties, and supposing them arranged otherwise than as they are. 'The cat is on the mat' gives me information, not simply because it is incompatible with 'The cat is somewhere other than on the mat' (one does not know what a sentence means by knowing that it is incompatible with its own negation), but because I can easily envisage situations which agree with the one and disagree with the other. Supposing I have never seen that cat anywhere but on that mat, then I have never encountered any situation excluded by 'The cat is on the mat'; and indeed perhaps there has never been one. But because cats can be in all kinds of places, the class of excluded situations may be said to exist, and I can easily envisage specimens, for example by combining the familiar elements: the cat, being on, and the sideboard. Because I know that being on the sideboard or under the sofa would not be a case of being on the mat, I know what is claimed by 'the cat is on the mat' (the non-existence of all the incompatible situations) and thus what it means. But in the case of 'God created the world', if I am to know what this means, I must have some idea of the incompatible situations, and if I am to be able in this way to envisage them, they must be situations which can be constructed by rearranging familiar elements, and in that case what the assertion we are considering rules out must be something which logically might be the case. But if something is such that it logically might be the case, then it is always possible that some observation, some day, will show that it is the case. Therefore on this view 'God created the world', if we are ever to discover what it means, must be a scientific hypothesis, subject to scientific refutation. Consider, as a fair parallel, 'The universe is expanding'. This is a fair parallel because it is, like the creation statement, completely general. If it is true, then there are no cases of a non-expanding universe, ever, anywhere. Nothing actual is excluded by the statement. When, then, an astronomer makes it, how do we discover what he means? By looking to see what evidence he brings in support of the view, what observations he admits would refute it. Perhaps the spectra of the heavenly bodies are such as they would be if observer and observed were moving rapidly away from each other; if this were not so he would withdraw his claim. We thus know what his claim amounts to. If 'God created the world' is allowed to be in similar case, then we can know what it means, and what it means must be something empirical. If it is not, then we cannot discover what it means, because it cannot literally mean anything, and we must conclude that its efficacy in discourse is not that of an ordinary factual statement.

Perhaps it is a myth that we tell in order to inculcate an attitude of reverence.

So much for the philosopher's perplexities about theological statements. To summarize them, the first is that these statements purport to be about a particular object, which it is in principle impossible to indicate' in any non-linguistic way, and which is thus different from all other particular objects in whose existence we have any ground for believing; the second that while it is claimed that these statements are true, and have determinate meaning, none the less the theist seems not to regard himself as embroiled in scientific dispute; he claims an immunity which belongs properly to persons who do not make statements of fact. In themselves, his sentences are perfectly intelligible. We all know what '... loves us' means, and 'God' is a proper name. Anybody, therefore, can understand the assertion 'God loves us' on its own. But as used in theological discourse it acquires formal properties which render it utterly baffling to the critic; the rules laid down about how such utterances are to be taken (e.g. that 'God' is indeed a proper name, but that it is in principle impossible to see God) are such that he cannot see either what its reference can be (the first perplexity) or what its content (the second).

3. WHAT FOLLOWS FROM THE FACT OF THESE ANOMALIES?

*The anomalous formal properties of theological statements
help to fix the reference of these statements*

We must now turn to see what we can do about these perplexities. Let us begin by considering what a theist might reply to such a critic. Might he not say something like this: None of the above arguments are compelling. You show that God is unlike all other individuals and expect us to conclude that therefore there is no such individual. You show that statements about him are not like ordinary contingent truths and so invite us to class them with tautologies and requests. Admittedly we might do these things, but we do not have to. Is it not clear, from the formal properties of our statements alone, that we believe in the existence of a being different in kind from all ordinary beings, and in some way detached from the events of the spatio-temporal universe; and that, therefore, we shall inevitably make statements having the *prima facie* peculiar, formal properties outlined above? Surely the formal properties of our statements delineate the object of our belief rather than furnish evidence that there is no such object.

For the formal properties of theological statements can themselves be expressed in higher-level statements having God as their subject, just as the formal properties of ordinary statements about triangles (such as that their interior angles total 180 degrees) can be expressed in higher-level statements having triangles as their subject (such as that triangles are not physical objects, but a shape). Thus we can express some of the formal properties of theological statements in the higher-level statement 'God is a transcendent, infinite and incomprehensible being, in incomprehensible relationship with the familiar universe'. Now is not this a tolerable statement of vague undifferentiated theism, not far from the kind of belief in God which we find, for example, in Aristotle? Too vague, indeed, for the needs of religion, but still the essential foundation on which religion must be built?

Up to a point this reply is justified, but we must tread carefully here. If some such higher-level statement is to be regarded as simply recording the formal properties of theological statements, then the words occurring in it must bear no sense beyond what is necessary to express these properties. 'God is a transcendent being' becomes something like 'There exists an object of discourse which is particular but not indicable.' But of course when stated thus, there is nothing religious about the formula. So the position is something like this: the theist may claim that if he wants to talk about a transcendent being, his statements will have to have the formal properties of theological statements, and that, therefore, there is nothing scandalous about their possession of such properties. The critic may reply that he still cannot see what talk about a transcendent being is talk about, and therefore the theist cannot claim that the formal properties of his statements are sufficient to delineate the object of his belief. The most the theist can claim for the consideration of the formal properties alone (or, if you prefer, the higher-level theological statements in which they are expressed) is that it diverts attention away from all irrelevant subject-matters; that it makes clear that all non-theological subject-matters are irrelevant—theology is not to be assimilated to anything else; and that, therefore, if anybody is to understand what religion is about, he must be willing to conceive the possibility of an object which is neither similar to, nor in any normal relation with, any spatio-temporal object.

What the argument so far has shown is that there is no direct inference from the paradoxicality of the formal properties of theological statements to their meaninglessness. The critic's case is a *probable* case, and the theist has a probable case on the other side. The critic, feeling no impulsion to talk about anything which would have to be talked about in such a fashion, judges it probable that such talk only occurs because theologians, valuing for various reasons the simple piety of simple people with their anthropomorphic God and geomorphic heaven, but aware that they cannot defend these beings against the advance of knowledge, protect them from scientific criticism by the assertion that they are beings of a peculiar order. The theist, on the contrary, believing in a mystery beyond experience, traces of which he claims to detect in experience, contends that he is obliged to use, for the expression of his beliefs, language governed by paradoxical rules.

The 'affinities' of theological statements help to fix their reference

But the theist cannot really rest there. The critic is open to be convinced of the validity of theological language, if someone can show him what such language is used about, and how it succeeds in communicating truth about it. Let us then continue with the argument and see how much further we can get towards meeting the first of these requirements; that is, how much further we can fix the reference of theological statements.

First we might ask the critic to bear in mind the formal properties of theological statements, as an essential negative clue, and then listen to people making use of theological statements. For, we may say, an important hint concerning their reference may be derived from observing the relationships which appear to obtain between theological statements and statements of other kinds. For although we do not regard the divine love as identical in kind with human love, divine creation as identical with human making, none the less the words which are chosen for use in theological predicates are chosen for some kind of appropriateness. Again, although we do not identify the divine activity with any set of finite events, and for that reason refuse to let statements about providence or grace be strictly equivalent to empirical generalizations of history or psychology, none the less we do maintain that statements about grace are about a subject-matter which overlaps at least with the subject-matter of psychology.[4] We do not regard the doctrine of divine love as a doctrine of exemption from suffering, and for that reason evidence to the effect that people suffer is not allowed to overrule the doctrine that God loves them. Yet the theist must be intellectually sensitive to the existence of suffering; if, for example, somebody said that our life was one of unalleviated misery the theist would be committed by doctrine as well as by common sense to disagree with him.

[4] Again the reader should turn to ch. VI [of *Faith and Logic*].

Against the rule that theological statements, not being empirical general-izations, cannot come into logical conflict with empirical generalizations, not being moral judgements, cannot come into logical conflict with moral judgements, and so on, you must set the rule that, since the subject-matter of theological statements overlaps with the subject-matters about which empirical generalizations and moral judgements are made, theo-logical statements are sensitive to, and have affinities and relationships with statements of other kinds.

Listen, then, we say, to religious discussion. You will find that religion is connected, in this loose way, with ethics, cosmology, history, psycho-logy; that it has nothing very direct to contribute to mathematics, literary criticism, or marine biology. Surely, if you do not pitch your demands too high, this will begin to fix for you the reference of theological state-ments? But first let us amplify the caution against pitching your demands too high. Imagine a game: one player leaves the room, and the rest select an object. On the return of the first player, the others utter the predicates only of true statements about the chosen object, and the first player must guess the object. Thus the players say '. . . invaded Britain', '. . . kept a log', '. . . required his wife to be above reproach'; and the first player guesses 'Julius Caesar'. Theists are not playing a game of that kind; God is not a familiar object cryptically named, as anti-fascist Italians used to speak of Mussolini as 'Mr. Smith'. God is a mystery, and therefore you cannot expect that knowing what statements about God are about will involve anything like having a precise conception of their subject. The most that can be hoped for is something much vaguer, of which the following may serve as an example.

I do not know what a quaternion is; for all I know it may be a measure of time, like a quinquennium, a dance, like a quadrille, a kind of lizard, a poem, an elementary particle, or anything whatsoever. But now sup-pose I listen (as we are advising the critic to listen) to people talking about quaternions. Fairly quickly I shall discover that they are not dances or lizards, and they hardly seem to be periods of time. Gradually they will place themselves for me somewhere in the region of the mathe-matical sciences. I shall still be very ignorant indeed of what they are; but I shall know what section of the library to go to look for a book about them. If you like, we might mark the extreme vagueness of my grasp of quaternions at this stage, by saying that while my listening has not fixed the reference of 'quaternion' for me (for I do not know what they are), it has fixed the reference-range (for I know what kind of thing they are). Surely, then, we may say to the critic, if you listen attentively to theological discourse, you will come to discover its reference-range?

Now the critic must, I think, concede that negatively such listening may be of considerable assistance. It is at least as useful as attending to the formal properties of theological statements for seeing what theological talk is not a contribution to. But for providing positive identification, it is a very different matter. Crudely put, identification by negation is only positive identification if one has a list and eliminates all the items but one. But the trouble is that God is not on the critic's list and therefore he cannot be enlightened by elimination. Let him put the point thus: the man who, from listening to talk about quaternions, comes to place them in the region of the mathematical sciences, only does so because he knows at least something among these latter, or at least can envisage their possibility. A child or a primitive, who had not yet abstracted the idea of number, could not place quaternions in the region of the mathematical sciences, because he would be absolutely without a notion of them. But, says the critic, with respect to God he is himself in the position of the unmathematical child with respect to quaternions. Nobody has ever taught him how to abstract the idea of God. Furthermore, he suspects that his listening has now made him unteachable; for it has shown him that religion is closely connected with such subjects as history, psychology, ethics, and cosmology. Theological vocabulary draws upon words commonly used in these subjects, innovations in these subjects are apt to upset theists and so forth. But if he is asked to find room for a further subject, related to these subjects as theology is apparently supposed to be related to them he simply cannot do it. How can anything underlie moral obligation as the divine will is supposed to do? How can grace be something which occurs in human souls and yet something which the psychologists can manage without? Again, he may say, it is no good saying that the reference-range of theological language is fixed by the language itself. For it is precisely fictions which are created by talking, and theology is not, apparently, a multi-volume novel. The reference-range of 'quaternion' may be fixed for me by listening to mathematicians talking, but it is fixed for mathematicians by the existence of the appropriate mathematical problems. If there were no such problems, there would be no talk about them. Theists cannot therefore content themselves with telling us to listen to them if we want to find out what they are talking about, for if they are talking about anything, then it must be possible to indicate what it is, or talk about it would never have begun. Unless they can indicate what their subject is, it is fair to ask them why they ever started uttering, and how it would matter if they stopped.

To some extent this reply is, certainly, justified. If theological talk has any valid use, then it must be possible to show in what kind of context one becomes conscious of the need to talk in this way; and this demonstration cannot be sufficiently given by disclosing that theological statements cannot be identified with statements of any other kinds, but have affinities and relationships with some of them. In so far as the critic believes that he can show that there could be no other subject-matter related to history, psychology and the rest, in the way in which theology is supposed to be related to them, there is no reason why we should agree with him. But in so far as he merely confesses a personal incapacity to see what this further subject is, he is, of course, perfectly justified. He is also perfectly justified if he stresses once more that the reference-range of theological statements is supposed to be fixed, and yet is not fixed by any normal kind of indication or conceptual description, that this is logically anomalous, and that he has a right to be given some account of it.

What is it that impels people to make theological statements? The short answer is, a conception of the divine. But what, asks the critic, is that? Is it not the remains of primitive myth, adorned by the feeling of awe in the face of natural phenomena? What are we to answer him? As we have seen above, a conception of the divine must be a conception of a being outside space and time, on whom the spatio-temporal universe is in some sense dependent. Given such a being, talk about him will have the formal properties theological talk has been found to have. It will not be possible, in any ordinary way, to indicate such a being, for indicating is selecting a region of space-time in which certain qualities are manifested. Again, it is natural to suppose that if the universe is dependent on God, then what is true of him will be, not exactly necessarily true (certainly not tautological) but, so to speak, less contingently true than truths about the dependent universe. It also seems natural to suppose that if God is conceived as the source of the space-time universe, himself outside space and time, his activity will not be manifested (at least normally) here rather than there (for then he would *be* here rather than there) and hence that statements about his relation to the created universe will not take the form of cosmological hypotheses, verifiable by observing the contents of particular spatio-temporal regions. So far, so good; given a conception of the divine it looks as if we might be able to smooth away the apparent logical anomalies of theological language; to show them to be necessary consequences of the purpose for which it is intended. But are we given such a conception?

We must acknowledge at once that in the ordinary sense we have no conception of the divine nature. We do not know God, and it would be absurd to claim that we know what kind of being he is. In so far as we use adjectives about him ('omniscient', 'eternal', and so on) they do not enable us to conceive what it is like to be God. Omniscience is not infinite erudition, and what it is must be beyond our comprehension. And yet people, whether they be theists, atheists, or agnostics do normally suppose themselves to know what people are talking about when they talk about God. The critic, of course, has his own explanation of this fact. According to him, what makes people suppose that they can grasp the reference of talk about God is nothing more than the old anthropomorphic conception of a superhuman being somewhere above the sky. No civilized person believes there to be such a being, but the picture serves, in unsophisticated minds, to conceal from us that we do not know what we are talking about.

This is certainly a possible account of how the reference-range of theological language is fixed for most people; whether it is, for you, a plausible account, will depend on your opinion of the critical powers of those who use such language. But our business, if we want to convince ourselves of the validity of theological language, is to show that the widespread readiness to attach sense to the notion of a being outside space and time has a more fundamental and more respectable origin than that.

4. THE REFERENCE OF THEOLOGICAL STATEMENTS

A 'conception of the divine' being necessary to fix their reference, what is this?

Can we, then, find a more fundamental and more respectable origin for our readiness to attach sense to the notion of a being outside space and time, a being whose nature would explain the anomalies of theological statements? To this we must now turn. What I propose to argue could be put like this: the conception of the divine is indeed in one sense an empty notion; but it is the notion of a complement which could fill in certain deficiencies in our experience, that could not be filled in by further experience or scientific theory-making; and its positive content is simply the idea of something (we know not what) which might supply those deficiencies. This bald account I must try to supplement, but not without a warning that what follows will be extremely sketchy and inadequate. The business of explaining the origin of the conception of God has provoked a very considerable literature, which passes under the name of natural theology. Often it has been held to be the task of natural theology to prove the existence of God. This seems to me to be a task which cannot, in any strict sense of 'prove', be accomplished. What however the arguments of the natural theologians do do is reveal the intellectual pressures which lead people to talk about God; and, in so doing, they illuminate the meaning of such talk. This being so, I must ask the reader to turn to the classical works on natural theology if he wants a more adequate treatment of the subject with which the following paragraphs are concerned.[5]

Our willingness to entertain the notion of a being outside space and time (of what I shall call a 'spirit') is perhaps most fundamentally based on our inability to accept with complete contentment the idea that we are ourselves normal spatio-temporal objects.[6] No doubt the point has often been put in extremely misleading ways, and many quite untenable claims have been made; but it remains true that you cannot adequately describe a human person with the range of concepts which is adequate for the description of a chair, a cabbage or even an electronic calculating machine. And the additional concepts which are needed for the adequate description of human experience—*loving, feeling,* even *seeing* are obvious examples—all have a relative independence of space, not in the sense that we can think of a loving being that is not somewhere, but in the sense that if you try to anatomize his loving you cannot think of it as rest or motion of parts, while you can think of his walking or digesting in such terms. One can of course think of the organic correlates of loving or hoping in physical, and therefore spatial terms; but while few would wish to distinguish the organic correlates of a psychical state, and the state itself, as two separate things, it remains true that we most of us feel uncomfortable about completely identifying them; not that we suppose that we are here dealing with two distinct, but accidentally conjoined, things, but that a full description of this one thing in terms of adrenalin glands, or whatever it may be, does not begin to do justice to the thing as it is known in experience, and has no logical connection with an adequate description of the latter. Much, that is, of what goes on in us is describable from two standpoints; the standpoint of the observer, who can see our muscles twitch, observe our brain-pulsations in an encephalograph; and the standpoint of the agent who is directly aware of himself; and what is described from this latter standpoint demands a distinct set of concepts. I would agree with the tradition from Aristotle to Professor Ryle which does not see in this duality of the human person

---

[5] See for example: Austin Farrer, *Finite and Infinite* (London: Dacre Press, 1943) and E. L. Mascall, *Existence and Analogy* (London: Darton, Longman and Todd, 1966).

[6] On this I must refer the reader to ch. V [of *Faith and Logic*].

any warrant for describing a man as a committee of two distinct entities, body and soul; but the duality remains, and is, as far as we know, a distinctive characteristic of our experience. We are not, nor is any part of ourselves, beings outside space and time, or spirits, but part of our experience of ourselves is only describable with the aid of concepts of a non-physical kind. What we should derive from this is not the grandiose view that we are spirits, but the ability to conceive the notion of a being independent of space, that is a being whose activity is not at all to be thought of in terms of colliding with this, or exercising a gravitational pull on that. We cannot of course form any kind of a lively idea of what it would be like to be such a being; but this is not the positive inability with which we are unable to conceive of a being corresponding to a self-contradictory or meaningless description. In the case of 'spirit' we do not know that there could not be a being like that, as we know that nothing could correspond to the description 'round square' or 'asymptotically democratic potato'. 'Spirit' is not an expression which affronts our logical conscience or leaves us with no clue at all. There are many different grades of 'not knowing what is meant by . . .' and our ignorance of the meaning of 'spirit' (that is, of what something would have to be like to conform to the requirements of this word) is not absolute. To say, then, that we conceive of God as a spirit, is to pitch our claims rather high; for the suggestion is of something parallel to conceiving of Tom as a sergeant-major, where there is some body to the conception. But because of the duality of our own nature, and of the applicability to ourselves of concepts which are not needed for the description of the material world, the formal properties of theological statements, requiring as they do that God be a spirit, leave us unable to conceive what it would be like to be God, but do not leave us without any inkling of the reference-range of such statements. It is not a conception, but a hint of the possibility of something we cannot conceive, but which lies outside the range of possible conception *in a determinate direction*.

But the duality of our human nature is of course a freakish characteristic in the world of space and time. If the world of common experience is all there is, then its purely 'material' contents form a sufficiently complete system on their own, with human spirituality a kind of alien intruder like the ornamentation on Victorian furniture. The pressure of this 'sense of alienation', this sense that we are strangers and sojourners upon earth, has led men for centuries to posit, what they cannot imagine, a spiritual world, to which we really belong; so that we are no longer bits of irrelevant ornament upon an independent structure, but the meeting point of two 'worlds', or interconnected systems of beings, to each of which we belong in one of our dual aspects.[7] Or, if you like our limited and imperfect spirituality—the fact that we are not spirits, but beings with a spiritual aspect—leads us to think of beings who are perfectly what we are imperfectly; not that we can properly conceive of such beings, but that we are forced to frame the abstract notion of them, by the feeling that the smattering of spirit which we find in ourselves must be a pointer to a pool from which it comes.

But, the reader may complain, I am talking of all this in terms appropriate to explaining the genesis of an illusion. I ought to be anatomizing the meaning of the word 'spirit', and that ought to mean listing those experienceable characteristics which we refer to in using the word. Instead of this I am apparently conceding that the word has no meaning (is used of something we cannot conceive of), and trying to explain why people use it as if it had. This I am doing because, in a sense, the notion of spirit is, not exactly an illusion, but an illegitimate notion; illegitimate because it is a kind of reified abstraction. For the words 'spirit', 'spiritual', and so forth, come to have specific meaning for us by being connected with particular characteristics of, or events in, human beings. We distinguish 'spirit' from 'influenza' or 'digestion' by showing to which aspects of men these words severally refer. 'Spirit' derives from 'spiritual' and 'spiritual' acquires specific meaning by correlation with thinking and other activities which only occur, in our experience, as activities of human beings. 'Spirit', then is not a common noun like 'mouse', because it is not the name of a distinct kind of being; it follows from the way the specific meaning of the word is learnt that it is an abstract noun like 'digestion', because it stands for activities of beings called men. We should all regard it absurd to speak of beings which were pure digestions; not the digestings of animals, but just digestings. Is it not equally absurd to speak of things which are pure spirits; not the spiritualizing of animate physical objects, but just spirits? Surely it must be a category mistake to use the word 'spirit' as anything but an abstract noun, or aspect-word?

[7] Friendly critics have objected to my use of the word 'aspect' here. While agreeing, more or less, with the arguments of this section, they hold it less misleading to talk, in the traditional way, of spirituality as a 'part' rather than an 'aspect' of men. For, they say, spirituality is at least an essential aspect; we identify ourselves with our spiritual activity in a way in which we do not identify ourselves with such other aspects as our height or weight. I agree that the word 'aspect' could be misleading; I use it for the reasons given below, and I think that if its meaning is confined to that which is required by these reasons it will not seriously mislead. In other contexts, I would quite agree, 'part' is often better.

Now, against a claim that we know what we mean by 'spirit' in the way in which we know what we mean by 'digestion' or 'smile', such an objection would be decisive. In the sense of 'meaning' in which the meaning of a word is those experienceable characteristics to which it refers, anybody who knows the meaning of 'spirit' can infer that, just as smiles can only be arrangements of features, so spirits can only be characteristics and activities of men. But I am not claiming that we 'know the meaning of spirit' (in the theological use) in this sense. In Berkeley's words, I admit that we have no idea of spirit, and claim only that it is extravagant to say that we have no notion whatsoever of how the word is used. How the word is used (and this, of course, defines such meaning as it has for us) in the theological context is by the deliberate commission of a category-mistake under the pressure of convictions which require us to depart from normal language-practice in this way. For if a man believes that there are beings, or one being, who are comparable to us only in so far as we are spiritual, then the following two things would appear inescapable: (1) that he cannot have any clear and distinct conception of the object of his belief; and (2) that, to express it, he will require some such noun as 'spirit' which will (*a*) retain specific meaning by connection with 'spirituality' as the name of a human aspect, but (*b*) be governed by a rule declaring that this noun is not to be taken as an abstract noun like 'smile' or 'bad temper', but as a concrete noun like 'man'. If you are prepared to accept the view that belief in the existence of purely spiritual beings is simply the result of logical illusion (like the belief in universals as independent entities), that theism is simply a category-mistake, then you need not sully your tongue with a word whose syntactical behaviour is incompatible with the way in which its meaning is learnt; but if you feel that you might entertain the view that there are purely spiritual beings, then you have to have the word. It does not seem to me at all plausible to regard theism as a category-mistake, for it is not pressures derived from logical theory that make people theists. People do not believe in *greenness*, existing independently of green things, until they have been subjected to philosophical reasoning, and told that, if A and B are both green, then there must be a common something in each of them, viz. the universal *greenness*. This is a pressure derived from (mistaken) logical theory. But theism has a quite different origin; we do not believe in God as a pure spirit because we are told that if Smith and Brown are spiritual beings, pure spirituality must exist—or anything of the kind. The notion of God as a spirit is indeed a category-mistake, or category-transgression, but one deliberately committed to express what we antecedently feel;

and if we antecedently feel something, the category-transgression we deliberately commit to express that feeling has some meaning—that namely, which it is designed to express. Disagreement with this conclusion must rest, I believe, on one or other of two general principles, for neither of which can I see any compelling argument: (1) that there can never be good grounds for committing category-transgressions; and (2) that there can be no 'meanings' which do not correspond to clear and distinct ideas.

Let me add, as a pendant to this discussion of 'spirit', that the sense that, in one aspect of our being, we belong to a country in which what is imperfectly realized in us is fully and perfectly realized is not, of course, a compelling argument for the existence of such a country. I claim only two things; the first, that it does not rest solely on inadvertence to logical grammar, but can even survive a clear realization of the logical anomalies of such a belief; the second, that it is this belief or feeling which fixes for us the reference-range of 'spirit' and related expressions as they occur in theological language.

But God is not only a spirit, but also Infinite Spirit. We have so far been discussing the noun; what of the adjective?

Here again an adequate discussion would be equally beyond my space and my powers. But by way of further illustration of the way in which the reference-range of theological language is fixed for us, I shall again venture something.

When we speak of God as an infinite being we are not, of course, using the word 'infinite' in its strict mathematical sense. We mean, negatively that he is unlimited; or, more positively, that, being the source of all limitation, there is nothing whatsoever to which he is conformed, or to which he must conform himself. 'Infinite', therefore, comes to very much the same thing as 'necessary', 'omnipotent', 'creator of all things', and other words of the same kind which we use about God. Now it is characteristic of all these words, that, in so far as they have any precise sense, they cannot be used about God. For, since we do not know God, they cannot acquire a precise sense by reference to his properties; if then they have a precise sense they must acquire it from reference to the properties of something else; and, since nothing else can be an adequate model for God, in so far as they have a precise sense, it cannot be applied to him. Suppose we say, then, that what we mean is something rather loose and vague, loosely and vaguely connected with the normal uses of these words (or, in the case of a word like 'omnipotent', with the result of combining the normal forces of their components). Even so, we have many difficulties to face. Take for example the formula

I used above, that God is 'the source of all limitation', and that, therefore, 'there is nothing whatsoever to which he is conformed, or to which
he must conform himself'. Now even supposing it is admitted on all
hands that we cannot expect to have any idea of what it would be like
to be, or encounter, such a being, we may still be asked to provide
some sense for the phrase 'source of all limitation'. What can we say?
Limitations are due to natural laws, natural laws to the natures, behaviour patterns, or whatnot, which things have. If then God is the
source of all limitations, he gave things their natures, or created them.
But although we can push the counters about in this way, and travel by
'bastard inference' from *infinite* to *creator*, where have we got to
when we arrive? What does a doctrine of Creation amount to? If you
think of God anthropomorphically, Creation is all very well. He took
some raw material, and by compounding and arranging it, gave it the
properties we see around us; he now sustains it, and will one day put
it on the bonfire. But if you think of God anthropomorphically, who
made God?

So far are we, in fact, from being able to argue from the contingency
of the world to the necessary being of God, that we cannot see how
to attach a clear sense to the claim that the world is contingent. The
logical sense of the word will not do: in that sense parts of the world
may be said to exist contingently—that only means that if *x* exists,
it might not have done so, and that only means that from what we know
of the rest of the world we cannot strictly deduce that *x* exists. But
the world as a whole cannot be contingent in this sense. We cannot
sensibly say that, from what we know of the rest, we cannot strictly
deduce that the world as a whole exists, for there is no 'rest' for us to
have knowledge about—unless indeed the rest be God. Yet although
we cannot find a clear sense for 'contingent', 'created' and so forth in
this context, the fact remains that people do persist in having beliefs
for the expression of which they call upon such terms. To some extent,
no doubt, these beliefs rest on theoretical errors. Thus people may hold
that there must be a God because, they say, the world can't have come
from nothing, for *ex nihilo nihil fit*. If you reply that either it is possible
for a thing to 'come from nothing', or it is not possible, and that in the
former case the world may have 'come from nothing', and in the latter
case God cannot have done (so that by parity of reasoning we must
ask: 'Who created God?'), you may or you may not dislodge the belief.
If it rests merely on the theoretical error of applying the principle *ex
nihilo nihil fit* to the entire universe, on the ground that it may be legitimately applied to particular portions of it, then no doubt you will. But

in some people on whom you employ this reasoning, you may encounter an obstinate conviction that none the less this is in fact a created universe, a conviction which involves the belief, not that, as a general 'truth of reason', everything whatsoever must have an origin outside itself (in which case God must, too, *ad infinitum*), but rather that *this* universe is something about which one is prompted to ask where it comes from, with the corollary that there might be something about which one was not prompted to ask this question.

What those features of this universe are which make us feel that it is not its own origin, I am not going to inquire. Many of the classical arguments for the existence of God are designed to draw attention to these features. Nor, of course, am I suggesting that because people feel that there might be a being about which one was not tempted to ask, 'What is its origin?' therefore such a being must exist. My claim is only that if you want to know what is meant by such expressions as 'infinite', 'omnipotent', or 'creator' when applied to God, then the sense that this is a derivative universe, with the corollary that a non-derivative might exist, is the nearest you can get to an understanding of their meaning.

'Finite' and 'infinite', 'contingent' and 'necessary', 'derivative' and 'non-derivative': all these are pairs. When we use either member of any of them in the theological context we cannot anatomize the meaning to be attached to it. When we speak of the world as finite we do not mean that it can be counted, or travelled across; when we speak of it as derivative, we do not think of it as extracted from its origin by any normal kind of derivation. But the meaning to be attached to the second member of each pair is to be got at by seeing what kind of judgement about the world is intended by the use of the first. The kind of judgement intended by the use of such expressions (or by the parallel use of less metaphysical language, such as 'There must be something behind all this passing show') is an intellectual dissatisfaction with the notion of this universe as a complete system, with, as corollary, the notion of a being with which one could not be thus dissatisfied.[8]

That is, you may say, of a being who could claim one's adoration. And many will hold that, to fix the reference-range of theological statements it is better to attend not to what religious people feel or say

[8] Professor Findlay's article: 'Can God's Existence be Disproved?' *Mind,* Vol. 57, 1948; reprinted in *New Essays in Philosophical Theology,* ed. Flew and MacIntyre (London: S.C.M., 1955), depends for its disproof of God's existence on taking necessary in 'Necessary Being' in the logician's sense; but seems to me to provide a very fair characterization of the theist's sense, by its characterization of 'the religious attitude'.

about the world, but to how they dispose themselves towards God—that is, to learn what worship is. It is the contrast between the attitude of worship, and the attitude which religion commends towards creatures (always to be valued, but never, absolutely, in themselves) which illuminates what religion takes the infinite–finite contrast to be. It was the ban on idolatry which taught the Jews what God is. Indeed, it may be said that the sense of contingency is psychologically a correlative of the attempt to worship; one does not begin to feel a sense of finitude until one has made an effort of self-surrender. I do not want to quarrel with any of this; I have tried a more theoretical approach, because I think one should be possible, and because one ought to be suspicious of the possible abuses of appealing to what a man does for the elucidation of what he believes. But I have no doubt that if any vividness of apprehension of the meaning of such terms as 'infinite' is required, then the activity of religion may best supply it.

Let me try to sum up this part of the argument. We are considering how the reference-range of theological statements is fixed—how we know what statements about God are about. The problem is posed by the fact that we neither know God nor know what kind of a being he is. God is neither 'that being', nor 'the being such that ...' More positively, we want to say that God is a being beyond the reach of our conception. Very well, then: God is inconceivable. But, it may be said, that is only a clumsy and misleading way of saying that the expression 'God' lacks meaning. We cannot *mean* inconceivables, for the meaning of any expression can only be those conceivables by reference to which we use it, by indicating which we could teach its use to others. I have tried to define a sense in which we *can* mean inconceivables, and that is when we use a word to refer to the postulated, though unimaginable, absence of limitations or imperfections of which we are aware. It is a little as if I were dissatisfied with a sentence I have written; it is inelegant, and somehow it does not express my meaning. Now the expression 'the correct version of that sentence' is not entirely without meaning to me, although, alas, I cannot at the moment conceive what it stands for. But I should recognize and welcome it if it came, and it would remove a fairly specific dissatisfaction from which I am suffering, or at least a dissatisfaction about a specific subject. This analogy must not be pressed,[9] but it may shed some little light on the sense in which it may be claimed that such an expression as 'Infinite Spirit' has

---

[9] There is no difficulty about the *sense* of 'the correct version of that sentence'; but only about its *reference*.

meaning for us. Such expressions stand for the abstract conception of the possibility of the removal of certain intellectual dissatisfactions which we may feel about the universe of common experience.

The critic complained that he could see neither what theological statements were about—how their reference-range was fixed—nor how they could be regarded as making statements about it—how one could extract their content. I have been trying to deal with the first problem, and must now pass to the second. But before I do so I have a caution to offer. In trying to fix the reference-range of theological statements I am trying to fix it for *the critic*, that is for the man who says that he cannot see what religious people are talking about, and does not believe that there is anything which can be talked about in such a way. It is only to him that one would ever think of answering the question, 'What does "God" stand for?' in such a way. To the religious man the natural answer to such a question is, ' "God" is the name of the Being who is worthy to be adored.' And, as I have said, that is perhaps the most illuminating answer one can give. The answer I have given is one which would only be given to a man from whom the other answer would provoke the retort that, as he did not know what 'adoration' referred to—certain actions apart—the phrase 'being worthy to be adored' could serve as no kind of identification for him. I have been trying to offer a neutral account of what 'God' stands for, one which does not employ any notions whose understanding presupposes a religious outlook. To put it another way, I have not been trying to describe what the Christian takes God to be, but merely to answer a logical challenge, to the effect that theological statements cannot be meaningful because they employ a proper name which seems to be such that it is logically impossible to indicate to an inquirer what it stands for.

III

THEOLOGY AND VERIFICATION

JOHN HICK

To ask 'Is the existence of God verifiable?' is to pose a question which is too imprecise to be capable of being answered.[1] There are many different concepts of God, and it may be that statements employing some of them are open to verification or falsification while statements employing others of them are not. Again, the notion of verifying is itself by no means perfectly clear and fixed; and it may be that on some views of the nature of verification the existence of God is verifiable, whereas on other views it is not.

Instead of seeking to compile a list of the various different concepts of God and the various possible senses of 'verify', I wish to argue with regard to one particular concept of deity, namely the Christian concept, that divine existence is in principle verifiable; and as the first stage of this argument I must indicate what I mean by 'verifiable'.

I

The central core of the concept of verification, I suggest, is the removal of ignorance or uncertainty concerning the truth of some proposition. That p is verified (whether p embodies a theory, hypothesis, prediction, or straightforward assertion) means that something happens which

From *Theology Today*, 17 (1960), 12–31. Reprinted by permission of the author and the Editor of *Theology Today*.

[1] In this article I assume that an indicative sentence expresses a factual assertion if and only if the state in which the universe would be if the putative assertion could correctly be said to be true differs in some experienceable way from the state in which the universe would be if the putative assertion could correctly be said to be false, all aspects of the universe other than that referred to in the putative assertion being the same in either case. This criterion acknowledges the important core of truth in the logical positivist verification principle. 'Experienceable' in the above formulation means, in the case of alleged subjective or private facts (e.g. pains, dreams, after-images, etc.), 'experienceable by the subject in question' and, in the case of alleged objective or public facts, 'capable in principle of being experienced by anyone'. My contention is going to be that 'God exists' asserts a matter of objective fact.

makes it clear that p is true. A question is settled so that there is no longer room for rational doubt concerning it. The way in which grounds for rational doubt are excluded varies, of course, with the subject-matter. But the general feature common to all cases of verification is the ascertaining of truth by the removal of grounds for rational doubt. Where such grounds are removed, we rightly speak of verification having taken place.

To characterize verification in this way is to raise the question whether the notion of verification is purely logical or is both logical and psychological. Is the statement that p is verified simply the statement that a certain state of affairs exists (or has existed), or is it the statement also that someone is aware that this state of affairs exists (or has existed) and notes that its existence establishes the truth of p? A geologist predicts that the earth's surface will be covered with ice in 15 million years time. Suppose that in 15 million years time the earth's surface *is* covered with ice, but that in the meantime the human race has perished, so that no one is left to observe the event or to draw any conclusion concerning the accuracy of the geologist's prediction. Do we now wish to say that his prediction has been verified, or shall we deny that it has been verified, on the ground that there is no one left to do the verifying?

The range of 'verify' and its cognates is sufficiently wide to permit us to speak in either way. But the only sort of verification of theological propositions which is likely to interest us is one in which human beings participate. We may therefore, for our present purposes, treat verification as a logico-psychological rather than as a purely logical concept. I suggest, then, that 'verify' be construed as a verb which has its primary uses in the active voice: I verify, you verify, we verify, they verify, or have verified. The impersonal passive, it is verified, now becomes logically secondary. To say that p has been verified is to say that (at least) someone has verified it, often with the implication that his or their report to this effect is generally accepted. But it is impossible, on this usage, for p to have been verified without someone having verified it. 'Verification' is thus primarily the name for an event which takes place in human consciousness.[2] It refers to an experience, the experience of ascertaining that a given proposition or set of propositions is true. To

[2] This suggestion is closely related to Carnap's insistence that, in contrast to 'true', 'confirmed' is time-dependent. To say that a statement is confirmed, or verified, is to say that it has been confirmed at a particular time—and, I would add, by a particular person. See Rudolf Carnap, 'Truth and Confirmation', *Readings in Philosophical Analysis*, ed. H. Feigl and W. Sellars (New York: Appleton-Century-Crofts, 1949), pp. 119f.

this extent verification is a psychological notion. But of course it is also a logical notion. For needless to say, not *any* experience is rightly called an experience of verifying *p*. Both logical and psychological conditions must be fulfilled in order for verification to have taken place. In this respect, 'verify' is like 'know'. Knowing is an experience which some-one has or undergoes, or perhaps a dispositional state in which someone is, and it cannot take place without someone having or undergoing it or being in it; but not by any means every experience which people have, or every dispositional state in which they are, is rightly called knowing.

With regard to this logico–psychological concept of verification, such questions as the following arise. When *A*, but nobody else, has ascer-tained that *p* is true, can *p* be said to have been verified; or is it required that others also have undergone the same ascertainment? How public, in other words, must verification be? Is it necessary that *p* could in principle be verified by anyone, without restriction, even though per-haps only *A* has in fact verified it? If so, what is meant here by 'in principle'; does it signify, for example, that *p* must be verifiable by any-one who performs a certain operation; and does it imply that to do this is within everyone's power?

These questions cannot, I believe, be given any general answer applic-able to all instances of the exclusion of rational doubt. The answers must be derived in each case from an investigation of the particular subject-matter. It will be the object of subsequent sections of this article to undertake such an investigation concerning the Christian concept of God.

Verification is often construed as the verification of a prediction. How-ever, verification, as the exclusion of grounds for rational doubt, does not necessarily consist in the proving correct of a prediction; a verify-ing experience does not always need to have been predicted in order to have the effect of excluding rational doubt. But when we are interested in the verifiability of propositions as the criterion for their having factual meaning, the notion of prediction becomes central. If a propo-sition contains or entails predictions which can be verified or falsified, its character as an assertion (though not of course its character as a true assertion) is thereby guaranteed.

Such predictions may be and often are conditional. For example, statements about the features on the dark side of the moon are rendered meaningful by the conditional predictions which they entail to the effect that if an observer comes to be in such a position in space, he will make such-and-such observations. It would in fact be more accurate to say that the prediction is always conditional, but that sometimes the conditions are so obvious and so likely to be fulfilled in any case that they require no special mention, while sometimes they require for their fulfilment some unusual expedition or operation. A prediction, for example, that the sun will rise within twenty-four hours is intended unconditionally, at least as concerns conditions to be fulfilled by the observer; he is not required by the terms of the prediction to perform any special operation. Even in this case, however, there is an implied negative condition that he shall not put himself in a situation (such as immuring himself in the depths of a coal mine) from which a sunrise would not be perceptible. Other predictions, however, are explicitly conditional. In these cases it is true for any particular individual that in order to verify the statement in question he must go through some specified course of action. The prediction is to the effect that if you conduct such an experiment you will obtain such a result; for example, if you go into the next room you will have such-and-such visual experiences, and if you then touch the table which you see you will have such-and-such tactual experiences, and so on. The content of the 'if' clause is of course always determined by the particular subject-matter. The logic of 'table' determines what you must do to verify statements about tables; the logic of 'molecule' determines what you must do to verify statements about molecules; and the logic of 'God' determines what you must do to verify statements about God.

In those cases in which the individual who is to verify a proposition must himself first perform some operation, it clearly cannot follow from the circumstance that the proposition is true that everybody has in fact verified it, or that everybody will at some future time verify it. For whether or not any particular person performs the requisite operation is a contingent matter.

II

What is the relation between verification and falsification? We are all familiar today with the phrase, 'theology and falsification'. A. G. N. Flew and others,[3] taking their cue from John Wisdom,[4] have raised instead of the question, 'What possible experiences would verify "God exists"?' the matching question, 'What possible experiences would falsify

---

[3] *New Essays in Philosophical Theology*, ed. Antony Flew and Alasdair MacIntyre (London: S.C.M., 1955), ch. VI.

[4] 'Gods', *Proceedings of the Aristotelian Society*, Vol. 45 (1944–5). Reprinted in *Logic and Language*, First Series, ed. Antony Flew (Oxford: Blackwell, 1955), and in John Wisdom, *Philosophy and Psycho-Analysis* (Oxford: Blackwell, 1952).

"God exists"? What conceivable state of affairs would be incompatible with the existence of God?' In posing the question in this way it was apparently assumed that verification and falsification are symmetrically related, and that the latter is apt to be the more accessible of the two.

In the most common cases, certainly, verification and falsification are symmetrically related. The logically simplest case of verification is provided by the crucial instance. Here it is integral to a given hypothesis that if, in specified circumstances, A occurs, the hypothesis is thereby shown to be true, whereas if B occurs the hypothesis is thereby shown to be false. Verification and falsification are also symmetrically related in the testing of such a proposition as 'There is a table in the next room.' The verifying experiences in this case are experiences of seeing and touching, predictions of which are entailed by the proposition in question, under the proviso that one goes into the next room; and the absence of such experiences in those circumstances serves to falsify the proposition.

But it would be rash to assume, on this basis, that verification and falsification must always be related in this symmetrical fashion. They do not necessarily stand to one another as do the two sides of a coin, so that once the coin is spun it must fall on one side or the other. There are cases in which verification and falsification each correspond to a side on a different coin, so that one can fail to verify without this failure constituting falsification.

Consider, for example, the proposition that 'there are three successive sevens in the decimal determination of π.' So far as the value of π has been worked out, it does not contain a series of three sevens, but it will always be true that such a series may occur at a point not yet reached in anyone's calculations. Accordingly, the proposition may one day be verified, if it is true, but can never be falsified, if it is false.

The hypothesis of continued conscious existence after bodily death provides an instance of a different kind of such asymmetry, and one which has a direct bearing upon the theistic problem. This hypothesis has built into it a prediction that one will after the date of one's bodily death have conscious experiences, including the experience of remembering that death. This is a prediction which will be verified in one's own experience if it is true, but which cannot be falsified if it is false. That is to say, it can be false, but *that* it is false can never be a fact which anyone has experimentally verified. But this circumstance does not undermine the meaningfulness of the hypothesis, since it is also such that if it be true, it will be known to be true.

It is important to remember that we do not speak of verifying logically necessary truths, but only propositions concerning matters of fact. Accordingly verification is not to be identified with the concept of logical certification or proof. The exclusion of rational doubt concerning some matter of fact is not equivalent to the exclusion of the logical possibility or error or illusion. For truths concerning fact are not logically necessary. Their contrary is never self-contradictory. But at the same time the bare logical possibility of error does not constitute ground for rational doubt as to the veracity of our experience. If it did, no empirical proposition could ever be verified, and indeed the notion of empirical verification would be without use and therefore without sense. What we rightly seek, when we desire the verification of a factual proposition, is not a demonstration of the logical impossibility of the proposition's being false (for this would be a self-contradictory demand), but such weight of evidence as suffices, in the type of case in question, to exclude rational doubt.

III

These features of the concept of verification—that verification consists in the exclusion of grounds for rational doubt concerning the truth of some proposition; that this means its exclusion from particular minds; that the nature of the experience which serves to exclude grounds for rational doubt depends upon the particular subject matter; that verification is often related to predictions and that such predictions are often conditional; that verification and falsification may be asymmetrically related; and finally, that the verification of a factual proposition is not equivalent to logical certification—are all relevant to the verification of the central religious claim, 'God exists.' I wish now to apply these discriminations to the notion of eschatological verification, which has been briefly employed by Ian Crombie in his contribution to *New Essays in Philosophical Theology*,[5] and by myself in *Faith and Knowledge*.[6] This suggestion has on each occasion been greeted with disapproval by both philosophers and theologians. I am, however, still of the opinion that the notion of eschatological verification is sound; and further, that no viable alternative to it has been offered to establish the factual character of theism.

The strength of the notion of eschatological verification is that it is not an *ad hoc* invention but is based upon an actually operative religious concept of God. In the language of the Christian faith, the word 'God'

[5] p. 126.   [6] (New York: Cornell, 1957), pp. 150–62.

stands at the centre of a system of terms, such as Spirit, grace, Logos, incarnation, Kingdom of God, and many more; and the distinctly Christian conception of God can only be fully grasped in its connection with these related terms.[7] It belongs to a complex of notions which together constitute a picture of the universe in which we live, of man's place therein, of a comprehensive divine purpose interacting with human purposes, and of the general nature of the eventual fulfilment of that divine purpose. This Christian picture of the universe, entailing as it does certain distinctive expectations concerning the future, is a very different picture from any that can be accepted by one who does not believe that the God of the New Testament exists. Further, these differences are such as to show themselves in human experience. The possibility of experiential confirmation is thus built into the Christian concept of God; and the notion of eschatological verification seeks to relate this fact to the logical problem of meaning.

Let me first give a general indication of this suggestion, by repeating a parable which I have related elsewhere,[8] and then try to make it more precise and eligible for discussion. Here, first, is the parable.

Two men are travelling together along a road. One of them believes that it leads to a Celestial City, the other that it leads nowhere; but since this is the only road there is, both must travel it. Neither has been this way before, and therefore neither is able to say what they will find around each next corner. During their journey they meet both with moments of refreshment and delight, and with moments of hardship and danger. All the time one of them thinks of his journey as a pilgrimage to the Celestial City and interprets the pleasant parts as encouragements and the obstacles as trials of his purpose and lessons in endurance, prepared by the king of that city and designed to make of him a worthy citizen of the place when at last he arrives there. The other, however, believes none of this and sees their journey as an unavoidable and aimless ramble. Since he has no choice in the matter, he enjoys the good and endures the bad. But for him there is no Celestial City to be reached, no all-encompassing purpose ordaining their journey; only the road itself and the luck of the road in good weather and in bad.

---

[7] Its clear recognition of this fact, with regard not only to Christianity but to any religion is one of the valuable features of Ninian Smart's *Reasons and Faiths* (London: Routledge and Kegan Paul, 1958). He remarks, for example, that 'the claim that God exists can only be understood by reference to many, if not all, other propositions in the doctrinal scheme from which it is extrapolated' (p. 12).

[8] *Faith and Knowledge*, pp. 150f.

During the course of the journey the issue between them is not an experimental one. They do not entertain different expectations about the coming details of the road, but only about its ultimate destination. And yet when they do turn the last corner it will be apparent that one of them has been right all the time and the other wrong. Thus although the issue between them has not been experimental, it has nevertheless from the start been a real issue. They have not merely felt differently about the road; for one was feeling appropriately and the other inappropriately in relation to the actual state of affairs. Their opposed interpretations of the road constituted genuinely rival assertions, though assertions whose assertion-status has the peculiar characteristic of being guaranteed retrospectively by a future crux.

This parable has of course (like all parables) strict limitations. It is designed to make only one point: that Christian doctrine postulates an ultimate unambiguous state of existence in *patria* as well as our present ambiguous existence *in via*. There is a state of having arrived as well as a state of journeying, an eternal heavenly life as well as an earthly pilgrimage. The alleged future experience of this state cannot, of course, be appealed to as evidence for theism as a present interpretation of our experience; but it does suffice to render the choice between theism and atheism a real and not a merely empty or verbal choice. And although this does not affect the logic of the situation, it should be added that the alternative interpretations are more than theoretical, for they render different practical plans and policies appropriate now.

The universe as envisaged by the theist, then, differs as a totality from the universe as envisaged by the atheist. This difference does not, however, from our present standpoint within the universe, involve a difference in the objective content of each or even any of its passing moments. The theist and the atheist do not (or need not) expect different events to occur in the successive details of the temporal process. They do not (or need not) entertain divergent expectations of the course of history viewed from within. But the theist does and the atheist does not expect that when history is completed it will be seen to have led to a particular end-state and to have fulfilled a specific purpose, namely that of creating 'children of God'.

IV

The idea of an eschatological verification of theism can make sense, however, only if the logically prior idea of continued personal existence after death is intelligible. A desultory debate on this topic has been going on for several years in some of the philosophical periodicals. C. I.

Lewis has contended that the hypothesis of immortality 'is an hypothesis about our own future experience. And our understanding of what would verify it has no lack of clarity.'[9] And Moritz Schlick agreed, adding, 'We must conclude that immortality, in the sense defined [i.e. "survival after death", rather than "never-ending life"], should not be regarded as a "metaphysical problem", but is an empirical hypothesis, because it possesses logical verifiability. It could be verified by following the prescription: "Wait until you die!"'[10] However, others have challenged this conclusion, either on the ground that the phrase 'surviving death' is self-contradictory in ordinary language or, more substantially, on the ground that the traditional distinction between soul and body cannot be sustained.[11] I should like to address myself to this latter view. The only self of which we know, it is said, is the empirical self, the walking, talking, acting, sleeping individual who lives, it may be, for some sixty to eighty years and then dies. Mental events and mental characteristics are analysed into the modes of behaviour and behavioural dispositions of this empirical self. The human being is described as an organism capable of acting in the 'high-level' ways which we characterize as intelligent, thoughtful, humorous, calculating, and the like. The concept of mind or soul is thus not the concept of a 'ghost in the machine' (to use Gilbert Ryle's loaded phrase[12]), but of the more flexible and sophisticated ways in which human beings behave and have it in them to behave. On this view there is no room for the notion of soul in distinction from body; and if there is no soul in distinction from body, there can be no question of the soul surviving the death of the body. Against this philosophical background the specifically Christian (and also Jewish) belief in the resurrection of the flesh, or body, in contrast to the Hellenic notion of the survival of a disembodied soul, might be expected to have attracted more attention than it has. For it is consonant with the conception of man as an indissoluble psycho–physical unity, and yet it also offers the possibility of an empirical meaning for the idea of 'life after death'.

Paul is the chief Biblical expositor of the idea of the resurrection of

[9] 'Experience and Meaning', *Philosophical Review*, Vol. 43 (1934), reprinted in Feigl and Sellars, op. cit., p. 142.

[10] 'Meaning and Verification', *Philosophical Review*, Vol. 45 (1936), reprinted in Feigl and Sellars, op. cit., p. 160.

[11] e.g. Antony Flew, 'Death', *New Essays in Philosophical Theology*, ed. Flew; 'Can a Man Witness his own Funeral?', *Hibbert Journal*, Vol. 54 (1956).

[12] *The Concept of Mind* (London: Hutchinson, 1949), which contains an important exposition of the interpretation of 'mental' qualities as characteristics of behaviour.

the body.[13] His view, as I understand it, is this. When someone has died he is, apart from any special divine action, extinct. A human being is by nature mortal and subject to annihilation by death. But in fact God, by an act of sovereign power, either sometimes or always resurrects or (better) reconstitutes or recreates him—not, however, as the identical physical organism that he was before death, but as a *soma pneumatikon* ('spiritual body') embodying the dispositional characteristics and memory traces of the deceased physical organism, and inhabiting an environment with which the *soma pneumatikon* is continuous as the *ante-mortem* body was continuous with our present world. In discussing this notion we may well abandon the word 'spiritual', as lacking today any precise established usage, and speak of 'resurrection bodies' and of 'the resurrection world'. The principal questions to be asked concern the relation between the physical world and the resurrection world, and the criteria of personal identity which are operating when it is alleged that a certain inhabitant of the resurrection world is the same person as an individual who once inhabited this world. The first of these questions turns out on investigation to be the more difficult of the two, and I shall take the easier one first.

Let me sketch a very odd possibility (concerning which, however, I wish to emphasize not so much its oddness as its possibility!), and then see how far it can be stretched in the direction of the notion of the resurrection body. In the process of stretching it will become even more odd than it was before; but my aim will be to show that, however odd, it remains within the bounds of the logically possible. This progression will be presented in three pictures, arranged in a self-explanatory order.

First picture: Suppose that at some learned gathering in this country one of the company were suddenly and inexplicably to disappear, and that at the same moment an exact replica of him were suddenly and inexplicably to appear at some comparable meeting in Australia. The person who appears in Australia is exactly similar, as to both bodily and mental characteristics, with the person who disappears in America. There is continuity of memory, complete similarity of bodily features, including even fingerprints, hair and eye colouration and stomach contents, and also of beliefs, habits, and mental propensities. In fact there is everything that would lead us to identify the one who appeared with the one who disappeared, except continuity of occupancy of space. We may suppose, for example, that a deputation of the colleagues of the man who disappeared fly to Australia to interview the replica of him which is

[13] I Cor. 15.

reported there, and find that he is in all respects but one exactly as though he had travelled from, say, Princeton to Melbourne by conventional means. The only difference is that he describes how, as he was sitting listening to Dr. Z reading a paper, on blinking his eyes he suddenly found himself sitting in a different room listening to a different paper by an Australian scholar. He asks his colleagues how the meeting had gone after he ceased to be there, and what they had made of his disappearance, and so on. He clearly thinks of himself as the one who was present with them at their meeting in the United States. I suggest that faced with all these circumstances his colleagues would soon, if not immediately, find themselves thinking of him and treating him as the individual who had so inexplicably disappeared from their midst. We should be extending our normal use of 'same person' in a way which the postulated facts would both demand and justify if we said that the one who appears in Australia is the same person as the one who disappears in America. The factors inclining us to identify them would far outweigh the factors disinclining us to do this. We should have no reasonable alternative but to extend our usage of 'the same person' to cover the strange new case.

Second picture: Now let us suppose that the event in America is not a sudden and inexplicable disappearance, indeed not a disappearance at all, but a sudden death. Only, at the moment when the individual dies, a replica of him as he was at the moment before his death, complete with memory up to that instant, appears in Australia. Even with the corpse on our hands, it would still, I suggest, be an extension of 'same person' required and warranted by the postulated facts, to say that the same person who died has been miraculously recreated in Australia. The case would be considerably odder than in the previous picture, because of the existence of the corpse in America contemporaneously with the existence of the living person in Australia. But I submit that, although the oddness of this circumstance may be stated as strongly as you please, and can indeed hardly be overstated, yet it does not exceed the bounds of the logically possible. Once again we must imagine some of the deceased's colleagues going to Australia to interview the person who has suddenly appeared there. He would perfectly remember them and their meeting, be interested in what had happened, and be as amazed and dumbfounded about it as anyone else; and he would perhaps be worried about the possible legal complications if he should return to America to claim his property; and so on. Once again, I believe, they would soon find themselves thinking of him and treating him as the same person as the dead Princetonian. Once again the factors inclining us to say that the one who died and the one who appeared are the same person would outweigh the factors inclining us to say that they are different people. Once again we should have to extend our usage of 'the same person' to cover this new case.

Third picture: My third supposal is that the replica, complete with memory, etc. appears, not in Australia, but as a resurrection replica in a different world altogether, a resurrection world inhabited by resurrected persons. This world occupies its own space, distinct from the space with which we are now familiar. That is to say, an object in the resurrection world is not situated at any distance or in any direction from an object in our present world, although each object in either world is spatially related to each other object in the same world.

Mr. X, then, dies. A Mr. X replica, complete with the set of memory traces which Mr. X had at the last moment before his death, comes into existence. It is composed of other material than physical matter, and is located in a resurrection world which does not stand in any spatial relationship with the physical world. Let us leave out of consideration St. Paul's hint that the resurrection body may be as unlike the physical body as is a full grain of wheat from the wheat seed, and consider the simpler picture in which the resurrection body has the same shape as the physical body.[14]

In these circumstances, how does Mr. X know that he has been resurrected or recreated? He remembers dying; or rather he remembers being on what he took to be his death-bed, and becoming progressively weaker until, presumably, he lost consciousness. But how does he know that (to put it Irishly) his 'dying' proved fatal; and that he did not, after losing consciousness, begin to recover strength, and has now simply waked up?

The picture is readily enough elaborated to answer this question. Mr. X meets and recognizes a number of relatives and friends and historical personages whom he knows to have died; and from the fact of their presence, and also from their testimony that he has only just now appeared in their world, he is convinced that he has died. Evidences of this kind could mount up to the point at which they are quite as strong as the evidence which, in pictures one and two, convince the individual in question that he has been miraculously translated to Australia. Resurrected persons would be individually no more in doubt about their own identity than we are now, and would be able to identify one another in the same kind of ways, and with a like degree of assurance, as we do now.

---

[14] As would seem to be assumed, for example, by Irenaeus (*Adversus Haereses*, Bk. II, ch. 34, s. 1).

If it be granted that resurrected persons might be able to arrive at a rationally founded conviction that their existence is *post-mortem*, how could they know that the world in which they find themselves is in a different space from that in which their physical bodies were? How could such a one know that he is not in a like situation with the person in picture number two, who dies in America and appears as a full-blooded replica in Australia, leaving his corpse in the U.S.A.—except that now the replica is situated, not in Australia, but on a planet of some other star?

It is of course conceivable that the space of the resurrection world should have properties which are manifestly incompatible with its being a region of physical space. But on the other hand, it is not of the essence of the notion of a resurrection world that its space should have properties different from those of physical space. And supposing it not to have different properties, it is not evident that a resurrected individual could learn from any direct observations that he was not on a planet of some sun which is at so great a distance from our own sun that the stellar scenery visible from it is quite unlike that which we can now see. The grounds that a resurrected person would have for believing that he is in a different space from physical space (supposing there to be no discernible difference in spatial properties) would be the same as the grounds that any of us may have now for believing this concerning resurrected individuals. These grounds are indirect and consist in all those considerations (e.g. Luke 16:26) which lead most of those who consider the question to reject as absurd the possibility of, for example, radio communication or rocket travel between earth and heaven.

V

In the present context my only concern is to claim that this doctrine of the divine creation of bodies, composed of a material other than that of physical matter, which bodies are endowed with sufficient correspondence of characteristics with our present bodies, and sufficient continuity of memory with our present consciousness, for us to speak of the same person being raised up again to life in a new environment, is not self-contradictory. If, then, it cannot be ruled out *ab initio* as meaningless, we may go on to consider whether and how it is related to the possible verification of Christian theism.

So far I have argued that a survival prediction such as is contained in the *corpus* of Christian belief is in principle subject to future verification. But this does not take the argument by any means as far as it must go if it is to succeed. For survival, simply as such, would not serve to verify theism. It would not necessarily be a state of affairs which is manifestly incompatible with the non-existence of God. It might be taken just as a surprising natural fact. The atheist, in his resurrection body, and able to remember his life on earth, might say that the universe has turned out to be more complex, and perhaps more to be approved of, than he had realized. But the mere fact of survival, with a new body in a new environment, would not demonstrate to him that there is a God. It is fully compatible with the notion of survival that the life to come be, so far as the theistic problem is concerned, essentially a continuation of the present life, and religiously no less ambiguous. And in this event, survival after bodily death would not in the least constitute a final verification of theistic faith.

I shall not spend time in trying to draw a picture of a resurrection existence which would merely prolong the religious ambiguity of our present life. The important question, for our purpose, is not whether one can conceive of after-life experiences which would *not* verify theism (and in point of fact one can fairly easily conceive them), but whether one can conceive of after-life experiences which *would* serve to verify theism.

I think that we can. In trying to do so I shall not appeal to the traditional doctrine, which figures especially in Catholic and mystical theology, of the Beatific Vision of God. The difficulty presented by this doctrine is not so much that of deciding whether there are grounds for believing it, as of deciding what it means. I shall not, however, elaborate this difficulty, but pass directly to the investigation of a different and, as it seems to me, more intelligible possibility. This is the possibility not of a direct vision of God, whatever that might mean, but of a *situation* which points unambiguously to the existence of a loving God. This would be a situation which, so far as its religious significance is concerned, contrasts in a certain important respect with our present situation. Our present situation is one which in some ways seems to confirm and in other ways to contradict the truth of theism. Some events around us suggest the presence of an unseen benevolent intelligence and others suggest that no such intelligence is at work. Our situation is religiously ambiguous. But in order for us to be aware of this fact we must already have some idea, however vague, of what it would be for our situation to be not ambiguous, but on the contrary wholly evidential of God. I therefore want to try to make clearer this presupposed concept of a religiously unambiguous situation.

There are, I suggest, two possible developments of our experience such that, if they occurred in conjunction with one another (whether in this life or in another life to come), they would assure us beyond rational doubt of the reality of God, as conceived in the Christian faith. These are, *first*, an experience of the fulfilment of God's purpose for ourselves, as this has been disclosed in the Christian revelation; in conjunction, *second*, with an experience of communion with God as he has revealed himself in the person of Christ.

The divine purpose for human life, as this is depicted in the New Testament documents, is the bringing of the human person, in society with his fellows, to enjoy a certain valuable quality of personal life, the content of which is given in the character of Christ—which quality of life (i.e. life in relationship with God, described in the Fourth Gospel as eternal life) is said to be the proper destiny of human nature and the source of man's final self-fulfilment and happiness. The verification situation with regard to such a fulfilment is asymmetrical. On the one hand, so long as the divine purpose remains unfulfilled, we cannot know that it never will be fulfilled in the future; hence no final falsification is possible of the claim that this fulfilment will occur—unless, of course, the prediction contains a specific time clause which, in Christian teaching, it does not. But on the other hand, if and when the divine purpose *is* fulfilled in our own experience, we must be able to recognize and rejoice in that fulfilment. For the fulfilment would not be for us the promised fulfilment without our own conscious participation in it.

It is important to note that one can say this much without being cognizant in advance of the concrete form which such fulfilment will take. The before-and-after situation is analogous to that of a small child looking forward to adult life and then, having grown to adulthood, looking back upon childhood. The child possesses and can use correctly in various contexts the concept of 'being grown up', although he does not know, concretely, what it is like to be grown-up. But when he reaches adulthood he is nevertheless able to know that he has reached it; he is able to recognize the experience of living a grown-up life even though he did not know in advance just what to expect. For his understanding of adult maturity grows as he himself matures. Something similar may be supposed to happen in the case of the fulfilment of the divine purpose for human life. That fulfilment may be as far removed from our present condition as is mature adulthood from the mind of a little child; nevertheless, we possess already a comparatively vague notion of this final fulfilment, and as we move towards it our concept will itself become more adequate; and if and when we finally reach that fulfilment, the problem of recognizing it will have disappeared in the process.

The other feature that must, I suggest, be present in a state of affairs that would verify theism, is that the fulfilment of God's purpose be apprehended *as* the fulfilment of God's purpose and not simply as a natural state of affairs. To this end it must be accompanied by an experience of communion with God as he has made himself known to men in Christ.

The specifically Christian clause, 'as he has made himself known to men in Christ', is essential, for it provides a solution to the problem of recognition in the awareness of God. Several writers have pointed out the logical difficulty involved in any claim to have encountered God.[15] How could one know that it was *God* whom one had encountered? God is described in Christian theology in terms of various absolute qualities, such as omnipotence, omnipresence, perfect goodness, infinite love, etc., which cannot as such be observed by us, as can their finite analogues, limited power, local presence, finite goodness, and human love. One can recognize that a being whom one 'encounters' has a given finite degree of power, but how does one recognize that he has *un*limited power? How does one observe that an encountered being is *omni*present? How does one perceive that his goodness and love, which one can perhaps see to exceed any human goodness and love, are actually infinite? Such qualities cannot be given in human experience. One might claim, then, to have encountered a Being whom one presumes, or trusts, or hopes to be God; but one cannot claim to have encountered a Being whom one recognized to be the infinite, almighty, eternal Creator.

This difficulty is met in Christianity by the doctrine of the Incarnation —although this was not among the considerations which led to the formulation of that doctrine. The idea of incarnation provides answers to the two related questions: 'How do we know that God has certain absolute qualities which, by their very nature, transcend human experience?' and 'How can there be an eschatological verification of theism which is based upon a recognition of the presence of God in his Kingdom?'

In Christianity God is known as 'the God and Father of our Lord Jesus Christ'.[16] God is the Being about whom Jesus taught; the Being in relation to whom Jesus lived, and into a relationship with whom he brought his disciples; the Being whose *agape* towards men was seen on earth in the life of Jesus. In short, God is the transcendent Creator who has revealed himself in Christ. Now Jesus's teaching about the Father is a part of that self-disclosure, and it is from this teaching (together with

[15] For example, R. W. Hepburn, *Christianity and Paradox* (London: C. A. Watts, 1958), pp. 56f.

[16] II Cor. 11:31.

that of the prophets who preceded him) that the Christian knowledge of God's transcendent being is derived. Only God himself knows his own infinite nature; and our human belief about that nature is based upon his self-revelation to men in Christ. As Karl Barth expresses it, 'Jesus Christ is the knowability of God.'[17] Our beliefs about God's infinite being are not capable of observational verification, being beyond the scope of human experience, but they are susceptible of indirect verification by the removal of rational doubt concerning the authority of Christ. An experience of the reign of the Son in the Kingdom of the Father would confirm that authority, and therewith, indirectly, the validity of Jesus's teaching concerning the character of God in his infinite transcendent nature.

The further question as to how an eschatological experience of the Kingdom of God could be known to be such has already been answered by implication. It is God's union with man in Christ that makes possible man's recognition of the fulfilment of God's purpose for man as being indeed the fulfilment of *God's* purpose for him. The presence of Christ in his Kingdom marks this as being beyond doubt the Kingdom of the God and Father of the Lord Jesus Christ.

It is true that even the experience of the realization of the promised Kingdom of God, with Christ reigning as Lord of the New Aeon, would not constitute a logical certification of his claims nor, accordingly, of the reality of God. But this will not seem remarkable to any philosopher in the empiricist tradition, who knows that it is only a confusion to demand that a factual proposition be an analytic truth. A set of expectations based upon faith in the historic Jesus as the incarnation of God, and in his teaching as being divinely authoritative, could be so fully confirmed in *post-mortem* experience as to leave no grounds for rational doubt as to the validity of that faith.

VI

There remains of course the problem (which falls to the New Testament scholar rather than to the philosopher) whether Christian tradition, and in particular the New Testament, provides a sufficiently authentic 'picture' of the mind and character of Christ to make such recognition possible. I cannot here attempt to enter into the vast field of Biblical criticism, and shall confine myself to the logical point, which only emphasizes the importance of the historical question, that a verification of theism made possible by the Incarnation is dependent upon the

[17] *Church Dogmatics*, Vol. II, Pt. I, p. 150.

Christian's having a genuine contact with the person of Christ, even though this is mediated through the life and tradition of the Church.

One further point remains to be considered. When we ask the question, '*To whom* is theism verified?' one is initially inclined to assume that the answer must be, 'To everyone.' We are inclined to assume that, as in my parable of the journey, the believer must be confirmed in his belief, and the unbeliever converted from his unbelief. But this assumption is neither demanded by the nature of verification nor by any means unequivocally supported by our Christian sources.

We have already noted that a verifiable prediction may be conditional. 'There is a table in the next room' entails conditional predictions of the form: if someone goes into the next room he will see, etc. But no one is compelled to go into the next room. Now it may be that the predictions concerning human experience which are entailed by the proposition that God exists are conditional predictions and that no one is compelled to fulfil those conditions. Indeed we stress in much of our theology that the manner of the divine self-disclosure to men is such that our human status as free and responsible beings is respected, and an awareness of God never is forced upon us. It may then be a condition of *post-mortem* verification that we be already in some degree conscious of God by an uncompelled response to his modes of revelation in this world. It may be that such a voluntary consciousness of God is an essential element in the fulfilment of the divine purpose for human nature, so that the verification of theism which consists in an experience of the final fulfilment of that purpose can only be experienced by those who have already entered upon an awareness of God by the religious mode of apperception which we call faith.

If this be so, it has the consequence that only the theistic believer can find the vindication of his belief. This circumstance would not of course set any restriction upon who can become a believer, but it would involve that while theistic faith can be verified—found by one who holds it to be beyond rational doubt—yet it cannot be proved to the non-believer. Such an asymmetry would connect with that strain of New Testament teaching which speaks of a division of mankind even in the world to come.

Having noted this possibility I will only express my personal opinion that the logic of the New Testament as a whole, though admittedly not always its explicit content, leads to a belief in ultimate universal salvation. However, my concern here is not to seek to establish the religious facts, but rather to establish that there are such things as religious facts, and in particular that the existence or non-existence of the God of the New Testament is a matter of fact, and claims as such eventual experiential verification.

IV

AN EMPIRICIST'S VIEW OF THE NATURE OF RELIGIOUS BELIEF

R. B. BRAITHWAITE

'THE meaning of a scientific statement is to be ascertained by reference to the steps which would be taken to verify it.' Eddington wrote this in 1939. Unlike his heterodox views of the *a priori* and epistemological character of the ultimate laws of physics, this principle is in complete accord with contemporary philosophy of science; indeed it was Eddington's use of it in his expositions of relativity theory in the early 1920s that largely contributed to its becoming the orthodoxy. Eddington continued his passage by saying: 'This [principle] will be recognized as a tenet of logical positivism—only it is there extended to all statements.'[1] Just as the tone was set to the empiricist tradition in British philosophy —the tradition running from Locke through Berkeley, Hume, Mill to Russell in our own time—by Locke's close association with the scientific work of Boyle and the early Royal Society, so the contemporary development of empiricism popularly known as logical positivism has been greatly influenced by the revolutionary changes this century in physical theory and by the philosophy of science which physicists concerned with these changes—Einstein and Heisenberg as well as Eddington—have thought most consonant with relativity and quantum physics. It is therefore, I think, proper for me to take the verification principle of meaning, and a natural adaptation of it, as that aspect of contemporary scientific thought whose bearing upon the philosophy of religion I shall discuss this afternoon. Eddington, in the passage from which I have quoted, applied the verificational principle to the meaning of scientific statements only. But we shall see that it will be necessary, and concordant with an empiricist way of thinking, to modify the principle by allowing *use* as well as *verifiability* to be a criterion for meaning; so I believe that all I say will be in the spirit of a remark with which Eddington concluded an

The ninth Arthur Stanley Eddington Memorial Lecture (November 1955). Reprinted by permission of the author and Cambridge University Press.

[1] A. S. Eddington, *The Philosophy of Physical Science* (Cambridge: Cambridge University Press, 1939), p. 189.

article published in 1926: 'The scientist and the religious teacher may well be content to agree that the *value* of any hypothesis extends just so far as it is verified by actual experience.'[2]

I will start with the verificational principle in the form in which it was originally propounded by logical positivists—that the meaning of any statement is given by its method of verification.[3]

The implication of this general principle for the problem of religious belief is that the primary question becomes, not whether a religious statement such as that a personal God created the world is true or is false, but how it could be known either to be true or to be false. Unless this latter question can be answered, the religious statement has no ascertainable meaning and there is nothing expressed by it to be either true or false. Moreover a religious statement cannot be believed without being understood, and it can only be understood by an understanding of the circumstances which would verify or falsify it. Meaning is not logically prior to the possibility of verification: we do not first learn the meaning of a statement, and afterwards consider what would make us call it true or false; the two understandings are one and indivisible.

It would not be correct to say that discussions of religious belief before this present century have always ignored the problem of meaning, but until recently the emphasis has been upon the question of the truth or the reasonableness of religious beliefs rather than upon the logically prior question as to the meaning of the statements expressing the beliefs. The argument usually proceeded as if we all knew what was meant by the statement that a personal God created the world; the point at issue was whether or not this statement was true or whether there were good reasons for believing it. But if the meaning of a religious statement has to be found by discovering the steps which must be taken to ascertain its truth-value, an examination of the methods for testing the statement for truth-value is an essential preliminary to any discussion as to which of the truth-values—truth or falsity—holds of the statement.

There are three classes of statement whose method of truth-value testing is in general outline clear: statements about particular matters of empirical fact, scientific hypotheses and other general empirical statements, and the logically necessary statements of logic and mathematics (and their contradictories). Do religious statements fall into any of these three classes? If they do, the problem of their meaningfulness will be

---

[2] *Science, Religion and Reality*, ed. by J. Needham (London: S.P.C.K., 1926), p. 218 (my italics).

[3] The principle was first explicitly stated by F. Waismann, in *Erkenntnis*, I (1930), 229.

solved: their truth-values will be testable by the methods appropriate to empirical statements, particular or general, or to mathematical statements. It seems to me clear that religious statements, as they are normally used, have no place in this trichotomy. I shall give my reasons very briefly, since I have little to add here to what other empiricist philosophers have said.

(1) Statements about particular empirical facts are testable by direct observation. The only facts that can be directly known by observation are that the things observed have certain observable properties or stand in certain observable relations to one another. If it is maintained that the *existence* of God is known by observation, for example, in the 'self-authenticating' experience of 'meeting God', the term 'God' is being used merely as part of the description of that particular experience. Any interesting theological proposition, e.g. that God is personal, will attribute a property to God which is not an observable one and so cannot be known by direct observation. Comparison with our knowledge of other people is an unreal comparison. I can get to know things about an intimate friend at a glance, but this knowledge is not self-authenticating; it is based upon a great deal of previous knowledge about the connection between facial and bodily expressions and states of mind.

(2) The view that would class religious statements with scientific hypotheses must be taken much more seriously. It would be very unplausible if a Baconian methodology of science had to be employed, and scientific hypotheses taken as simple generalizations from particular instances, for then there could be no understanding of a general theological proposition unless particular instances of it could be directly observed. But an advanced science has progressed far beyond its natural history stage; it makes use in its explanatory hypotheses of concepts of a high degree of abstractness and at a far remove from experience. These theoretical concepts are given a meaning by the place they occupy in a deductive system consisting of hypotheses of different degrees of generality in which the least general hypotheses, deducible from the more general ones, are generalizations of observable facts. So it is no valid criticism of the view that would treat God as an empirical concept entering into an explanatory hypothesis to say that God is not directly observable. No more is an electric field of force or a Schrödinger wave-function. There is no *prima facie* objection to regarding such a proposition as that there is a God who created and sustains the world as an explanatory scientific hypothesis.

But if a set of theological propositions are to be regarded as scientific explanations of facts in the empirical world, they must be refutable by experience. We must be willing to abandon them if the facts prove different from what we think they are. A hypothesis which is consistent with every possible empirical fact is not an empirical one. And though the theoretical concepts in a hypothesis need not be explicitly definable in terms of direct observation—indeed they must not be if the system is to be applicable to novel situations—yet they must be related to some and not to all of the possible facts in the world in order to have a non-vacuous significance. If there is a personal God, how would the world be different if there were not? Unless this question can be answered God's existence cannot be given an empirical meaning.

At earlier times in the history of religion God's personal existence has been treated as a scientific hypothesis subjectable to empirical test. Elijah's contest with the prophets of Baal was an experiment to test the hypothesis that Jehovah and not Baal controlled the physical world. But most educated believers at the present time do not think of God as being detectable in this sort of way, and hence do not think of theological propositions as explanations of facts in the world of nature in the way in which established scientific hypotheses are.

It may be maintained, however, that theological propositions explain facts about the world in another way. Not perhaps the physical world, for physical science has been so successful with its own explanations; but the facts of biological and psychological development. Now it is certainly the case that a great deal of traditional Christian language—phrases such as 'original sin', 'the old Adam', 'the new man', 'growth in holiness'—can be given meanings within statements expressing general hypotheses about human personality. Indeed it is hardly too much to say that almost all statements about God as immanent, as an indwelling spirit, can be interpreted as asserting psychological facts in metaphorical language. But would those interpreting religious statements in this way be prepared to abandon them if the empirical facts were found to be different? Or would they rather re-interpret them to fit the new facts? In the latter case the possibility of interpreting them to fit experience is not enough to give an empirical meaning to the statements. Mere consistency with experience without the possibility of inconsistency does not determine meaning. And a metaphorical description is not in itself an explanation. This criticism also holds against attempts to interpret theism as an explanation of the course of history, unless it is admitted (which few theists would be willing to admit) that, had the course of history been different in some specific way, God would not have existed.

Philosophers of religion who wish to make empirical facts relevant to the meaning of religious statements but at the same time desire to hold

on to these statements whatever the empirical facts may be are indulg-
ing, I believe, in a sort of *doublethink* attitude: they want to hold that
religious statements both are about the actual world (i.e. are empirical
statements) and also are not refutable in any possible world, the
characteristic of statements which are logically necessary.

(3) The view that statements of natural theology resemble the propositions of logic and mathematics in being logically necessary would
have as a consequence that they make no assertion of existence. Whatever exactly be the status of logically necessary propositions, Hume and
Kant have conclusively shown that they are essentially hypothetical.
$2+3=5$ makes no assertion about there being any things in the world;
what it says is that, *if* there is a class of five things in the world, *then*
this class is the union of two mutually exclusive subclasses one comprising two and the other comprising three things. The logical positivist
thesis, due to Wittgenstein, that the truth of this hypothetical proposi-
ion is verified not by any logical fact about the world but by the way in
which we use numerical symbols in our thinking goes further than Kant
did in displacing logic and mathematics from the world of reality. But it
is not necessary to accept this more radical thesis in order to agree with
Kant that no logically necessary proposition can assert existence; and
this excludes the possibility of regarding theological propositions as
logically necessary in the way in which the hypothetical propositions of
mathematics and logic are necessary.

The traditional arguments for a Necessary God—the ontological and
the cosmological—were elaborated by Anselm and the scholastic philosophers before the concurrent and inter-related development of natural
science and of mathematics had enabled necessity and contingency to
be clearly distinguished. The necessity attributed by these arguments to
the being of God may perhaps be different from the logical necessity of
mathematical truths; but, if so, no method has been provided for testing
the truth-value of the statement that God is necessary being, and conse-
quently no way given for assigning meaning to the terms 'necessary
being' and 'God'.

If religious statements cannot be held to fall into any of these three
classes, their method of verification cannot be any of the standard
methods applicable to statements falling in these classes. Does this imply
that religious statements are not verifiable, with the corollary, according
to the verificational principle, that they have no meaning and, though
they purport to say something, are in fact nonsensical sentences? The
earlier logical positivists thought so: they would have echoed the
demand of their precursor Hume that a volume ('of divinity or school

metaphysics') which contains neither 'any abstract reasoning concerning quantity or number' nor 'any experimental reasoning concerning matter of fact and existence' should be committed to the flames; though their justification for the holocaust would be even more cogent than Hume's. The volume would not contain even 'sophistry and illusion': it would contain nothing but meaningless marks of printer's ink.

Religious statements, however, are not the only statements which are unverifiable by standard methods; moral statements have the same peculiarity. A moral principle, like the utilitarian principle that a man ought to act so as to maximize happiness, does not seem to be either a logically necessary or a logically impossible proposition. But neither does it seem to be an empirical proposition, all the attempts of ethical empiricists to give naturalistic analyses having failed. Though a tough-minded logical positivist might be prepared to say that all religious statements are sound and fury, signifying nothing, he can hardly say that of all moral statements. For moral statements have a use in guiding conduct; and if they have a use they surely have a meaning—in some sense of meaning. So the verificational principle of meaning in the hands of empiricist philosophers in the 1930s became modified either by a glossing of the term 'verification' or by a change of the verification principle into the use principle: the meaning of any statement is given by the way in which it is used.[4]

Since I wish to continue to employ verification in the restricted sense of ascertaining truth-value, I shall take the principle of meaning in this new form in which the word 'verification' has disappeared. But in removing this term from the statement of the principle, there is no desertion from the spirit of empiricism. The older verificational principle is subsumed under the new use principle: the use of an empirical statement derives from the fact that the statement is empirically verifiable, and the logical positivist thesis of the 'linguistic' character of logical and mathematical statements can be equally well, if not better, expressed in terms of their use than of their method of verification. Moreover the only way of discovering how a statement is used is by an empirical inquiry; a statement need not itself be empirically verifiable, but that it is used in a particular way is always a straightforward empirical proposition.

The meaning of any statement, then, will be taken as being given by the way it is used. The kernel for an empiricist of the problem of the nature of religious belief is to explain, in empirical terms, how a religious

[4] See L. Wittgenstein, *Philosophical Investigations* (Oxford: Blackwell. 1953), especially §§ 340, 353, 559, 560.

statement is used by a man who asserts it in order to express his religious conviction.

Since I shall argue that the primary element in this use is that the religious assertion is used as a moral assertion, I must first consider how moral assertions are used. According to the view developed by various moral philosophers since the impossibility of regarding moral statements as verifiable propositions was recognized, a moral assertion is used to express an *attitude* of the man making the assertion. It is not used to assert the proposition that he has the attitude—a verifiable psychological proposition; it is used to show forth or evince his attitude. The attitude is concerned with the action which he asserts to be right or to be his duty, or the state of affairs which he asserts to be good; it is a highly complex state, and contains elements to which various degrees of importance have been attached by moral philosophers who have tried to work out an 'ethics without propositions'. One element in the attitude is a feeling of approval towards the action; this element was taken as the fundamental one in the first attempts, and views of ethics without propositions are frequently lumped together as 'emotive' theories of ethics. But discussion of the subject during the last twenty years has made it clear, I think, that no emotion of feeling of approval is fundamental to the use of moral assertions; it may be the case that the moral asserter has some specific feeling directed on to the course of action said to be right, but this is not the most important element in his 'pro-attitude' towards the course of action: what is primary is his intention to perform the action when the occasion for it arises.

The form of ethics without propositions which I shall adopt is therefore a conative rather than an emotive theory: it makes the primary use of a moral assertion that of expressing the intention of the asserter to act in a particular sort of way specified in the assertion. A utilitarian, for example, in asserting that he ought to act so as to maximize happiness, is thereby declaring his intention to act, to the best of his ability, in accordance with the policy of utilitarianism: he is not asserting any proposition, or necessarily evincing any feeling of approval; he is subscribing to a policy of action. There will doubtless be empirical propositions which he may give as reasons for his adherence to the policy (e.g. that happiness is what all, or what most people, desire), and his having the intention will include his understanding what is meant by pursuing the policy, another empirically verifiable proposition. But there will be no specifically moral proposition which he will be asserting when he declares his intention to pursue the policy. This account is fully in accord with the spirit of empiricism, for whether or not a man has the intention of pursuing a particular behaviour policy can be empirically tested, both by observing what he does and by hearing what he replies when he is questioned about his intentions.

Not all expressions of intentions will be moral assertions: for the notion of morality to be applicable it is necessary either that the policy of action intended by the asserter should be a general policy (e.g. the policy of utilitarianism) or that it should be subsumable under a general policy which the asserter intends to follow and which he would give as the reason for his more specific intention. There are difficulties and vaguenesses in the notion of a general policy of action, but these need not concern us here. All that we require is that, when a man asserts that he ought to do so-and-so, he is using the assertion to declare that he resolves, to the best of his ability, to do so-and-so. And he will not necessarily be insincere in his assertion if he suspects, at the time of making it, that he will not have the strength of character to carry out his resolution.

The advantage this account of moral assertions has over all others, emotive non-propositional ones as well as cognitive propositional ones, is that it alone enables a satisfactory answer to be given to the question: What is the reason for my doing what I think I ought to do? The answer it gives is that, since my thinking that I ought to do the action is my intention to do it if possible, the reason why I do the action is simply that I intend to do it, if possible. On every other ethical view there will be a mysterious gap to be filled somehow between the moral judgement and the intention to act in accordance with it: there is no such gap if the primary use of a moral assertion is to declare such an intention.

Let us now consider what light this way of regarding moral assertions throws upon assertions of religious conviction. The idealist philosopher McTaggart described religion as 'an emotion resting on a conviction of a harmony between ourselves and the universe at large',[5] and many educated people at the present time would agree with him. If religion is essentially concerned with emotion, it is natural to explain the use of religious assertions on the lines of the original emotive theory of ethics and to regard them as primarily evincing religious feelings or emotions. The assertion, for example, that God is our Heavenly Father will be taken to express the asserter's feeling secure in the same way as he would feel secure in his father's presence. But explanations of religion in terms of feeling, and of religious assertions as expressions of such feelings, are usually propounded by people who stand outside any

[5] J. M. E. McTaggart, *Some Dogmas of Religion* (London: Arnold, 1906), p. 3.

religious system; they rarely satisfy those who speak from inside. Few religious men would be prepared to admit that their religion was a matter merely of feeling: feelings—of joy, of consolation, of being at one with the universe—may enter into their religion, but to evince such feelings is certainly not the primary use of their religious assertions.

This objection, however, does not seem to me to apply to treating religious assertions in the conative way in which recent moral philosophers have treated moral statements—as being primarily declarations of adherence to a policy of action, declarations of commitment to a way of life. That the way of life led by the believer is highly relevant to the sincerity of his religious conviction has been insisted upon by all the moral religions, above all, perhaps, by Christianity. 'By their fruits ye shall know them.' The view which I put forward for your consideration is that the intention of a Christian to follow a Christian way of life is not only the criterion for the sincerity of his belief in the assertions of Christianity; it is the criterion for the meaningfulness of his assertions. Just as the meaning of a moral assertion is given by its use in expressing the asserter's intention to act, so far as in him lies, in accordance with the moral principle involved, so the meaning of a religious assertion is given by its use in expressing the asserter's intention to follow a specified policy of behaviour. To say that it is belief in the dogmas of religion which is the cause of the believer's intending to behave as he does is to put the cart before the horse: it is the intention to behave which constitutes what is known as religious conviction.

But this assimilation of religious to moral assertions lays itself open to an immediate objection. When a moral assertion is taken as declaring the intention of following a policy, the form of the assertion itself makes it clear what the policy is with which the assertion is concerned. For a man to assert that a certain policy ought to be pursued, which on this view is for him to declare his intention of pursuing the policy, presupposes his understanding what it would be like for him to pursue the policy in question. I cannot resolve not to tell a lie without knowing what a lie is. But if a religious assertion is the declaration of an intention to carry out a certain policy, what policy does it specify? The religious statement itself will not explicitly refer to a policy, as does a moral statement; how then can the asserter of the statement know what is the policy concerned, and how can he intend to carry out a policy if he does not know what the policy is? I cannot intend to do something I know not what.

The reply to this criticism is that, if a religious assertion is regarded as representative of a large number of assertions of the same religious system, the body of assertions of which the particular one is a representative specimen is taken by the asserter as implicitly specifying a particular way of life. It is no more necessary for an empiricist philosopher to explain the use of a religious statement taken in isolation from other religious statements than it is for him to give a meaning to a scientific hypothesis in isolation from other scientific hypotheses. We understand scientific hypotheses, and the terms that occur in them, by virtue of the relation of the whole system of hypotheses to empirically observable facts; and it is the whole system of hypotheses, not one hypothesis in isolation, that is tested for its truth-value against experience. So there are good precedents, in the empiricist way of thinking, for considering a system of religious assertions as a whole, and for examining the way in which the whole system is used.

If we do this the fact that a system of religious assertions has a moral function can hardly be denied. For to deny it would require any passage from the assertion of a religious system to a policy of action to be mediated by a moral assertion. I cannot pass from asserting a fact, of whatever sort, to intending to perform an action, without having the hypothetical intention to intend to do the action if I assert the fact. This holds however widely fact is understood—whether as an empirical fact or as a non-empirical fact about goodness or reality. Just as the intention-to-act view of moral assertions is the only view that requires no reason for my doing what I assert to be my duty, so the similar view of religious assertions is the only one which connects them to ways of life without requiring an additional premiss. Unless a Christian's assertion that God is love (*agape*)—which I take to epitomize the assertions of the Christian religion—be taken to declare his intention to follow an agapeistic way of life, he could be asked what is the connection between the assertion and the intention, between Christian belief and Christian practice. And this question can always be asked if religious assertions are separated from conduct. Unless religious principles are moral principles, it makes no sense to speak of putting them into practice.

The way to find out what are the intentions embodied in a set of religious assertions, and hence what is the meaning of the assertions, is by discovering what principles of conduct the asserter takes the assertions to involve. These may be ascertained both by asking him questions and by seeing how he behaves, each test being supplemental to the other. If what is wanted is not the meaning of the religious assertions made by a particular man but what the set of assertions would mean were they to be made by anyone of the same religion (which I will call their *typical* meaning), all that can be done is to specify the form of behaviour which is in accordance with what one takes to be the fundamental moral principles of the religion in question. Since different people will take different views as to what these fundamental moral principles are, the typical meaning of religious assertions will be different for different people. I myself take the typical meaning of the body of Christian assertions as being given by their proclaiming intentions to follow an agapeistic way of life, and for a description of this way of life—a description in general and metaphorical terms, but an empirical description nevertheless—I should quote most of the thirteenth chapter of I Corinthians. Others may think that the Christian way of life should be described somewhat differently, and will therefore take the typical meaning of the assertions of Christianity to correspond to their different view of its fundamental moral teaching.

My contention then is that the primary use of religious assertions is to announce allegiance to a set of moral principles: without such allegiance there is no 'true religion'. This is borne out by all the accounts of what happens when an unbeliever becomes converted to a religion. The conversion is not only a change in the propositions believed— indeed there may be no specifically intellectual change at all; it is a change in the state of will. An excellent instance is C. S. Lewis's recently published account of his conversion from an idealist metaphysic—'a religion [as he says] that cost nothing'—to a theism where he faced (and he quotes George MacDonald's phrase) 'something to be neither more nor less nor other than *done*'. There was no intellectual change, for (as he says) 'there had long been an ethic (theoretically) attached to my Idealism': it was the recognition that he had to do something about it, that 'an attempt at complete virtue must be made'.[6] His conversion was a re-orientation of the will.

In assimilating religious assertions to moral assertions I do not wish to deny that there are any important differences. One is the fact already noticed that usually the behaviour policy intended is not specified by one religious assertion in isolation. Another difference is that the fundamental moral teaching of the religion is frequently given, not in abstract terms, but by means of concrete examples—of how to behave, for instance, if one meets a man set upon by thieves on the road to Jericho. A resolution to behave like the good Samaritan does not, in itself, specify the behaviour to be resolved upon in quite different circumstances. However, absence of explicitly recognized general principles does not prevent a man from acting in accordance with such principles; it only makes it

---

[6] C. S. Lewis, *Surprised by Joy* (London: Bles, 1955), pp. 198, 212–13.

more difficult for a questioner to discover upon what principles he is acting. And the difficulty is not only one way round. If moral principles are stated in the most general form, as most moral philosophers have wished to state them, they tend to become so far removed from particular courses of conduct that it is difficult, if not impossible, to give them any precise content. It may be hard to find out what exactly is involved in the imitation of Christ; but it is not very easy to discover what exactly is meant by the pursuit of Aristotle's *eudaemonia* or of Mill's *happiness*. The tests for what it is to live agapeistically are as empirical as are those for living in quest of happiness; but in each case the tests can best be expounded in terms of examples of particular situations.

A more important difference between religious and purely moral principles is that, in the higher religions at least, the conduct preached by the religion concerns not only external but also internal behaviour. The conversion involved in accepting a religion is a conversion, not only of the will, but of the heart. Christianity requires not only that you should behave towards your neighbour as if you loved him as yourself: it requires that you should love him as yourself. And though I have no doubt that the Christian concept of *agape* refers partly to external behaviour—the agapeistic behaviour for which there are external criteria—yet being filled with *agape* includes more than behaving agapeistically externally: it also includes an agapeistic frame of mind. I have said that I cannot regard the expression of a feeling of any sort as the primary element in religious assertion; but this does not imply that intention to feel in a certain way is not a primary element, nor that it cannot be used to discriminate religious declarations of policy from declarations which are merely moral. Those who say that Confucianism is a code of morals and not, properly speaking, a religion are, I think, making this discrimination.

The resolution proclaimed by a religious assertion may then be taken as referring to inner life as well as to outward conduct. And the superiority of religious conviction over the mere adoption of a moral code in securing conformity to the code arises from a religious conviction changing what the religious man wants. It may be hard enough to love your enemy, but once you have succeeded in doing so it is easy to behave lovingly towards him. But if you continue to hate him, it requires a heroic perseverance continually to behave as if you loved him. Resolutions to feel, even if they are only partly fulfilled, are powerful reinforcements of resolutions to act.

But though these qualifications may be adequate for distinguishing religious assertions from purely moral ones, they are not sufficient to discriminate between assertions belonging to one religious system and those belonging to another system in the case in which the behaviour policies, both of inner life and of outward conduct, inculcated by the two systems are identical. For instance I have said that I take the fundamental moral teaching of Christianity to be the preaching of an agapeistic way of life. But a Jew or a Buddhist may, with considerable plausibility, maintain that the fundamental moral teaching of his religion is to recommend exactly the same way of life. How then can religious assertions be distinguished into those which are Christian, those which are Jewish, those which are Buddhist, by the policies of life which they respectively recommend if, on examination, these policies turn out to be the same?

Many Christians will, no doubt, behave in a specifically Christian manner in that they will follow ritual practices which are Christian and neither Jewish nor Buddhist. But though following certain practices may well be the proper test for membership of a particular religious society, a church, not even the most ecclesiastically-minded Christian will regard participation in a ritual as the fundamental characteristic of a Christian way of life. There must be some more important difference between an agapeistically policied Christian and an agapeistically policied Jew than that the former attends a church and the latter a synagogue.

The really important difference, I think, is to be found in the fact that the intentions to pursue the behaviour policies, which may be the same for different religions, are associated with thinking of different *stories* (or sets of stories). By a story I shall here mean a proposition or set of propositions which are straightforwardly empirical propositions capable of empirical test and which are thought of by the religious man in connection with his resolution to follow the way of life advocated by his religion. On the assumption that the ways of life advocated by Christianity and by Buddhism are essentially the same, it will be the fact that the intention to follow this way of life is associated in the mind of a Christian with thinking of one set of stories (the Christian stories) while it is associated in the mind of a Buddhist with thinking of another set of stories (the Buddhist stories) which enables a Christian assertion to be distinguished from a Buddhist one.

A religious assertion will, therefore, have a propositional element which is lacking in a purely moral assertion, in that it will refer to a story as well as to an intention. The reference to the story is not an assertion of the story taken as a matter of empirical fact: it is a telling of the story, or an alluding to the story, in the way in which one can tell, or allude to, the story of a novel with which one is acquainted. To assert the whole set of assertions of the Christian religion is both to tell the Christian doctrinal story and to confess allegiance to the Christian way of life.

The story, I have said, is a set of empirical propositions, and the language expressing the story is given a meaning by the standard method of understanding how the story-statements can be verified. The empirical story-statements will vary from Christian to Christian; the doctrines of Christianity are capable of different empirical interpretations, and Christians will differ in the interpretations they put upon the doctrines. But the interpretations will all be in terms of empirical propositions. Take, for example, the doctrine of Justification by means of the Atonement. Matthew Arnold imagined it in terms of

a sort of infinitely magnified and improved Lord Shaftesbury, with a race of vile offenders to deal with, whom his natural goodness would incline him to let off, only his sense of justice will not allow it; then a younger Lord Shaftesbury, on the scale of his father and very dear to him, who might live in grandeur and splendour if he liked, but who prefers to leave his home, to go and live among the race of offenders, and to be put to an ignominious death, on condition that his merits shall be counted against their demerits, and that his father's goodness shall be restrained no longer from taking effect, but any offender shall be admitted to the benefit of it on simply pleading the satisfaction made by the son;—and then, finally, a third Lord Shaftesbury, still on the same high scale, who keeps very much in the background, and works in a very occult manner, but very efficaciously nevertheless, and who is busy in applying everywhere the benefits of the son's satisfaction and the father's goodness.[7]

Arnold's 'parable of the three Lord Shaftesburys' got him into a lot of trouble: he was 'indignantly censured' (as he says) for wounding 'the feelings of the religious community by turning into ridicule an august doctrine, the object of their solemn faith'.[8] But there is no other account of the Anselmian doctrine of the Atonement that I have read which puts it in so morally favourable a light. Be that as it may, the only way in which the doctrine can be understood verificationally is in terms of human beings—mythological beings, it may be, who never existed, but who nevertheless would have been empirically observable had they existed.

For it is not necessary, on my view, for the asserter of a religious assertion to believe in the truth of the story involved in the assertions:

[7] Matthew Arnold, *Literature and Dogma* (London: Smith, Elder, and Co., 1873), pp. 306–7.

[8] Matthew Arnold, *God and the Bible* (London: Smith, Elder, and Co., 1875), pp. 18–19.

what is necessary is that the story should be entertained in thought, i.e. that the statement of the story should be understood as having a meaning. I have secured this by requiring that the story should consist of empirical propositions. Educated Christians of the present day who attach importance to the doctrine of the Atonement certainly do not believe an empirically testable story in Matthew Arnold's or any other form. But it is the fact that entertainment in thought of this and other Christian stories forms the context in which Christian resolutions are made which serves to distinguish Christian assertions from those made by adherents of another religion, or of no religion.

What I am calling a *story* Matthew Arnold called a *parable* and a *fairy-tale*. Other terms which might be used are *allegory*, *fable*, *tale*, *myth*. I have chosen the word 'story' as being the most neutral term, implying neither that the story is believed nor that it is disbelieved. The Christian stories include straightforward historical statements about the life and death of Jesus of Nazareth; a Christian (unless he accepts the unplausible Christ-myth theory) will naturally believe some or all of these. Stories about the beginning of the world and of the Last Judgment as facts of past or of future history are believed by many unsophisticated Christians. But my contention is that belief in the truth of the Christian stories is not the proper criterion for deciding whether or not an assertion is a Christian one. A man is not, I think, a professing Christian unless he both proposes to live according to Christian moral principles and associates his intention with thinking of Christian stories; but he need not believe that the empirical propositions presented by the stories correspond to empirical fact.

But if the religious stories need not be believed, what function do they fulfil in the complex state of mind and behaviour known as having a religious belief? How is entertaining the story related to resolving to pursue a certain way of life? My answer is that the relation is a psychological and causal one. It is an empirical psychological fact that many people find it easier to resolve upon and to carry through a course of action which is contrary to their natural inclinations if this policy is associated in their minds with certain stories. And in many people the psychological link is not appreciably weakened by the fact that the story associated with the behaviour policy is not believed. Next to the Bible and the Prayer Book the most influential work in English Christian religious life has been a book whose stories are frankly recognized as fictitious—Bunyan's *Pilgrim's Progress*; and some of the most influential works in setting the moral tone of my generation were the novels of Dostoevsky. It is completely untrue, as a matter of psychological fact, to think that the only intellectual considerations which affect action are beliefs: it is *all* the thoughts of a man that determine his behaviour; and these include his phantasies, imaginations, ideas of what he would wish to be and do, as well as the propositions which he believes to be true.

This important psychological fact, a commonplace to all students of the influence of literature upon life, has not been given sufficient weight by theologians and philosophers of religion. It has not been altogether ignored; for instance, the report of the official Commission on Doctrine in the Church of England, published in 1938, in a section entitled 'On the application to the Creeds of the conception of symbolic truth', says: 'Statements affirming particular facts may be found to have value as pictorial expressions of spiritual truths, even though the supposed facts themselves did not actually happen. ... It is not therefore of necessity illegitimate to accept and affirm particular clauses of the Creeds while understanding them in this symbolic sense.'[9] But the patron saint whom I claim for my way of thinking is that great but neglected Christian thinker Matthew Arnold, whose parable of the three Lord Shaftesburys is a perfect example of what I take a religious story to be. Arnold's philosophy of religion has suffered from his striking remarks being lifted from their context: his description of religion as *morality touched by emotion* does not adequately express his view of the part played by imagination in religion. Arnold's main purpose in his religious writings was that of 'cementing the alliance between the imagination and con- duct'[10] by regarding the propositional element in Christianity as 'literature' rather than as 'dogma'. Arnold was not prepared to carry through his programme completely; he regarded *the Eternal not our- selves that makes for righteousness* more dogmatically than fictionally. But his keen insight into the imaginative and poetic element in religious belief as well as his insistence that religion is primarily concerned with guiding conduct make him a profound philosopher of religion as well as a Christian teacher full of the 'sweet reasonableness' he attributed to Christ.

> *God's wisdom and God's goodness!*—Ay, but fools
> Mis-define these till God knows them no more.
> *Wisdom and goodness, they are God!*—what schools
> Have yet so much as heard this simpler lore?[11]

---

[9] *Doctrine in the Church of England* (London: S.P.C.K., 1938), pp. 37–8.
[10] Arnold, *God and the Bible*, p. xiii.
[11] From Matthew Arnold's sonnet 'The Divinity' (1867).

To return to our philosophizing. My contention that the propositional element in religious assertions consists of stories interpreted as straightforwardly empirical propositions which are not, generally speaking, believed to be true has the great advantage of imposing no restriction whatever upon the empirical interpretation which can be put upon the stories. The religious man may interpret the stories in the way which assists him best in carrying out the behaviour policies of his religion. He can, for example, think of the three persons of the Trinity in visual terms, as did the great Christian painters, or as talking to one another, as in the poems of St. John of the Cross. And since he need not believe the stories he can interpret them in ways which are not consistent with one another. It is disastrous for anyone to try to believe empirical propositions which are mutually inconsistent, for the courses of action appropriate to inconsistent beliefs are not compatible. The needs of practical life require that the body of believed propositions should be purged of inconsistency. But there is no action which is appropriate to thinking of a proposition without believing it; thinking of it may, as I have said, produce a state of mind in which it is easier to carry out a particular course of action, but the connection is causal: there is no intrinsic connection between the thought and the action. Indeed a story may provide better support for a long-range policy of action if it contains inconsistencies. The Christian set of stories, for example, contains both a pantheistic sub-set of stories in which everything is a part of God, and a dualistic Manichaean sub-set of stories well represented by St. Ignatius Loyola's allegory of a conflict between the forces of righteousness under the banner of Christ and the forces of darkness under Lucifer's banner. And the Marxist religion's set of stories contains both stories about an inevitable perfect society and stories about a class war. In the case of both religions the first sub-set of stories provides confidence, the second spurs to action.

There is one story common to all the moral theistic religions which has proved of great psychological value in enabling religious men to persevere in carrying out their religious behaviour policies—the story that in so doing they are doing the will of God. And here it may look as if there is an intrinsic connection between the story and the policy of conduct. But even when the story is literally believed, when it is believed that there is a magnified Lord Shaftesbury who commands or desires the carrying out of the behaviour policy, that in itself is no reason for carrying out the policy: it is necessary also to have the intention of doing what the magnified Lord Shaftesbury commands or desires. But the intention to do what a person commands or desires, irrespective of what this command or desire may be, is no part of a higher religion; it is when the religious man finds that what the magnified Lord Shaftesbury commands or desires accords with his own moral judgement that he decides to obey or to accede to it. But this is no new decision, for his own moral judgement is a decision to carry out a behaviour policy; all that is happening is that he is describing his old decision in a new way. In religious conviction the resolution to follow a way of life is primary; it is not derived from believing, still less from thinking of, any empirical story. The story may psychologically support the resolution, but it does not logically justify it.

In this lecture I have been sparing in my use of the term 'religious belief' (although it occurs in the title), preferring instead to speak of religious assertions and of religious conviction. This was because for me the fundamental problem is that of the meaning of statements used to make religious assertions, and I have accordingly taken my task to be that of explaining the use of such assertions, in accordance with the principle that meaning is to be found by ascertaining use. In disentangling the elements of this use I have discovered nothing which can be called 'belief' in the senses of this word applicable either to an empirical or to a logically necessary proposition. A religious assertion, for me, is the assertion of an intention to carry out a certain behaviour policy, subsumable under a sufficiently general principle to be a moral one, together with the implicit or explicit statement, but not the assertion, of certain stories. Neither the assertion of the intention nor the reference to the stories includes belief in its ordinary senses. But in avoiding the term 'belief' I have had to widen the term 'assertion', since I do not pretend that either the behaviour policy intended or the stories entertained are adequately specified by the sentences used in making isolated religious assertions. So assertion has been extended to include elements not explicitly expressed in the verbal form of the assertion. If we drop the linguistic expression of the assertion altogether the remainder is what may be called religious belief. Like moral belief, it is not a species of ordinary belief, of belief in a proposition. A moral belief is an intention to behave in a certain way: a religious belief is an intention to behave in a certain way (a moral belief) together with the entertainment of certain stories associated with the intention in the mind of the believer. This solution of the problem of religious belief seems to me to do justice both to the empiricists's demand that meaning must be tied to empirical use and to the religious man's claim for his religious beliefs to be taken seriously.

Seriously, it will be retorted, but not objectively. If a man's religion is all a matter of following the way of life he sets before himself and of strengthening his determination to follow it by imagining exemplary fairy tales, it is purely subjective: his religion is all in terms of his own private ideals and of his own private imaginations. How can he even try to convert others to his religion if there is nothing objective to convert them to? How can he argue in its defence if there is no religious proposition which he believes, nothing which he takes to be the fundamental truth about the universe? And is it of any public interest what mental techniques he uses to bolster up his will? Discussion about religion must be more than the exchange of autobiographies.

But we are all social animals; we are all members one of another. What is profitable to one man in helping him to persevere in the way of life he has decided upon may well be profitable to another man who is trying to follow a similar way of life; and to pass on information that might prove useful would be approved by almost every morality. The autobiography of one man may well have an influence upon the life of another, if their basic wants are similar.

But suppose that these are dissimilar, and that the two men propose to conduct their lives on quite different fundamental principles. Can there be any reasonable discussion between them? This is the problem that has faced the many moral philosophers recently who have been forced, by their examination of the nature of thinking, into holding non-propositional theories of ethics. All I will here say is that to hold that the adoption of a set of moral principles is a matter of the personal decision to live according to these principles does not imply that beliefs as to what are the practical consequences of following such principles are not relevant to the decision. An intention, it is true, cannot be logically based upon anything except another intention. But in considering what conduct to intend to practise, it is highly relevant whether or not the consequences of practising that conduct are such as one would intend to secure. As R. M. Hare has well said, an ultimate decision to accept a way of life, 'far from being arbitrary, ... would be the most well-founded of decisions, because it would be based upon a consideration of everything upon which it could possibly be founded'.[12] And in this consideration there is a place for every kind of rational argument.

Whatever may be the case with other religions Christianity has always been a personal religion demanding personal commitment to a personal way of life. In the words of another Oxford philosopher, 'the questions

[12] R. M. Hare, *The Language of Morals* (Oxford: Clarendon Press, 1952), p. 69.

"What shall I do?" and "What moral principles should I adopt?" must be answered by each man for himself'.[13] Nowell-Smith takes this as part of the meaning of morality: whether or not this is so, I am certain that it is of the very essence of the Christian religion.

[13] P. H. Nowell-Smith, *Ethics* (Harmondsworth: Penguin, 1954), p. 320.

V

EVIL AND OMNIPOTENCE

J. L. MACKIE

THE traditional arguments for the existence of God have been fairly thoroughly criticized by philosophers. But the theologian can, if he wishes, accept this criticism. He can admit that no rational proof of God's existence is possible. And he can still retain all that is essential to his position, by holding that God's existence is known in some other, non-rational way. I think, however, that a more telling criticism can be made by way of the traditional problem of evil. Here it can be shown, not that religious beliefs lack rational support, but that they are positively irrational, that the several parts of the essential theological doctrine are inconsistent with one another, so that the theologian can maintain his position as a whole only by a much more extreme rejection of reason than in the former case. He must now be prepared to believe, not merely what cannot be proved, but what can be *disproved* from other beliefs that he also holds.

The problem of evil, in the sense in which I shall be using the phrase, is a problem only for someone who believes that there is a God who is both omnipotent and wholly good. And it is a logical problem, the problem of clarifying and reconciling a number of beliefs: it is not a scientific problem that might be solved by further observations, or a practical problem that might be solved by a decision or an action. These points are obvious; I mention them only because they are sometimes ignored by theologians, who sometimes parry a statement of the problem with such remarks as 'Well, can you solve the problem yourself?' or 'This is a mystery which may be revealed to us later' or 'Evil is something to be faced and overcome, not to be merely discussed.'

In its simplest form the problem is this: God is omnipotent; God is wholly good; and yet evil exists. There seems to be some contradiction between these three propositions, so that if any two of them were true the third would be false. But at the same time all three are essential parts of most theological positions: the theologian, it seems, at once *must*

From *Mind*, 64 (1955), 200–12. Reprinted by permission of the author and the Editor of *Mind*.

adhere and *cannot consistently* adhere to all three. (The problem does not arise only for theists, but I shall discuss it in the form in which it presents itself for ordinary theism.)

However, the contradiction does not arise immediately; to show it we need some additional premisses, or perhaps some quasi-logical rules connecting the terms 'good', 'evil', and 'omnipotent'. These additional principles are that good is opposed to evil, in such a way that a good thing always eliminates evil as far as it can, and that there are no limits to what an omnipotent thing can do. From these it follows that a good omnipotent thing eliminates evil completely, and then the propositions that a good omnipotent thing exists, and that evil exists, are incompatible.

A. ADEQUATE SOLUTIONS

Now once the problem is fully stated it is clear that it can be solved, in the sense that the problem will not arise if one gives up at least one of the propositions that constitute it. If you are prepared to say that God is not wholly good, or not quite omnipotent, or that evil does not exist, or that good is not opposed to the kind of evil that exists, or that there are limits to what an omnipotent thing can do, then the problem of evil will not arise for you.

There are, then, quite a number of adequate solutions of the problem of evil, and some of these have been adopted, or almost adopted, by various thinkers. For example, a few have been prepared to deny God's omnipotence, and rather more have been prepared to keep the term 'omnipotence' but severely to restrict its meaning, recording quite a number of things that an omnipotent being cannot do. Some have said that evil is an illusion, perhaps because they held that the whole world of temporal, changing things is an illusion, and that what we call evil belongs only to this world, or perhaps because they held that although temporal things *are* much as we see them, those that we call evil are not really evil. Some have said that what we call evil is merely the privation of good, that evil in a positive sense, evil that would really be opposed to good, does not exist. Many have agreed with Pope that disorder is harmony not understood, and that partial evil is universal good. Whether any of these views is *true* is, of course, another question. But each of them gives an adequate solution of the problem of evil in the sense that if you accept it this problem does not arise for you, though you may, of course, have *other* problems to face.

But often enough these adequate solutions are only *almost* adopted. The thinkers who restrict God's power, but keep the term 'omnipotence', may reasonably be suspected of thinking, in other contexts, that his power is really unlimited. Those who say that evil is an illusion may also be thinking, inconsistently, that this illusion is itself an evil. Those who say that 'evil' is merely privation of good may also be thinking, inconsistently, that privation of good is an evil. (The fallacy here is akin to some forms of the 'naturalistic fallacy' in ethics, where some think, for example, that 'good' is just what contributes to evolutionary progress, and that evolutionary progress is itself good.) If Pope meant what he said in the first line of his couplet, that 'disorder' is only harmony not understood, the 'partial evil' of the second line must, for consistency, mean 'that which, taken in isolation, falsely appears to be evil', but it would more naturally mean 'that which, in isolation, really is evil'. The second line, in fact, hesitates between two views, that 'partial evil' isn't really evil, since only the universal quality is real, and that 'partial evil' is really an evil, but only a little one.

In addition, therefore, to adequate solutions, we must recognize unsatisfactory inconsistent solutions, in which there is only a half-hearted or temporary rejection of one of the propositions which together constitute the problem. In these, one of the constituent propositions is explicitly rejected, but it is covertly re-asserted or assumed elsewhere in the system.

B. FALLACIOUS SOLUTIONS

Besides these half-hearted solutions, which explicitly reject but implicitly assert one of the constituent propositions, there are definitely fallacious solutions which explicitly maintain all the constituent propositions, but implicitly reject at least one of them in the course of the argument that explains away the problem of evil.

There are, in fact, many so-called solutions which purport to remove the contradiction without abandoning any of its constituent propositions. These must be fallacious, as we can see from the very statement of the problem, but it is not so easy to see in each case precisely where the fallacy lies. I suggest that in all cases the fallacy has the general form suggested above: in order to solve the problem one (or perhaps more) of its constituent propositions is given up, but in such a way that it appears to have been retained, and can therefore be asserted without qualification in other contexts. Sometimes there is a further complication: the supposed solution moves to and fro between, say, two of the constituent propositions, at one point asserting the first of these but covertly abandoning the second, at another point asserting the second but covertly abandoning the first. These fallacious solutions often turn upon some equivocation with the words 'good' and 'evil', or upon some vagueness about the way in which good and evil are opposed to one another, or about how much is meant by 'omnipotence'. I propose to examine some of these so-called solutions, and to exhibit their fallacies in detail. Incidentally, I shall also be considering whether an adequate solution could be reached by a minor modification of one or more of the constituent propositions, which would, however, still satisfy all the essential requirements of ordinary theism.

1. 'Good cannot exist without evil' or 'Evil is necessary as a counterpart to good.'

It is sometimes suggested that evil is necessary as a counterpart to good, that if there were no evil there could be no good either, and that this solves the problem of evil. It is true that it points to an answer to the question 'Why should there be evil?' But it does so only by qualifying some of the propositions that constitute the problem.

First, it sets a limit to what God can do, saying that God *cannot* create good without simultaneously creating evil, and this means either that God is not omnipotent or that there are *some* limits to what an omnipotent thing can do. It may be replied that these limits are always presupposed, that omnipotence has never meant the power to do what is logically impossible, and on the present view the existence of good without evil would be a logical impossibility. This interpretation of omnipotence may, indeed, be accepted as a modification of our original account which does not reject anything that is essential to theism, and I shall in general assume it in the subsequent discussion. It is, perhaps, the most common theistic view, but I think that some theists at least have maintained that God can do what is logically impossible. Many theists, at any rate, have held that logic itself is created or laid down by God, that logic is the way in which God arbitrarily chooses to think. (This is, of course, parallel to the ethical view that morally right actions are those which God arbitrarily chooses to command, and the two views encounter similar difficulties.) And *this* account of logic is clearly inconsistent with the view that God is bound by logical necessities—unless it is possible for an omnipotent being to bind himself, an issue which we shall consider later, when we come to the Paradox of Omnipotence. This solution of the problem of evil cannot, therefore, be consistently adopted along with the view that logic is itself created by God.

But, secondly, this solution denies that evil is opposed to good in our original sense. If good and evil are counterparts, a good thing will not 'eliminate evil as far as it can'. Indeed, this view suggests that good and evil are not strictly qualities of things at all. Perhaps the suggestion is that good and evil are related in much the same way as great and small. Certainly, when the term 'great' is used relatively as a condensation of 'greater than so-and-so', and 'small' is used correspondingly, greatness and smallness are counterparts and cannot exist without each other. But in this sense greatness is not a quality, not an intrinsic feature of anything; and it would be absurd to think of a movement in favour of greatness and against smallness in this sense. Such a movement would be self-defeating, since relative greatness can be promoted only by a simultaneous promotion of relative smallness. I feel sure that no theists would be content to regard God's goodness as analogous to this—as if what he supports were not the *good* but the *better*, and as if he had the paradoxical aim that all things should be better than other things.

This point is obscured by the fact that 'great' and 'small' seem to have an absolute as well as a relative sense. I cannot discuss here whether there is absolute magnitude or not, but if there is, there could be an absolute sense for 'great', it could mean of at least a certain size, and it would make sense to speak of all things getting bigger, of a universe that was expanding all over, and therefore it would make sense to speak of promoting greatness. But in *this* sense great and small are not logically necessary counterparts : either quality could exist without the other. There would be no logical impossibility in everything's being small or in everything's being great.

Neither in the absolute nor in the relative sense, then, of 'great' and 'small' do these terms provide an analogy of the sort that would be needed to support this solution of the problem of evil. In neither case are greatness and smallness *both* necessary counterparts *and* mutually opposed forces or possible objects for support or attack.

It may be replied that good and evil are necessary counterparts in the same way as any quality and its logical opposite : redness can occur, it is suggested, only if non-redness also occurs. But unless evil is merely the privation of good, they are not logical opposites, and some further argument would be needed to show that they are counterparts in the same way as genuine logical opposites. Let us assume that this could be given. There is still doubt of the correctness of the metaphysical principle that a quality must have a real opposite : I suggest that it is not really impossible that everything should be, say, red, that the truth is merely that if everything were red we should not notice redness, and so we should have no word 'red'; we observe and give names to qualities only if they have real opposites. If so, the principle that a term must have an opposite would belong only to our language or to our thought, and would not be an ontological principle, and, correspondingly, the rule that good cannot exist without evil would not state a logical necessity of a sort that God would just have to put up with. God might have made everything good, though *we* should not have noticed it if he had.

But, finally, even if we concede that this *is* an ontological principle, it will provide a solution for the problem of evil only if one is prepared to say, 'Evil exists, but only just enough evil to serve as the counterpart of good.' I doubt whether any theist will accept this. After all, the *ontological* requirement that non-redness should occur would be satisfied even if all the universe, except for a minute speck, were red, and, if there were a corresponding requirement for evil as a counterpart to good, a minute dose of evil would presumably do. But theists are not usually willing to say, in all contexts, that all the evil that occurs is a minute and necessary dose.

2. 'Evil is necessary as a means to good.'

It is sometimes suggested that evil is necessary for good not as a counterpart but as a means. In its simple form this has little plausibility as a solution of the problem of evil, since it obviously implies a severe restriction of God's power. It would be a *causal* law that you cannot have a certain end without a certain means, so that if God has to introduce evil as a means to good, he must be subject to at least some causal laws. This certainly conflicts with what a theist normally means by omnipotence. This view of God as limited by causal laws also conflicts with the view that causal laws are themselves made by God, which is more widely held than the corresponding view about the laws of logic. This conflict would, indeed, be resolved if it were possible for an omnipotent being to bind himself, and this possibility has still to be considered. Unless a favourable answer can be given to this question, the suggestion that evil is necessary as a means to good solves the problem of evil only by denying one of its constituent propositions, either that God is omnipotent or that 'omnipotent' means what it says.

3. 'The universe is better with some evil in it than it could be if there were no evil.'

Much more important is a solution which at first seems to be a mere variant of the previous one, that evil may contribute to the goodness of a whole in which it is found, so that the universe as a whole is better as it is, with some evil in it, than it would be if there were no evil. This solution may be developed in either of two ways. It may be supported by an aesthetic analogy, by the fact that contrasts heighten beauty, that in a musical work, for example, there may occur discords which somehow add to the beauty of the work as a whole. Alternatively, it may be worked out in connection with the notion of progress, that the best possible organization of the universe will not be static, but progressive, that the gradual overcoming of evil by good is really a finer thing than would be the eternal unchallenged supremacy of good.

In either case, this solution usually starts from the assumption that the evil whose existence gives rise to the problem of evil is primarily what is called physical evil, that is to say, pain. In Hume's rather half-hearted presentation of the problem of evil, the evils that he stresses are pain and disease, and those who reply to him argue that the existence of pain and disease makes possible the existence of sympathy, bene-volence, heroism, and the gradually successful struggle of doctors and reformers to overcome these evils. In fact, theists often seize the oppor-tunity to accuse those who stress the problem of evil of taking a low, materialistic view of good and evil, equating these with pleasure and pain, and of ignoring the more spiritual goods which can arise in the struggle against evils.

But let us see exactly what is being done here. Let us call pain and misery 'first order evil' or 'evil (1)'. What contrasts with this, namely, pleasure and happiness, will be called 'first order good' or 'good (1)'. Distinct from this is 'second order good' or 'good (2)' which somehow emerges in a complex situation in which evil (1) is a necessary com-ponent—logically, not merely causally, necessary. (Exactly *how* it emerges does not matter: in the crudest version of this solution good (2) is simply the heightening of happiness by the contrast with misery, in other versions it includes sympathy with suffering, heroism in facing danger, and the gradual decrease of first order evil and increase of first order good.) It is also being assumed that second order good is more important than first order good or evil, in particular that it more than outweighs the first order evil it involves.

Now this is a particularly subtle attempt to solve the problem of evil. It defends God's goodness and omnipotence on the ground that (on a sufficiently long view) this is the best of all logically possible worlds, because it includes the important second order goods, and yet it admits that real evils, namely first order evils, exist. But does it still hold that good and evil are opposed? Not, clearly, in the sense that we set out originally: good does not tend to eliminate evil in general. Instead, we have a modified, a more complex pattern. First order good (e.g. happi-ness) *contrasts with* first order evil (e.g. misery): these two are opposed in a fairly mechanical way; some second order goods (e.g. benevolence) try to maximize first order good and minimise first order evil; but God's goodness is not this, it is rather the will to maximize *second* order good. We might, therefore, call God's goodness an example of a third order goodness, or good (3). While this account is different from our original one, it might well be held to be an improvement on it, to give a more accurate description of the way in which good is opposed to evil, and to be consistent with the essential theist position.

There might, however, be several objections to this solution.

First, some might argue that such qualities as benevolence—and *a fortiori* the third order goodness which promotes benevolence—have a merely derivative value, that they are not higher sorts of good, but merely means to good (1), that is, to happiness, so that it would be absurd for God to keep misery in existence in order to make possible the virtues of benevolence, heroism, etc. The theist who adopts the present solution must, of course, deny this, but he can do so with some plausibility, so I should not press this objection.

Secondly, it follows from this solution that God is not in our sense benevolent or sympathetic: he is not concerned to minimize evil (1), but only to promote good (2), and this might be a disturbing conclusion for some theists.

But, thirdly, the fatal objection is this. Our analysis shows clearly the possibility of the existence of a *second* order evil, an evil (2) contrasting with good (2) as evil (1) contrasts with good (1). This would include malevolence, cruelty, callousness, cowardice, and states in which good (1) is decreasing and evil (1) increasing. And just as good (2) is held to be the important kind of good, the kind that God is concerned to promote, so evil (2) will, by analogy, be the important kind of evil, the kind which God, if he were wholly good and omnipotent, would eliminate. And yet evil (2) plainly exists, and indeed most theists (in other contexts) stress its existence more than that of evil (1). We should, therefore, state the problem of evil in terms of second order evil, and against this form of the problem the present solution is useless.

An attempt might be made to use this solution again, at a higher level, to explain the occurrence of evil (2): indeed the next main solution that we shall examine does just this, with the help of some new notions. Without any fresh notions, such a solution would have little plausibility: for example, we could hardly say that the really important good was a good (3), such as the increase of benevolence in proportion to cruelty, which logically required for its occurrence the occurrence of some second order evil. But even if evil (2) could be explained in this way, it is fairly clear that there would be third order evils contrasting with this third order good: and we should be well on the way to an infinite regress, where the solution of a problem of evil, stated in terms of evil (*n*), indicated the existence of an evil (*n*+1), and a further problem to be solved.

4. 'Evil is due to human free will.'

Perhaps the most important proposed solution of the problem of evil is that evil is not to be ascribed to God at all, but to the independent actions of human beings, supposed to have been endowed by God with freedom of the will. This solution may be combined with the preceding one: first order evil (e.g. pain) may be justified as a logically necessary component in second order good (e.g. sympathy) while second order evil (e.g. cruelty) is not *justified*, but is so ascribed to human beings that God cannot be held responsible for it. This combination evades my third criticism of the preceding solution.

The free will solution also involves the preceding solution at a higher level. To explain why a wholly good God gave men free will although it would lead to some important evils, it must be argued that it is better on the whole that men should act freely, and sometimes err, than that they should be innocent automata, acting rightly in a wholly determined way. Freedom, that is to say, is now treated as a third order good, and as being more valuable than second order goods (such as sympathy and heroism) would be if they were deterministically produced, and it is being assumed that second order evils, such as cruelty, are logically necessary accompaniments of freedom, just as pain is a logically necessary pre-condition of sympathy.

I think that this solution is unsatisfactory primarily because of the incoherence of the notion of freedom of the will: but I cannot discuss this topic adequately here, although some of my criticisms will touch upon it.

First I should query the assumption that second order evils are logically necessary accompaniments of freedom. I should ask this: if God has made men such that in their free choices they sometimes prefer what is good and sometimes what is evil, why could he not have made men such that they always freely choose the good? If there is no logical impossibility in a man's freely choosing the good on one, or on several occasions, there cannot be a logical impossibility in his freely choosing the good on every occasion. God was not, then, faced with a choice between making innocent automata and making beings who, in acting freely, would sometimes go wrong: there was open to him the obviously better possibility of making beings who would act freely but always go

right. Clearly, his failure to avail himself of this possibility is inconsistent with his being both omnipotent and wholly good.

If it is replied that this objection is absurd, that the making of some
wrong choices is logically necessary for freedom, it would seem that
'freedom' must here mean complete randomness or indeterminacy, including randomness with regard to the alternatives good and evil, in
other words that men's choices and consequent actions can be 'free'
only if they are not determined by their characters. Only on this assumption can God escape the responsibility for men's actions; for if he made
them as they are, but did not determine their wrong choices, this can
only be because the wrong choices are not determined by men as they
are. But then if freedom is randomness, how can it be a characteristic of
will? And, still more, how can it be the most important good? What
value or merit would there be in free choices if these were random
actions which were not determined by the nature of the agent?

I conclude that to make this solution plausible two different senses of
'freedom' must be confused, one sense which will justify the view that
freedom is a third order good, more valuable than other goods would
be without it, and another sense, sheer randomness, to prevent us from
ascribing to God a decision to make men such that they sometimes go
wrong when he might have made them such that they would always
freely go right.

This criticism is sufficient to dispose of this solution. But besides this
there is a fundamental difficulty in the notion of an omnipotent God
creating men with free will, for if men's wills are really free this must
mean that even God cannot control them, that is, that God is no longer
omnipotent. It may be objected that God's gift of freedom to men does
not mean that he *cannot* control their wills, but that he always *refrains*
from controlling their wills. But why, we may ask, should God refrain
from controlling evil wills? Why should he not leave men free to will
rightly, but intervene when he sees them beginning to will wrongly?
If God could do this, but does not, and if he is wholly good, the only
explanation could be that even a wrong free act of will is not really
evil, that its freedom is a value which outweighs its wrongness, so that
there would be a loss of value if God took away the wrongness and the
freedom together. But this is utterly opposed to what theists say about
sin in other contexts. The present solution of the problem of evil, then,
can be maintained only in the form that God has made men so free
that he *cannot* control their wills.

This leads us to what I call the Paradox of Omnipotence: can an
omnipotent being make things which he cannot subsequently control?

Or, what is practically equivalent to this, can an omnipotent being make rules which then bind himself? (These are practically equivalent because any such rules could be regarded as setting certain things beyond his control and *vice versa*.) The second of these formulations is relevant to the suggestions that we have already met, that an omnipotent God creates the rules of logic or causal laws, and is then bound by them.

It is clear that this is a paradox: the questions cannot be answered satisfactorily either in the affirmative or in the negative. If we answer 'Yes', it follows that if God actually makes things which he cannot control, or makes rules which bind himself, he is not omnipotent once he has made them: there are *then* things which he cannot do. But if we answer 'No', we are immediately asserting that there are things which he cannot do, that is to say that he is already not omnipotent.

It cannot be replied that the question which sets this paradox is not a proper question. It would make perfectly good sense to say that a human mechanic has made a machine which he cannot control: if there is any difficulty about the question it lies in the notion of omnipotence itself.

This, incidentally, shows that although we have approached this paradox from the free will theory, it is equally a problem for a theological determinist. No one thinks that machines have free will, yet they may well be beyond the control of their makers. The determinist might reply that anyone who makes anything determines its ways of acting, and so determines its subsequent behaviour: even the human mechanic does this by his *choice* of materials and structure for his machine, though he does not know all about either of these: the mechanic thus determines, though he may not foresee, his machine's actions. And since God is omniscient, and since his creation of things is total, he both determines and foresees the ways in which his creatures will act. We may grant this, but it is beside the point. The question is not whether God *originally* determined the future actions of his creatures, but whether he can *subsequently* control their actions, or whether he was able in his original creation to put things beyond his subsequent control. Even on determinist principles the answers 'Yes' and 'No' are equally irreconcilable with God's omnipotence.

Before suggesting a solution of this paradox, I would point out that there is a parallel Paradox of Sovereignty. Can a legal sovereign make a law restricting its own future legislative power? For example, could the British parliament make a law forbidding any future parliament to socialize banking, and also forbidding the future repeal of this law itself? Or could the British parliament, which was legally sovereign in

Australia in, say, 1899, pass a valid law, or series of laws, which made it no longer sovereign in 1933? Again, neither the affirmative nor the negative answer is really satisfactory. If we were to answer 'Yes', we should be admitting the validity of a law which, if it were actually made, would mean that parliament was no longer sovereign. If we were to answer 'No', we should be admitting that there is a law, not logically absurd, which parliament cannot validly make, that is, that parliament is not now a legal sovereign. This paradox can be solved in the following way. We should distinguish between first order laws, that is laws governing the actions of individuals and bodies other than the legislature, and second order laws, that is laws about laws, laws governing the actions of the legislature itself. Correspondingly, we should distinguish between two orders of sovereignty, first order sovereignty (sovereignty (1)) which is unlimited authority to make first order laws, and second order sovereignty (sovereignty (2)) which is unlimited authority to make second order laws. If we say that parliament is sovereign we might mean that any parliament at any time has sovereignty (1), or we might mean that parliament has both sovereignty (1) and sovereignty (2) at present, but we cannot without contradiction mean both that the present parliament has sovereignty (2) and that every parliament at every time has sovereignty (1), for if the present parliament has sovereignty (2) it may use it to take away the sovereignty (1) of later parliaments. What the paradox shows is that we cannot ascribe to any continuing institution legal sovereignty in an inclusive sense.

The analogy between omnipotence and sovereignty shows that the paradox of omnipotence can be solved in a similar way. We must distinguish between first order omnipotence (omnipotence (1)), that is unlimited power to act, and second order omnipotence (omnipotence (2)), that is unlimited power to determine what powers to act things shall have. Then we could consistently say that God all the time has omnipotence (1), but if so no beings at any time have powers to act independently of God. Or we could say that God at one time had omnipotence (2), and used it to assign independent powers to act to certain things, so that God thereafter did not have omnipotence (1). But what the paradox shows is that we cannot consistently ascribe to any continuing being omnipotence in an inclusive sense.

An alternative solution to this paradox would be simply to deny that God is a continuing being, that any times can be assigned to his actions at all. But on this assumption (which also has difficulties of its own) no meaning can be given to the assertion that God made men with wills so free that he could not control them. The paradox of omnipotence can be avoided by putting God outside time, but the free will solution of the problem of evil cannot be saved in this way, and equally it remains impossible to hold that an omnipotent God *binds himself* by causal or logical laws.

CONCLUSION

Of the proposed solutions of the problem of evil which we have examined, none has stood up to criticism. There may be other solutions which require examination, but this study strongly suggests that there is no valid solution of the problem which does not modify at least one of the constituent propositions in a way which would seriously affect the essential core of the theistic position.

Quite apart from the problem of evil, the paradox of omnipotence has shown that God's omnipotence must in any case be restricted in one way or another, that unqualified omnipotence cannot be ascribed to any being that continues through time. And if God and his actions are not in time, can omnipotence, or power of any sort, be meaningfully ascribed to him?

VI

THE FREE WILL DEFENCE

ALVIN PLANTINGA

SINCE the days of Epicurus many philosophers have suggested that the existence of evil constitutes a problem for those who accept theistic belief.[1] Those contemporaries who follow Epicurus here claim, for the most part, to detect logical inconsistency in such belief. So McCloskey:

Evil is a problem for the theist in that a *contradition* is involved in the fact of evil, on the one hand, and the belief in the omnipotence and perfection of God on the other.[2]

and Mackie:

I think, however, that a more telling criticism can be made by way of the traditional problem of evil. Here it can be shown, not that religious beliefs lack rational support, but that they are positively irrational, that the several parts of the essential theological doctrine are *inconsistent* with one another ...[3]

and essentially the same charge is made by Professor Aiken in an article entitled 'God and Evil'.[4]

These philosophers, then, and many others besides, hold that traditional theistic belief is self-contradictory and that the problem of evil, for the theist, is that of deciding which of the relevant propositions he is to abandon. But just which propositions are involved? What is the set of theistic beliefs whose conjunction yields a contradiction? The authors referred to above take the following five propositions to be essential to traditional theism: (*a*) that God exists, (*b*) that God is

From *Philosophy in America*, ed. M. Black (London: Allen and Unwin, 1965), pp. 204–20. © 1965 by George Allen & Unwin Ltd. Reprinted by permission of George Allen & Unwin Ltd., and Cornell University Press.

[1] David Hume and some of the French encyclopedists, for example, as well as F. H. Bradley, J. McTaggart, and J. S. Mill.

[2] H. J. McCloskey, 'God and Evil', *The Philosophical Quarterly*, 10 (1960), 97.

[3] J. L. Mackie, 'Evil and Omnipotence', *Mind*, 64 (1955), 200 [included as ch. V of this volume.]

[4] *Ethics*, 48 (1957–8), 79.

omnipotent, (c) that God is omniscient, (d) that God is wholly good, and (e) that evil exists. Here they are certainly right: each of these propositions is indeed an essential feature of orthodox theism. And it is just these five propositions whose conjunction is said, by our atheologians,[5] to be self-contradictory.

Apologists for theism, of course, have been quick to repel the charge. A line of resistance they have often employed is called *The Free Will Defence*; in this paper I shall discuss and develop that idea.

First of all, a distinction must be made between *moral evil* and *physical evil*. The former, roughly, is the evil which results from human choice or volition; the latter is that which does not. Suffering due to an earthquake, for example, would be a case of physical evil; suffering resulting from human cruelty would be a case of moral evil. This distinction, of course, is not very clear and many questions could be raised about it; but perhaps it is not necessary to deal with these questions here. Given this distinction, the Free Will Defence is usually stated in something like the following way. A world containing creatures who freely perform both good and evil actions—and do more good than evil—is more valuable than a world containing quasi-automata who always do what is right because they are unable to do otherwise. Now God can create free creatures, but he cannot causally or otherwise determine them to do only what is right; for if he does so they do not do what is right *freely*. To create creatures capable of moral good, therefore, he must create creatures capable of moral evil; but he cannot create the possibility of moral evil and at the same time prohibit its actuality. And as it turned out, some of the free creatures God created exercised their freedom to do what is wrong: hence moral evil. The fact that free creatures sometimes err, however, in no way tells against God's omnipotence or against his goodness; for he could forestall the occurrence of moral evil only by removing the possibility of moral good.

In this way some traditional theists have tried to explain or justify part of the evil that occurs by ascribing it to the will of man rather than to the will of God. At least three kinds of objections to this idea are to be found both in the tradition and in the current literature. I shall try to develop and clarify the Free Will Defence by restating it in the face of these objections.

---

[5] *Natural theology* is the attempt to infer central religious beliefs from premisses that are either obvious to common sense (e.g. *that some things are in motion*) or logically necessary. *Natural atheology* is the attempt to infer the falsity of such religious beliefs from premisses of the same sort.

I

The first objection challenges the assumption, implicit in the above statement of the Free Will Defence, that free will and causal determinism are logically incompatible. So Flew:

> ... to say that a person could have helped doing something is not to say that what he did was in principle unpredictable nor that there were no causes anywhere which determined that he would as a matter of fact act in this way. It is to say that if he had chosen to do otherwise he would have been able to do so; that there were alternatives, within the capacities of one of his physical strength, of his I.Q., of his knowledge, open to a person in his situation.

> There is no contradiction involved in saying that a particular action or choice was: *both* free, and could have been helped, and so on; and predictable, or even foreknown, and explicable in terms of caused causes.

> ... if it is really logically possible for an action to be both freely chosen and yet fully determined by caused causes, then the keystone argument of the Free Will Defence, that there is contradiction in speaking of God so arranging the laws of nature that all men always as a matter of fact freely choose to do the right, cannot hold.[6]

Flew's objection, I think, can be dealt with in a fairly summary fashion. He does not, in the paper in question, explain what he means by 'causal determination' (and of course in that paper this omission is quite proper and justifiable). But presumably he means to use the locution in question in such a way that to say of Jones's action A that it is *causally determined* is to say that the action in question has causes and that, given these causes, Jones could not have refrained from doing A. That is to say, Flew's use of 'causally determined', presumably, is such that one or both of the following sentences, or some sentences very much like them, express necessarily true propositions:

(*a*) If Jones's action A is causally determined, then a set S of events has occurred prior to Jones's doing A such that, given S, it is causally impossible for Jones to refrain from doing A.

(*b*) If Jones's action A is causally determined, then there is a set S of propositions describing events occurring before A and a set L of propositions expressing natural laws such that

(1) the conjunction of S's members does not entail that Jones does A, and

[6] 'Divine Omnipotence and Human Freedom', in *New Essays in Philosophical Theology*, ed. Antony Flew and Alasdair MacIntyre, (London: S.C.M., 1955), pp. 150, 151, 153.

(2) the conjunction of the members of S with the members of L does entail that Jones does A.

And Flew's thesis, then, is that there is no contradiction in saying of a man, both that all of his actions are causally determined (in the sense just explained) and that some of them are free.

Now it seems to me altogether paradoxical to say of anyone all of whose actions are causally determined, that on some occasions he acts freely. When we say that Jones acts freely on a given occasion, what we say entails, I should think, that either his action on that occasion is not causally determined, or else he has previously performed an undetermined action which is a causal ancestor of the one in question. But this is a difficult and debatable issue; fortunately we need not settle it in order to assess the force of Flew's objection to the Free Will Defence. The Free Will Defender claims that the sentence 'Not all free actions are causally determined' expresses a necessary truth; Flew denies this claim. This strongly suggests that Flew and the Free Will Defender are not using the words 'free' and 'freedom' in the same way. The Free Will Defender, apparently, uses the words in question in such a way that sentences 'Some of Jones's actions are free' and 'Jones did Action A freely' express propositions which are inconsistent with the proposition that all of Jones's actions are causally determined. Flew, on the other hand, claims that with respect to the ordinary use of these words, there is no such inconsistency. It is my opinion that Flew is mistaken here; I think it is he who is using these words in a non-standard, unordinary way. But we need not try to resolve that issue; for the Free Will Defender can simply make Flew a present of the word 'freedom' and state his case using other locutions. He might now hold, for example, not that God made men free and that a world in which men freely do both good and evil is more valuable than a world in which they unfreely do only what is good; but rather that God made men such that some of their actions are *unfettered* (both free in Flew's sense and also causally undetermined) and that a world in which men perform both good and evil unfettered actions is superior to one in which they perform only good, but fettered, actions. By substituting 'unfettered' for 'free' throughout this account, the Free Will Defender can elude Flew's objection altogether.[7] So whether Flew is right or wrong about the ordinary sense of 'freedom' is of no consequence; his objection is in

[7] And since this is so in what follows I shall continue to use the words 'free' and 'freedom' in the way the Free Will Defence uses them.

an important sense merely verbal and thus altogether fails to damage the Free Will Defence.

II

Flew's objection, in essence, is the claim that an omnipotent being could have created men in such a way that although free they would be *causally determined* to perform only right actions. According to a closely allied objection, an omnipotent being could have made men in such a way that although free, and free from any such causal determination, they would none the less *freely refrain* from performing any evil actions. Here the contemporary spokesman is Mackie:

if God has made men such that in their free choices they sometimes prefer what is good and sometimes what is evil, why could he not have made men such that they always freely choose the good? If there is no logical impossibility in a man's freely choosing the good on one, or on several occasions, there cannot be a logical impossibility in his freely choosing the good on every occasion. God was not, then, faced with a choice between making innocent automata and making beings who, in acting freely, would sometimes go wrong; there was open to him the obviously better possibility of making beings who would act freely but always go right. Clearly, his failure to avail himself of this possibility is inconsistent with his being both omnipotent and wholly good.[8]

This objection is more serious than Flew's and must be dealt with more fully. Now the Free Will Defence is an argument for the conclusion that (*a*) is not contradictory or necessarily false:[9]

(*a*) God is omnipotent, omniscient, and all-good and God creates free men who sometimes perform morally evil actions.

What Mackie says, I think, may best be construed as an argument for the conclusion that (*a*) is necessarily false; in other words, that *God is omnipotent, omniscient and all-good* entails *no free men he creates ever perform morally evil actions*. Mackie's argument seems to have the following structure:

(1) God is omnipotent and omniscient and all-good.

(2) If God is omnipotent, he can create any logically possible state of affairs.

∴ (3) God can create any logically possible state of affairs. (1, 2)

(4) That all free men do what is right on every occasion is a logically possible state of affairs.

[8] Op. cit., p. 209 [p. 100 above].
[9] And of course if (*a*) is consistent, so is the set (*a*)–(*e*) mentioned on pp. 105–6 for (*a*) entails each member of that set.

∴ (5) God can create free men such that they always do what is right. (4, 3)

(6) If God can create free men such that they always do what is right and God is all-good, then any free men created by God always do what is right.

∴ (7) Any free men created by God always do what is right. (1, 5, 6)

∴ (8) No free men created by God ever perform morally evil actions. (7)

Doubtless the Free Will Defender will concede the truth of (4); there is a difficulty with (2), however; for

(a) that there are men who are not created by God is a logically possible state of affairs

is clearly true. But (2) and (a) entail

(b) If God is omnipotent, God can create men who are not created by God.

And (b), of course, is false; (2) must be revised. The obvious way to repair it seems to be something like the following:

(2') If God is omnipotent, then God can create any state of affairs S such that *God creates S* is consistent.

Similarly, (3) must be revised:

(3') God can create any state of affairs S such that *God creates S* is consistent.

(1') and (3') do not seem to suffer from the faults besetting (1) and (3); but now it is not at all evident that (3') and (4) entail

(5) God can create free men such that they always do what is right

as the original argument claims. To see this, we must note that (5) is true only if

(5a) God creates free men such that they always do what is right

is consistent. But (5a), one might think, is equivalent to:

(5b) God creates free men and brings it about that they always freely do what is right.

And (5b), of course, is *not* consistent; for if God *brings it about* that the men he creates always do what is right, then they do not do what is right *freely*. So if (5a) is taken to express (5b), then (5) is clearly false and clearly not entailed by (3') and (4).

On the other hand, (5a) could conceivably be used to express:

(5c) God creates free men and these free men always do what is right.

(5c) is surely consistent; it is indeed logically possible that God creates free men and that the free men created by him always do what is right. And conceivably the objector is using (5) to express this possibility— i.e., it may be that (5) is meant to express:

(5d) the proposition *God creates free men and the free men created by God always do what is right* is consistent.

If (5) is equivalent to (5d), then (5) is true—in fact necessarily true (and hence trivially entailed by (3′) and (4)). But now the difficulty crops up with respect to (6) which, given the equivalence of (5) and (5d) is equivalent to

(6′) If God is all-good and the proposition *God creates free men and the free men he creates always do what is right* is consistent, then any free men created by God always do what is right.

Now Mackie's aim is to show that the proposition *God is omnipotent, omniscient and all-good* entails the proposition *no free men created by God ever perform morally evil actions*. His attempt, as I outlined it, is to show this by constructing a valid argument whose premiss is the former and whose conclusion is the latter. But then any additional premiss appealed to in the deduction must be necessarily true if Mackie's argument is to succeed. (6′) is one such additional premiss; but there seems to be no reason for supposing that (6′) is true at all, let alone necessarily true. Whether the free men created by God would always do what is right would presumably be up to them; for all we know they might sometimes exercise their freedom to do what is wrong. Put in a nutshell the difficulty with the argument is the following. (5a) (God creates free men such that they always freely do what is right) is susceptible of two interpretations ((5b) and (5c)). Under one of these interpretations (5) turns out to be false and the argument therefore fails. Under the other interpretation (6) turns out to be utterly groundless and question begging, and again the argument fails.

So far, then, the Free Will Defence has emerged unscathed from Mackie's objection. One has the feeling, however, that more can be said here; that there is something to Mackie's argument. What more? Well, perhaps something along the following lines. It is agreed that it is logically possible that all men always do only what is right. Now God is said to be omniscient and hence knows, with respect to any person he proposes to create, whether that person would or would not commit morally evil acts. For every person P who in fact performs morally evil actions, there is, evidently, a possible person P' who is exactly like P in every respect except that P' never performs any evil actions. If God is omnipotent, he could have created these possible persons instead of the persons he in fact did create. And if he is also all-good, he *would*, presumably, have created them, since they differ from the persons he did create only in being morally better than they are.

Can we make coherent sense out of this revised version of Mackie's objection? What, in particular, could the objector mean by 'possible person'? and what are we to make of the suggestion that God could have created possible persons? I think these questions can be answered. Let us consider first the set of all those properties it is logically possible for human beings to have. Examples of properties *not* in this set are the properties of *being over a mile long; being a hippopotamus; being a prime number; being divisible by four;* and the like. Included in the set are such properties as *having red hair; being present at the Battle of Waterloo; being the President of the United States; being born in 1889;* and *being a pipe-smoker.* Also included are such moral properties as *being kind to one's maiden aunt, being a scoundrel, performing at least one morally wrong action,* and so on. Let us call the properties in this set H properties. The complement $\bar{P}$ of an H property P is the property a thing has just in case it does not have P. And a *consistent set* of H properties is a set of H properties such that it is logically possible that there be a human being having every property in the set. Now we can define 'possible person' in the following way:

> x is a possible person $= x$ is a consistent set of H properties such that for every H property P, either P or $\bar{P}$ is a member of x.

To *instantiate* a possible person P is to create a human being having every property in P. And a set S of possible persons is a *co-possible set of possible persons* just in case it is logically possible that every member of S is instantiated.[10]

Given this technical terminology, Mackie's objection can be summarily restated. It is granted by everyone that there is no absurdity in the claim that some man who is free to do what is wrong never, in fact, performs any wrong action. It follows that there are many possible persons containing the property *is free to do wrong but always does right.* And since it is logically possible that all men always freely do what is right, there are presumably several co-possible sets of possible

---

[10] The definiens must not be confused with: For every member M of S, it is logically possible that M is instantiated.

persons such that each member of each set contains the property in question. Now God, if he is omnipotent, can instantiate any possible person and any co-possible set of possible persons he chooses. Hence, if he were all good, he would have instantiated one of the sets of co-possible persons all of whose members freely do only what is right.

In spite of its imposing paraphernalia the argument, thus restated, suffers from substantially the same defect that afflicts Mackie's original version. There are *some* possible persons God obviously cannot instantiate—those, for example, containing the property *is not created by God*. Accordingly it is *false* that God can instantiate just any possible person he chooses. But of course the interesting question is whether

> (1) God can instantiate possible persons containing the property of always freely doing what is right

is true; for perhaps Mackie could substitute (1) for the premiss just shown to be false.

Is (1) true? Perhaps we can approach this question in the following way. Let P be any possible person containing the property *always freely does what is right*. Then there must be some action A such that P contains the property of being free with respect to A (i.e. the property of being free to perform A and free to refrain from performing A). The *instantiation* of a possible person S, I shall say, is a person having every property in S; and let us suppose that if P were instantiated, its instantiation would be doing something morally wrong in performing A. And finally, let us suppose that God wishes to instantiate P. Now P contains many properties, in addition to the ones already mentioned. Among them, for example, we might find the following: *is born in 1910, has red hair, is born in Stuttgart, has feeble-minded ancestors, is six feet tall at the age of fourteen*, and the like. And there is no difficulty in God's creating a person with these properties. Further, there is no difficulty in God's bringing it about that this person (let's call him Smith) is free with respect to A. But if God *also* brings it about that Smith refrains from performing A (as he must to be the instantiation of P) then Smith is no longer free with respect to A and is hence not the instantiation of P after all. God cannot cause Smith to refrain from performing A, while allowing him to be free with respect to A; and therefore whether or not Smith does A will be entirely up to Smith; it will be a matter of free choice for him. Accordingly, whether God can instantiate P depends upon what Smith would freely decide to do.

This point may be put more accurately as follows: First, we shall say that an H property Q is *indeterminate* if *God creates a person and causes him to have Q* is necessarily false; an H property is *determinate* if it is not indeterminate. Of the properties we ascribed to P, all are determinate except *freely refrains from doing A* and *always freely does what is right*. Now consider P_1, the subset of P containing just the determinate members of P. In order to instantiate P God must instantiate P_1. It is evident that there is at most one instantiation of P_1, for among the members of P_1 will be some such individuating properties as for example, *is the third son of Richard and Lena Dykstra*. P_1 also contains the property of being free with respect to A; and if P_1 is instantiated, its instantiation will either perform A or refrain from performing A. It is, of course, possible that P_1 is such that if it is instantiated its instantiation I will perform A. If so, then if God allows I to remain free with respect to A, I will do A; and if God prevents I from doing A, then I is not free with respect to A and hence not the instantiation of P after all. Hence in neither case does God succeed in instantiating P. And accordingly God can instantiate P only if P_1 is *not* such that if it is instantiated, its instantiation will perform A. Hence it is possible that God cannot instantiate P. And evidently it is also possible, further, that *every* possible person containing the property *always freely does what is right* is such that neither God nor anyone else can instantiate it.

Now we merely supposed that P_1 is such that if it is instantiated, its instantiation will perform A. And this supposition, if true at all, is merely contingently true. It might be suggested, therefore, that God could instantiate P by instantiating P_1 and bringing it about that P_1 is *not* such that if it is instantiated, its instantiation will perform A. But to do this God must instantiate P_1 and bring it about that P_1 is such that if it is instantiated, its instantiation I will *refrain* from performing A. And if God does this then God brings it about that I will not perform A. But then I is not free to perform A and hence once more is not the instantiation of P.

It is possible, then, that God cannot instantiate any possible person containing the property *always freely does what is right*. It is also possible, of course, that he *can* instantiate some such possible persons. But *that* he can, if indeed he can, is a contingent truth. And since Mackie's project is to prove an entailment, he cannot employ any contingent propositions as added premisses. Hence the reconstructed argument fails.

Now the difficulty with the reconstructed argument is the fact that God cannot instantiate just any possible person he chooses, and the possibility that God cannot instantiate any possible persons containing the property of always freely doing what is right. But perhaps the objector can circumvent this difficulty.

The H properties that make trouble for the objector are the indeterminate properties—those which God cannot cause anyone to have. It is because possible persons contain indeterminate properties that God cannot instantiate just any possible person he wishes. And so perhaps the objector can reformulate his definition of 'possible person' in such a way that a possible person is a consistent set S of *determinate* properties such that for any determinate H property P, either P or P is a member of S. Unfortunately the following difficulty arises. Where I is any indeterminate H property and D a determinate H property, D or I (the property a person has if he has either D or I) is determinate And so, of course, is D. The same difficulty, accordingly, arises all over again—there will be some possible persons God can't instantiate (those containing the properties *is not created by God or has red hair* and *does not have red hair*, for example). We must add, therefore, that no possible person *entails* an indeterminate property.[11]

Even so our difficulties are not at an end. For the definition as now stated entails that there are no *possible free persons*, i.e. possible persons containing the property *on some occasions free to do what is right and free to do what is wrong*.[12] We may see this as follows: Let P be any possible free person. P then contains the property of being free with respect to some action A. Furthermore, P would contain either the property of performing A (since that is a determinate property) or the property of refraining from performing A. But if P contains the property of performing A and the property of being free with respect to A, then P entails the property of freely performing A—which is an indeterminate property. And the same holds in case P contains the property of refraining from performing A. Hence in either case P entails an indeterminate property and accordingly is not a possible person.

Clearly the objector must revise the definition of 'possible person' in such a way that for any action with respect to which a given possible person P is free, P contains neither the property of performing that action nor the property of refraining from performing it. This may be accomplished in the following way. Let us say that a person S is *free with respect to a property P* just in case there is some action A with respect to which S is free and which is such that S has P if and only if he performs A. So, for example, if a person is free to leave town and free to stay, then he is free with respect to the property *leaves town*. And let us say that a set of properties is free with respect to a given property P just in case it contains the property *is free with*

[11] Where a set S of properties entails a property P if and only if it is necessarily true that anything having every property in S also has P.

[12] This was pointed out to me by Mr. Lewis Creary.

respect to P. Now we can restate the definition of 'possible person' as follows:

> *x* is a possible person = *x* is a consistent set of determinate *H* properties such that (1) for every determinate *H* property *P* with respect to which *x* is not free, either *P* or *P̄* is a member of *x*, and (2) *x* does not entail any indeterminate property.

Now let us add the following new definition:

> Possible person *P* has indeterminate property *I* = if *P* were instantiated, *P*'s instantiation would have *I*.

Under the revised definition of 'possible person' is seems apparent that God, if he is omnipotent, can instantiate any possible person, and any co-possible set of possible persons, he chooses. But, the objector continues, if God is also all-good, he will, presumably, instantiate only those possible persons who have some such indeterminate *H* property as that of *always freely doing what is right*. And here the Free Will Defender can no longer make the objection which held against the previous versions of Mackie's argument. For if God can instantiate any possible person he chooses, he can instantiate any possible free person he chooses.

The Free Will Defender can, however, raise what is essentially the same difficulty in a new guise: what reason is there for supposing that there are *any* possible persons, in the present sense of 'possible person', having the indeterminate property in question? For it is clear that, given any indeterminate *H* property *I*, the proposition *no possible person has I* is a contingent proposition. Further, the proposition *every possible free person freely performs at least one morally wrong action* is possibly true. But if every *possible* free person performs at least one wrong action, then every *actual* free person also freely performs at least one wrong action; hence if every possible free person performs at least one wrong action, God could create a universe without moral evil only by refusing to create any free persons at all. And, the Free Will Defender adds, a world containing free persons and moral evil (provided that it contained more moral good than moral evil) would be superior to one lacking both free persons and moral good and evil. Once again, then, the objection seems to fail.

The definitions offered during the discussion of Mackie's objection afford the opportunity of stating the Free Will Defence more formally. I said above (p. 109) that the Free Will Defence is in essence an argument for the conclusion that (*a*) is consistent:

(a) God is omnipotent, omniscient, and all-good and God creates persons who sometimes perform morally evil actions.
One way of showing (a) to be consistent is to show that its first conjunct does not entail the negation of its second conjunct, i.e. that
(b) God is omnipotent omniscient and all good
does not entail
(c) God does not create persons who perform morally evil actions.

Now one can show that a given proposition p does not entail another proposition q by producing a third proposition r which is such that (1) the conjunction of p and r is consistent and (2) the conjunction of p and r entails the negation of q. What we need here, then, is a proposition whose conjunction with (b) is both logically consistent and a logically sufficient condition of the denial of (c).
Consider the following argument:

    (b) God is omnipotent, omniscient and all-good.
    (r1) God creates some free persons.
    (r2) Every possible free person performs at least one wrong action.
∴ (d) Every actual free person performs at least one wrong action. (r2)
∴ (e) God creates persons who perform morally evil actions. ((r1), (d))

This argument is valid (and can easily be expanded so that it is *formally* valid). Furthermore, the conjunction of (b), (r1), and (r2) is evidently consistent. And as the argument shows, (b), (r1), and (r2) jointly entail (e). But (e) is the denial of (c); hence (b) and (r) jointly entail the denial of (c). Accordingly (b) does not entail (c), and (a) (God is omnipotent, omniscient and all-good and God creates persons who perform morally evil acts) is shown to be consistent. So stated, therefore, the Free Will Defence appears to be successful.
At this juncture it might be objected that even if the Free Will Defence, as explained above, shows that there is no contradiction in the supposition that God, who is all-good, omnipotent and omniscient, creates persons who engage in moral evil, it does nothing to show that an all-good, omnipotent and omniscient Being could create a universe containing as *much* moral evil as this one seems to contain. The objection has a point, although the fact that there seems to be no way of measuring or specifying amounts of moral evil makes it exceedingly hard to state the objection in any way which does not leave it vague and merely suggestive. But let us suppose, for purposes of argument, that there is a

way of measuring moral evil (and moral good) and that the moral evil present in the universe amounts to ϕ. The problem then is to show that

(b) God is omnipotent, omniscient and all-good

is consistent with

(f) God creates a set of free persons who produce ϕ moral evil. Here the Free Will Defender can produce an argument to show that (b) is consistent with (f) which exactly parallels the argument for the consistency of (b) and (c):

(b) God is omnipotent, omniscient and all-good.

(r3) God creates a set S of free persons such that there is a balance of moral good over moral evil with respect to the members of S.

(r4) There is exactly one co-possible set S' of free possible persons such that there is a balance of moral good over moral evil with respect to its members; and the members of S' produce ϕ moral evil.

Set S is evidently the instantiation of S' (i.e. every member of S is an instantiation of some members of S' and every member of S' is instanstatiated by some member of S); hence the members of S produce ϕ moral evil. Accordingly, (b), (r3) and (r4) jointly entail (f); but the conjunction of (b), (r3) and (r4) is consistent; hence (b) is consistent with (f).

III

The preceding discussion enables us to conclude, I believe, that the Free Will Defence succeeds in showing that there is no inconsistency in the assertion that God creates a universe containing as much moral evil as the universe in fact contains. There remains but one objection to be considered. McCloskey, Flew and others charge that the Free Will Defence, even if it is successful, accounts for only *part* of the evil we find; it accounts only for moral evil, leaving physical evil as intractable as before. The atheologian can therefore restate his position, maintaining that the existence of *physical evil*, evil which cannot be ascribed to the free actions of human beings, is inconsistent with the existence of an omniscient, omnipotent and all-good Deity.

To make this claim, however, is to overlook an important part of traditional theistic belief; it is part of much traditional belief to attribute a good deal of the evil we find to Satan, or to Satan and his cohorts. Satan, so the traditional doctrine goes, is a mighty non-human spirit, who, along with many other angels, was created long before God created men. Unlike most of his colleagues, Satan rebelled against God and has since been creating whatever havoc he could; the result, of course, is physical evil. But now we see that the moves available to the Free Will Defender in the case of moral evil are equally available to him in the case of physical evil. First he provides definitions of 'possible non-human spirit', 'free non-human spirit', etc., which exactly parallel their counterparts where it was moral evil that was at stake. Then he points out that it is logically possible that

(r5) God creates a set S of free non-human spirits such that the members of S do more good than evil,

and

(r6) there is exactly one co-possible set S' of possible free non-human spirits such that the members of S' do more good than evil,

and

(r7) all of the physical evil in the world is due to the actions of the members of S.

He points out further that (r5), (r6), and (r7) are jointly consistent and that their conjunction is consistent with the proposition that God is omnipotent, omniscient, and all-good. But (r5) through (r7) jointly entail that God creates a universe containing as much physical evil as the universe in fact contains; it follows then, that the existence of physical evil is not inconsistent with the existence of an omniscient, omnipotent, all-good Deity.

Now it must be conceded that views involving devils and other non-human spirits do not at present enjoy either the extensive popularity or the high esteem of (say) the Theory of Relativity. Flew, for example, has this to say about the view in question:

To make this more than just another desperate *ad hoc* expedient of apologetic it is necessary to produce independent evidence for launching such an hypothesis (if 'hypothesis' is not too flattering a term for it).[13]

But in the present context this claim is surely incorrect; to rebut the charge of contradiction the theist need not hold that the hypothesis in question is probable or even true. He need hold only that it is not inconsistent with the proposition that God exists. Flew suspects that 'hypothesis' may be too flattering a term for the sort of view in question. Perhaps this suspicion reflects his doubts as to the meaningfulness of the proposed view. But it is hard to see how one could plausibly argue that the views in question are nonsensical (in the requisite sense) without invoking some version of the Verifiability Criterion, a doctrine whose harrowing vicissitudes are well known. Furthermore, it is likely that any premisses worth considering which yield the conclusion that hypo-

---

[13] Op. cit., p. 17.

theses about devils are nonsensical will yield the same conclusion about the hypothesis that God exists. And if *God exists* is nonsensical, then presumably theism is not self-contradictory after all.

We may therefore conclude that the Free Will Defence successfully rebuts the charge of contradiction brought against the theist. The Problem of Evil (if indeed evil constitutes a problem for the theist) does not lie in any inconsistency in the belief that God, who is omniscient, omnipotent and all-good, has created a world containing moral and physical evil.

VII

RELIGIOUS BELIEFS AND LANGUAGE-GAMES

D. Z. PHILLIPS

RECENTLY, many philosophers of religion have protested against the philosophical assertion that religious beliefs must be recognized as distinctive language-games. They feel that such an assertion gives the misleading impression that these language-games are cut off from all others. This protest has been made by Ronald Hepburn, John Hick, and Kai Nielsen, to give but three examples. Hepburn says, 'Within traditional Christian theology ... questions about the divine existence cannot be deflected into the question "Does 'God' play an intelligible role in the language-game?"'[1] Hick thinks that there is something wrong in saying that 'The logical implications of religious statements do not extend across the border of the *Sprachspiel* into assertions concerning the character of the universe beyond that fragment of it which is the religious speech of human beings.'[2] Nielsen objects to the excessive compartmentalization of modes of social life involved in saying that religious beliefs are distinctive language-games and argues that 'Religious discourse is not something isolated, sufficient unto itself'.[3] Although '"Reality" may be systematically ambiguous ... what constitutes evidence, or tests for the truth or reliability of specific claims, is not completely idiosyncratic to the context or activity we are talking about. Activities are not that insulated.'[4] I do not want to discuss the writings of these philosophers in this paper. I have already tried to meet some of their objections elsewhere.[5] Rather, I want to treat their remarks as

From *Ratio*, 12 (1970), 26–46. Reprinted by permission of the author and the Editor of *Ratio*.

[1] R. W. Hepburn, 'From World to God', *Mind*, 72 (1963), 41.

[2] John Hick, 'Sceptics and Believers', *Faith and the Philosophers*, ed. J. Hick, (London: Macmillan, 1964), p. 239.

[3] Kai Nielsen, 'Wittgensteinian Fideism', *Philosophy*, 42 (1967), 207.

[4] Ibid., p. 208.

[5] 'Religion and Epistemology: Some Contemporary Confusions' in *The Australasian Journal of Philosophy*, Dec. 1966.

symptoms of a general misgiving about talking of religious beliefs in the way I have indicated which one comes across with increasing frequency in philosophical writings and in philosophical discussions. I write this paper as one who has talked of religious beliefs as distinctive language-games, but also as one who has come to feel misgivings in some respects about doing so.

What do these misgivings amount to? Partly, at least, they amount to a feeling that if religious beliefs are isolated, self-sufficient language-games, it becomes difficult to explain why people *should* cherish religious beliefs in the way they do. On the view suggested, religious beliefs seem more like esoteric games, enjoyed by the initiates no doubt, but of little significance outside the internal formalities of their activities. Religious activities begin to look like hobbies; something with which men occupy themselves at week-ends. From other directions, the misgivings involve the suspicion that religious beliefs are being placed outside the reach of any possible criticism, and that the appeal of the internality of religious criteria of meaningfulness can act as a quasi-justification for what would otherwise be recognized as nonsense.

There is little doubt that talk about religious beliefs as distinctive language-games has occasioned these misgivings. As I shall try to show later in the paper, to some extent, there is good reason for these misgivings. It is also true, however, that these misgivings must be handled with great care. Some attempts at removing them lead to confusions about the logical grammar of certain religious beliefs. In the first sections of the paper I shall consider some of these.

I

In face of the misgiving that talk of religious beliefs as distinctive language-games may make them appear to be self-contained esoteric games, some philosophers of religion have denied that such talk is legitimate. What must be established, they argue, is the importance of religious beliefs. People must be given reasons why they ought to believe in God. In this way, religious beliefs are given a basis; they are shown to be reasonable. My difficulty is that I do not understand what is involved in this enterprise.

In his 'Lecture On Ethics', Wittgenstein emphasizes the difference between absolute judgements of value, and relative judgements of value. Words such as 'good', 'important', 'right', have a relative and an absolute use. For example, if I say that this is a *good* chair, I may be referring to its adequacy in fulfilling certain purposes. If I say it is *important* not to catch cold, I may be referring to the unpleasant consequences of doing so. If I say that this is the *right* road, I may be referring to the fact that it would get me to my destination if I follow it.[6] Now, in these instances, I can reverse my judgement as follows: 'This is not a good chair since I no longer want to relax, but to work', 'It is not important that I do not catch a cold since I don't care about the consequences. Doing what I want to do will be worth it', 'This is not the right road for me, since I no longer want to get to where it would take me.' But as well as a relative use of words like 'good', 'important', 'right', or 'ought', there is an absolute use of the words. Wittgenstein illustrates, the difference where 'ought' is concerned in the following example:

Supposing that I could play tennis and one of you saw me playing and said, 'Well, you play pretty badly', and suppose I answered, 'I know, I'm playing badly but I don't want to play any better', all the other man could say would be 'Ah, then that's all right.' But suppose I had told one of you a preposterous lie and he came up to me and said, 'You're behaving like a beast' and then I were to say, 'I know I behave badly, but then I don't want to behave any better', could he then say, 'Ah (then that's all right? Certainly not; he would say, 'Well you *ought* to want to behave better.' Here you have an absolute judgement of value, whereas the first instance was one of a relative judgement.[7]

Many religious apologists feel that if religious beliefs are not to appear as esoteric games they must be shown to be important. This is true as far as it goes. What remains problematic is the way in which the apologists think the importance of religion can be established. When they say it is important to believe in God, how are they using the word 'important'? Are they making a relative or an absolute judgement of value? Sometimes it seems as if relative judgements of value are being made. We are told to believe in God because he is the most powerful being. We are told to believe in God because only those who believe flourish in the end. We are told to believe in God because history is in his hand, and that despite appearances, the final victory is his. All these advocacies are founded on relative judgements of value. As in the other case we mentioned, the judgements are reversible. If the Devil happened to be more powerful than God, he would have to be worshipped. If believers are not to flourish in the end belief becomes pointless. Belief in God is pointless if historical development goes in one direction rather than another.

But need religious beliefs be thought of in this way? Belief in God is represented as a means to a further end. The end is all important, the means relatively unimportant. Belief in God has a point only if certain consequences follow. This seems to falsify the absolute character which belief in God has for many believers. They would say that God's divinity cannot be justified by external considerations. If we can see nothing in it, there is nothing apart from it which will somehow establish its point. Rush Rhees made a similar observation when he compared an absolute judgement of value in morality with a relative judgement of value:

'You ought to make sure that the strip is firmly clamped before you start drilling.' 'What if I don't?' 'When I tell you what will happen if you don't, you see what I mean.'
But, 'You ought to want to behave better.' 'What if I don't?' 'What more could I tell you?'[8]

We cannot give a man reasons why he should be good. Similarly, if a man urges someone to come to God, and he asks, 'What if I don't?' what more is there to say? Certainly, one could not get him to believe by telling him that terrible things will happen to him if he does not believe. Even if it were true that these things are going to happen, and even if a person believed because of them, he would not be believing in God. He would be believing in the best thing for himself. He would have a policy, not a faith. Furthermore, if religious beliefs have only a relative value, one can no longer give an account of the distinction between other-worldliness and worldliness, a distinction which is important in most religions. The distinction cannot be accounted for if one assumes that the value of religious beliefs can be assessed by applying them to a wider common measure. Consider the following arguments: (i) We should believe in God. He is the most powerful of all beings. We are all to be judged by him in the end. He is to determine our fate. In this argument, there is only one concept of power: worldly power. *As it happens* God is more powerful than we are, but it is the same kind of power; (ii) Many battles are fought. At times it looks as if the good is defeated and evil triumphs. But there is no reason to fear, the ultimate victory is God's. Here a common measure is applied to God and the powers of evil, as if God's victory is demonstrable, something recognized by good and evil alike. The man who says God is not victorious would be contradicting the man who says he is victorious.

These apologetic manœuvres remind one of Polus in Plato's *Gorgias*.

[8] Rush Rhees, 'Some Developments in Wittgenstein's View of Ethics', *The Philosophical Review*, 74 (1965), 18–19.

Polus did not understand Socrates when the latter said that goodness is to a man's advantage. He pointed to Archelaus the Tyrant of Macedonia. Surely, here was a wicked man who flourished. Is it not easy for even a child to show that Socrates is mistaken? But the fallacy in Polus's argument is his supposition that he and Socrates can only mean one thing when they speak of advantage, namely, what he, Polus, means by it. For Socrates, however, it is not the world's view of advantage which is to determine what is good, but what is good which is to determine what is to count as advantage. In what way are some apologists similar to Polus? In this way: when someone shows them how much power the forces ranged against religion have, they reply, 'But our God is more powerful!' But they use the same concept of power. Their idea of power is not qualitatively different from that of their opponents. On the contrary, in their view, the world and God share the same kind of power, only God has more of it. But, like Polus, they need to realize that for many believers, it is not the outcome, the course of events, which is to determine whether God is victorious, but faith in God which determines what is regarded as victory. If this were not so, there would be no tension between the world's ways of regarding matters, and religious reactions to them. The same tension exists in ethics. There are those for whom justice, to be worth pursuing, must be acceptable to a thousand tough characters. Others, like Socrates, recognizing that in Athens or any other city, anything may happen to one, can say without contradiction, that all will be well. In the eyes of the world, all cannot be well if anything will happen to one. Things must go in one way rather than another. Since, for many believers, love of God determines what is to count as important, there will be situations where what the believer calls success will be failure in the eyes of the world, what he calls joy will seem like grief, what he calls victory will seem like certain defeat. So it was, Christians believe, at the Cross of Christ. In drawing attention to this tension between two points of view my aim is not to advocate either, but to show that any account of religious beliefs which seems to deny that such a tension exists, falsifies the nature of the beliefs in question.

What we have seen in the first section of the paper is how, if philosophers are not careful, misgivings about treating religious beliefs as esoteric games can lead to an attempt to show why religious beliefs are important which distorts the nature of the values involved in such beliefs.

II

Misgivings about the philosophical characterization of religious beliefs as distinctive language-games not only lead to attempts to give an external justification of religious values, but also to attempts both by philosophers who are sympathetic and by philosophers who are unsympathetic to religion to show that their conclusions are reached by criteria of rationality which their opponents do or ought to accept. Unless believers and non-believers can be shown to be using common criteria of rationality, it is said, then the misgivings about religious beliefs being esoteric games cannot be avoided.

Wittgenstein raised the question whether, in relation to religion, the non-believer contradicts the believer when he says that he does not believe what the believer believes.[9] If one man contradicts another, they can be said to share a common understanding, to be playing the same game. Consider the following examples. The man who says that the sun is ninety million miles away from the earth contradicts the man who says that the sun is only twenty million miles away from the earth. The man who says that the profit from a business venture is one hundred thousand pounds, is contradicted by the man who says that the profit is fifty thousand pounds. The man who says that there are unicorns contradicts the man who says that there are no unicorns. In these examples, the disputants participate in a common understanding. The disputants about the distance of the sun from the earth share a common understanding, namely, methods of calculation in astronomy. The disputants about the business profit share a common understanding, namely, business methods of calculating gain and loss. The disputants about the unicorns share a common understanding, namely, methods of verifying the existence of various kinds of animals. The disputants differ about the facts, but they are one in logic, that is, they appeal to the same criteria to settle the disagreement. But what if one man says that handling the ball is a foul, and another says that handling the ball is not a foul? Are they contradicting each other? Surely, they are only doing so if they are playing the same game, referring to the same rules.

In the light of these examples, what are we to say about the man who believes in God and the man who does not? Are they contradicting each other? Are two people, one of whom says there is a God and the other

⁹ Ludwig Wittgenstein *Lectures and Conversations on Aesthetics, Psychology and Religious Belief,* ed. Cyril Barrett (Oxford: Blackwell, 1966), pp. 53–72. The lectures are selections from notes taken by Wittgenstein's students. They do not claim to be a verbatim report of his words.

of whom says he does not believe in God, like two people who disagree about the existence of unicorns? Wittgenstein shows that they are not.[10] The main reason for the difference is that God's reality is not one of a kind; he is not a being among beings. The word 'God' is not the name of a thing. Thus, the reality of God cannot be assessed by a common measure which also applies to things other than God. But these are conclusions for which reasons must be given.

If I say that something exists, it makes sense to think of that something ceasing to exist. But religious believers do not want to say that God might cease to exist. This is not because, as a matter of fact, they think God will exist for ever, but because it is meaningless to speak of God's ceasing to exist. Again, we cannot ask of God the kinds of questions we can ask of things which come to be and pass away, 'What brought him into existence?' 'When will he cease to exist?' 'He was existing yesterday, how about today?' Again, we find religious believers saying that it is a terrible thing not to believe in God. But if believing in God is to believe in the existence of a thing, an object, one might wonder why it is so terrible to say that the thing in question does not exist?[11] Or one might be puzzled as to why there is such a fuss about these matters anyway, since religious believers only *believe* them to be true. We might say, as we would normally in such cases, 'You only believe—oh well. ...'[11] But is this the way in which the word 'belief' is used in religion? Is it not queer to say of worshippers, 'They only believe there is a God'?

What is the reaction of philosophers to these differences? They are not unaware of them. On the contrary, we have quarterly reminders of their multiplicity. But most philosophers who write on the subject see these differences as an indication that serious blunders have been committed in the name of religion for some reason or another. Once the differences are seen as blunders, it is assumed that what are sometimes called 'the logical peculiarities' of religious discourse, are deviations from or distortions of non-religious ways of speaking with which we are familiar. Thus, the reality of God is made subject to wider criteria of intelligibility. Like the particular hypotheses about the distance of the sun from the earth, the profit in business, or the existence of unicorns, beliefs about God are thought to have a relative reality; that is, the reality of a hypothesis which is relative to the criteria by which it is

---

[10] I have tried to argue for a similar conclusion in *The Concept of Prayer* (London: Routledge and Kegan Paul, 1965). See chs. 1 and 2.

[11] Wittgenstein's examples. See *Lectures and Conversations on Aesthetics*, pp. 59–60.

assessed. In the case of religious beliefs, it is said that when they are brought into relation with the relevant criteria of assessment, they are shown to be mistakes, distortions, illusions, or blunders. If I understand Wittgenstein, he is saying that this conclusion arises, partly, at least, from a deep philosophical prejudice. One characteristic of this prejudice is the craving for generality, the insistence that what constitutes an intelligible move in one context, must constitute an intelligible move in all contexts; the insistence, to take our examples, that the use of 'existence' and 'belief' is the same in all contexts, and the failure to recognize this as an illegitimate elevation of *one* use of these words as a paradigm for *any* use of the words. What Wittgenstein shows us in his remarks on religious belief, is why there is good reason to note the different uses which 'belief' and 'existence' have, and to resist the craving for generality.

One of the ways of generalizing which has serious implications, and leads to a host of misunderstandings in philosophical discussions of religion, is to think that nothing can be believed unless there is evidence or grounds for that belief. Of course, where certain religious beliefs are concerned, for example, belief in the authenticity of a holy relic, grounds and evidence for the belief are relevant. But one cannot conclude that it makes sense to ask for the evidence or grounds of every religious belief. Wittgenstein considers belief in the Last Judgement. Now one way of proceeding is to ask what evidence there is for believing in the Last Judgement. One could imagine degrees of belief concerning it: some say that they are sure about it, others say that possibly there will be a Last Judgement, others do not believe in it. But despite these disagreements, we can say as we did of our earlier examples, that the disputants are one in logic. The Last Judgement seems to be thought of as a future event which may or may not occur. Those who feel sure it will occur, those who think it might possibly occur, and those who do not think it will occur, are all, logically, on the same level. They are all playing the same game: they are expressing their belief, half-belief, or unbelief, in a hypothesis. So this religious belief is taken to be a hypothesis.

But need religious beliefs always be hypotheses? Clearly not. Wittgenstein points out that the word 'God' is among the earliest learnt. We learn it through pictures, stories, catechisms, etc. But, Wittgenstein warns us, this does not have 'the same consequences as with pictures of aunts. I wasn't shown that which the picture pictured.'[12] Later, Wittgenstein illustrates the point as follows:

[12] Ibid., p. 59.

Take 'God created man.' Pictures of Michelangelo showing the creation of the world. In general, there is nothing which explains the meanings of words as well as a picture, and I take it that Michelangelo was as good as anyone can be and did his best, and here is the picture of the Deity creating Adam.

If we ever saw this, we certainly wouldn't think this the Deity. The picture has to be used in an entirely different way if we are to call the man in that queer blanket 'God', and so on. You could imagine that religion was taught by means of these pictures. 'Of course we can only express ourselves by means of pictures.' This is rather queer ... I could show Moore the pictures of a tropical plant. There is a technique of comparison between picture and plant. If I showed him the picture of Michelangelo and said: 'Of course, I can't show you the real thing, only the picture....' The absurdity is, I've never taught him the technique of using this picture.[13]

So the difference between a man who does and a man who does not believe in God, is like the difference between a man who does and a man who does not believe in a picture. But what does believing in a picture amount to? Is it like believing in a hypothesis? Certainly not. As Wittgenstein says, 'The whole *weight* may be in the picture.'[14] A man's belief in the Last Judgement may show itself in a way a man has this before his mind when he takes any decisions of importance, in the way it determines his attitude to his aspirations and failures, or to the fortunes or misfortunes which befall him. In referring to these features of the religious person's beliefs, Wittgenstein is stressing the grammar of belief in this context. He is bringing out what 'recognition of a belief' amounts to here. It does not involve the weighing of evidence, or reasoning to a conclusion. What it does involve is seeing how the belief regulates a person's life. 'Here believing obviously plays much more this role: suppose we said that a certain picture might play the role of constantly admonishing me, or I always think of it. Here, an enormous difference would be between those people for whom the picture is constantly in the foreground, and the others who just didn't use it at all.'[15] What, then, are we to say of those who do not use the picture, who do not believe in it? Do they contradict those who do? Wittgenstein shows that they do not.

Suppose someone is ill and he says: 'This is a punishment', and I say: 'If I'm ill, I don't think of punishment at all.' If you say: 'Do you believe the opposite?'—you can call it believing the opposite, but it is entirely different from what we would normally call believing the opposite.

I think differently, in a different way. I say different things to myself. I have different pictures.

It is this way: if someone said: 'Wittgenstein, you don't take illness as

[13] Ibid., p. 63.   [14] Ibid., p. 72.   [15] Ibid., p. 56.

punishment, so what do you believe?'—I'd say: 'I don't have any thoughts of punishment.'[16]

Those who do not use the picture cannot be compared, therefore, with those who do not believe in a hypothesis. Believing in the picture means, for example, putting one's trust in it, sacrificing for it, letting it regulate one's life, and so on. Not believing in the picture means that the picture plays no part in one's thinking. Wittgenstein brings out the difference between this and disputants over a hypothesis very neatly when he says, 'Suppose someone were a believer and said: "I believe in a Last Judgement", and I said: "Well, I'm not so sure. Possibly." You would say that there is an enormous gulf between us. If he said "There is a German aeroplane overhead", and I said "Possibly, I'm not so sure", you'd say we were fairly near.'[17]

Beliefs, such as belief in the Last Judgement, are not testable hypotheses but absolutes for believers in so far as they predominate in and determine much of their thinking. The absolute beliefs are the criteria not the object of assessment. To construe these beliefs as hypotheses which may or may not be true is to falsify their character. As Wittgenstein says, 'The point is that if there were evidence, this would in fact destroy the whole business.'[18] The difficulty is in seeing what might be meant in saying that absolute religious beliefs could turn out to be mistakes or blunders. As Wittgenstein points out, 'Whether a thing is a blunder or not—it is a blunder in a particular system. Just as something is a blunder in a particular game and not in another.'[19] Some blunders may be pretty fundamental. Others may be elementary. We can see what has gone wrong if, when asked to go on in the same way, someone continues the series 2, 4, 6, 8, 10 ... by repeating it. But, Wittgenstein says, 'If you suddenly wrote numbers down on the blackboard, and then said: "Now I'm going to add," and then said: "2 and 21 is 13," etc. I'd say: "This is no blunder." '[20] We do not say that the person has made a blunder in adding. We say that he is not adding at all. We may say that he is fooling, or that he is insane. Consider now the view that evidence for religious beliefs is very slender. Wittgenstein considers the example of a man who dreams of the Last Judgement and then says he knows what it must be like.[21] If we think of this as we think of attempts to assess next week's weather, it is queer to think of the dream as slender evidence. 'If you compare it with anything in Science which we call evidence, you can't credit that anyone could soberly argue: "Well, I had this dream ... therefore ... Last Judge-

[16] Ibid., p. 55.   [18] Ibid., p. 56.   [20] Ibid., p. 62.
[17] Ibid., p. 53.   [19] Ibid., p. 59.   [21] See Ibid., p. 61.

ment." You might say: "For a blunder, that's too big." '[22] As in the other case, you might look for other explanations. You might say that the believer is joking or insane. But this brings us precisely to the heart of the misgivings I mentioned at the outset: how do we know that religious practices aren't forms of disguised nonsense, which, for some reason or another, believers do not recognize as such? This question brings us to the final section of the paper.

III

So far, I have been stressing how certain philosophers, because they have feared the implications of describing religious beliefs as distinctive language-games, have tried to show why religious beliefs are important in much the same way as one might show a certain course of action to be prudential; or have tried to show the rationality of religious beliefs by assuming that the existence of God is to be established by reference to criteria under which it falls as *one* appropriate instance among many. Such attempts, I argued, falsify the absolute character of many religious beliefs and values.

Against this, it might be urged that, in my view, religious believers can say what they like. Such a reaction is strengthened when philosophers talk of language-games as having criteria of intelligibility within them, and of the impossibility of rendering one language-game unintelligible in terms of criteria of intelligibility taken from another. It is important, however, not to confuse the view I have argued for with another which has superficial resemblances to it. The view I have in mind was once put forward by T. H. McPherson, 'Religion belongs to the sphere of the unsayable, so it is not to be wondered at that in theology there is much nonsense (i.e. many absurdities); this is the natural result of trying to put into words—and to discuss—various kinds of inexpressible "experiences", and of trying to say things about God.'[23] J. A. Passmore comments on this observation, 'One difficulty with this line of reasoning considered as a defence of religion, is that it "saves" religion only at the cost of leaving the door open to any sort of transcendental metaphysics—and indeed to superstition and nonsense of the most arrant sort.'[24] One difference between calling religious beliefs dis-

[22] Ibid., p. 61–2.
[23] T. H. McPherson 'Religion as the Inexpressible', in *New Essays in Philosophical Theology,* ed. by A. Flew and A. MacIntyre (London: S.C.M., 1955), p. 142.
[24] J. A. Passmore, 'Christianity and Positivism' in the *Australasian Journal of Philosophy,* 35 (1957), 128.

tinctive language-games and McPherson's observations, is that there is no talk of incomprehensibility in the former. On the contrary, within religious practices there will be criteria for what can and cannot be said. So a believer can commit blunders within his religion. But this observation might not satisfy the critics, since they might argue that a set of pointless rules could have an internal consistency. People can follow, and therefore fail to follow, pointless rules. In that way they may make mistakes. But the possibility of their being correct or incorrect would not of itself confer a point on a set of pointless rules. To argue, therefore, that religious beliefs are distinctive language-games with rules which their adherents may follow or fail to follow, does not, of itself, show that the rules have any point.

I think the misgivings I have outlined are justified. They point to a strain in the analogy between religious beliefs and games. The point of religious beliefs, why people *should* cherish them in the way they do, cannot be shown simply by *distinguishing between* religious beliefs and other features of human existence. What I am saying is that the importance of religion in people's lives cannot be understood simply by distinguishing between religion and other modes of social life, although, as we have seen, there are important distinctions to be made in this way. I had said elsewhere that if religion were thought of as cut off from other modes of social life it could not have the importance it has, but I had not realized the full implications of these remarks.[25] I have been helped to see them more clearly by Rush Rhees's important paper, 'Wittgenstein's Builders'.[26]

In the *Tractatus* Wittgenstein thought that all propositions must, simply by being propositions, have a general form. Rhees says that although Wittgenstein had given up the idea of 'all propositions' in the *Investigations*, he was still interested in human language and in what belonging to a common language meant.

When he says that any language is a family of language-games, and that any of these might be a complete language by itself, he does not say whether people who might take part in several such games would be speaking the same language in each of them. In fact I find it hard to see on this view that they would *ever* be speaking a language.[27]

[25] 'Philosophy, Theology and the Reality of God', *The Philosophical Quarterly*, Vol. 13 (1963).
[26] R. Rhees, 'Wittgenstein's Builders', *Proceedings of the Aristotelian Society*, Vol. 60 (1959–60). Reprinted in *Ludwig Wittgenstein: the Man and his Philosophy*, ed. K. T. Fann (New York: Dell, 1967).
[27] Ibid., p. 253.

Why does Rhees say this? One important reason, as he says, is that Wittgenstein takes it for granted that the same language is being spoken in the different language-games. But if this is so, the sameness or unity of that language cannot be explained by describing the way any *particular* language-game is played. The problem becomes acute when Wittgenstein says that each language-game could be a complete language in itself. One reason why Wittgenstein said that each language-game is complete is that he wanted to rid us of the supposition that all propositions have a general form. The different language-games do not make up one big game. For the most part, this is what I have been stressing in relation to religious language-games in this paper, but it gives rise to new problems. The different games do not make up a game, and yet Wittgenstein wants to say that a language, the same language, *is* a family of language-games; that is, that this is the kind of unity a language has. At this point, there is a strain in the analogy between language and a game.

In the example of the builders at the beginning of the *Investigations*, Wittgenstein says that the language of orders and response, one man shouting 'Slab!' and another bringing one, could be the entire language of a tribe. Rhees says, 'But I feel that there is something wrong here. The trouble is not to imagine a people with a language of such a limited vocabulary. The trouble is to imagine that they spoke the language only to give these special orders on this job and otherwise never spoke at all. I do not think it would be speaking a language.'[28]

As Rhees points out, Wittgenstein imagines the children of the tribe being taught these shouts by adults. But such teaching would not be part of the technique of order and response on the actual job. Presumably, men go home and sometimes discuss their work with their families. Sometimes one has to discuss snags which crop up in the course of a job. These things are not part of a technique either. What Wittgenstein describes, Rhees argues, is more like a game with building-stones and the correct methods of reacting to signals, than people actually building a house. What Rhees is stressing is that learning a language cannot be equated with learning what is generally done. 'It has more to do with what it makes sense to answer or what it makes sense to ask, or what sense one remark may have in connection with another.'[29] The expressions used by the builders cannot have their meaning entirely within the job. We would not be able to grasp the meaning of expressions, see the bearing of one expression on another, appreciate why something

---

[28] Ibid., p. 256.   [29] Ibid., p. 260.

can be said here but not there, unless expressions were connected with contexts other than those in which we are using them now. Rhees says that when a child comes to learn the differences between sensible discourse and a jumble of words, this

is not something you can teach him by any sort of drill, as you might perhaps teach him the names of objects. I think he gets it chiefly from the way in which the members of his family speak to him and answer him. In this way he gets an idea of how remarks may be connected, and of how what people say to one another makes sense. In any case, it is not like learning the meaning of this or that expression. And although he can go on speaking, this is not like going on with the use of any particular expression or set of expressions, although of course it includes that.[30]

What Rhees says of the builders can also be said of worshippers. If the orders and responses of the builders are cut off from everything outside the techniques on the job, we seem to be talking about a game with building-blocks, a system of responses to signs, rather than about the building of an actual house. Similarly, if we think of religious worship as cut off from everything outside the formalities of worship, it ceases to be worship and becomes an esoteric game. What is the difference between a rehearsal for an act of worship and the actual act of worship? The answer cannot be in terms of responses to signs, since the responses to signs may be correct in the rehearsal. The difference has to do with the point the activity has in the life of the worshippers, the bearing it has on other features of their lives. Religion has something to say about aspects of human existence which are quite intelligible without reference to religion: birth, death, joy, misery, despair, hope, fortune, and misfortune. The connection between these and religion is not contingent. A host of religious beliefs could not be what they are without them. The force of religious beliefs depends, in part, on what is outside religion. Consider, for example, Jesus's words, 'Not as the world giveth give I unto you.' Here, the force of the contrast between the teaching of Jesus and worldliness, depends, logically, on both parts of the contrast. One could not understand the sense in which Jesus gives, unless one also understands the sense in which the world gives. So far from it being true that religious beliefs can be thought of as isolated language-games, cut off from all other forms of life, the fact is that religious beliefs cannot be understood at all unless their relation to other modes of life is taken into account. Suppose someone were to say in objection to this, 'No, what you need to understand is religious language,' what

[30] Ibid., p. 262.

would one think of it? One could not be blamed if it reminded one of those who think that all will be well if an acceptable liturgy is devised—a piece of empty aestheticism. Religious beliefs could then be described literally as a game, a neat set of rules with ever increasing refinements in their interpretation and execution. It would be impossible to distinguish between genuine and sham worship. As long as the moves and responses in the liturgical game were correct, nothing more could be said. In fact, we should have described what religious practices often do become for those for whom they have lost their meaning: a charming game which provides a welcome contrast to the daily routine, but which has no relevance to anything outside the doors of the church. I suppose that Father Sergius knew more about religious language, the formalities of worship, than Pashenka. She was so absorbed in her day to day duties in cleaning the church, that she never had time to read the Bible herself or to attend worship. But her devotion, sacrifice and humility were such, that Sergius was led to say that she lived for God and imagined she lived for men, while he, versed in religious rite and language, lived for men and imagined he lived for God.

Religion must take the world seriously. I have argued that religious reactions to various situations cannot be assessed according to some external criteria of adequacy. On the other hand, the connections between religious beliefs and such situations must not be fantastic. This in no way contradicts the earlier arguments, since whether the connections are fantastic is decided by criteria which are not in dispute. For example, some religious believers may try to explain away the reality of suffering, or try to say that all suffering has some purpose. When they speak like this, one may accuse them of not taking suffering seriously. Or if religious believers talk of death as if it were a sleep of long duration, one may accuse them of not taking death seriously. In these examples, what is said about suffering and death can be judged in terms of what we already know and believe about these matters. The religious responses are fantastic because they ignore or distort what we already know. What is said falls under standards of judgement with which we are already acquainted. When what is said by religious believers does violate the facts or distort our apprehension of situations, no appeal to the fact that what is said is said in the name of religion can justify or excuse the violation and distortion.

Furthermore, one must stress the connection between religious beliefs and the world, not only in bringing out the force which these beliefs have, but also in bringing out the nature of the difficulties which the beliefs may occasion. If religious beliefs were isolated language-games, cut off from everything which is not formally religious, how could there be any of the characteristic difficulties connected with religious beliefs? The only difficulties which could arise would be akin to the difficulties connected with mastering a complex technique. But these are not the kind of difficulties which do arise in connection with religious beliefs. Is not *striving* to believe itself an important feature of religious belief? Why should this be so?

Consider, for example, difficulties which arise because of a tension between a believer's beliefs and his desires. He may find it difficult to overcome his pride, his envy, or his lust. But these difficulties cannot be understood unless serious account is taken of what pride, envy and lust involve. Neither can the positive virtues be understood without reference to the vices to which they are contrasted.

Consider also difficulties of another kind, not difficulties in holding to one's beliefs in face of temptation, but difficulties in believing. The problem of evil occasions the most well known of these. One might have heard someone talk of what it means to accept a tragedy as the will of God. He might have explained what Jesus meant when he said that a man must be prepared to leave his father and mother for his sake, by pointing out that this does not imply that children should forsake their parents. What Jesus was trying to show, he might say, is that for the believer, the death of a loved one must not make life meaningless. If it did, he would have given the loved one a place in his life which should only be given to God. The believer must be able to leave his father and mother, that is, face parting with them, and still be able to find the meaning of his life in God. Listening to this exposition, one might have thought it expressed what one's own beliefs amounted to. But then, suddenly, one has to face the death of one's child, and one realizes that one cannot put into practice, or find any strength or comfort in, the beliefs one had said were one's own. The untimely death of one's child renders talk of God's love meaningless for one. One might want to believe, but one simply cannot. This is not because a hypothesis has been assessed or a theory tested, and found wanting. It would be nearer the truth to say that a person cannot bring himself to react in a certain way, he has no use for a certain picture of the situation. The point I wish to stress, however, is that no sense can be made of this difficulty unless due account is taken of the tragedy. If religious beliefs were esoteric games, why should the tragedy have any bearing on them at all? Why should the tragedy be a difficulty for faith or a trial of faith?

From the examples we have considered, it can be seen that the meaning and force of religious beliefs depend in part on the relation of these beliefs with features of human existence other than religion. Without such dependence, religion would not have the importance it does have in people's lives. It is an awareness of these important truths which in part accounts for the philosophical objections to talking of religious beliefs as distinctive language-games. But these objections are confused. They are the result of drawing false conclusions from important truths. Having recognized, correctly, that the meaning of religious beliefs is partly dependent on features of human life outside religion, philosophers conclude, wrongly, that one would be contradicting oneself if one claimed to recognize this dependence, and also claimed that religious beliefs are distinctive language-games. They are led to this conclusion *only because they assume that the relation between religious beliefs and the non-religious facts, is that between what is justified and its justification, or that between a conclusion and its grounds.* This is a far-reaching confusion. To say that the meaning of religious beliefs is partly dependent on non-religious facts, is not to say that those beliefs are justified by, or could be inferred from, the facts in question.

The main points I have been trying to emphasize in this paper can be summed up in terms of some examples.

A boxer crosses himself before the fight—a mother places a garland on a statue of the Virgin Mary—parents pray for their child lost in a wreck. Are these blunders or religious activities? What decides the answer to this question is the surroundings, what the people involved say about their actions, what their expectations are, what, if anything, would render the activity pointless, and so on. Does the boxer think that anyone who crosses himself before a fight will not come to serious harm in it? Does the mother think that the garland's value is prudential? Do the parents believe that all true prayers for the recovery of children lead to that recovery? If these questions are answered in the affirmative, the beliefs involved become testable hypotheses. They are, as a matter of fact, blunders, mistakes, regarding causal connections of a kind. We can say that the people involved are reasoning wrongly, meaning by this that they contradict what we already know. The activities are brought under a system where theory, repeatability, explanatory force, etc. are important features, and they are shown to be wanting, shown to be blunders. But perhaps the activities have a different meaning. Perhaps the boxer is dedicating his performance in crossing himself, expressing the hope that it be worthy of what he believes in, and so on. The mother may be venerating the birth of her child as God's gift, thanking him for it and contemplating the virtues of motherhood as found in the mother of Jesus. The parents may be making their desires known to God, wanting the situation which has occasioned them to be met in him. The beliefs involved are not testable hypotheses, but ways of reacting to and meeting such situations. They are expressions of faith and trust. Not to use these objects of faith, not to have any time for the reactions involved, is not to believe. The distinction between religious belief and superstition is extremely important. I want to emphasize it by considering one of the above examples in a little more detail.

Consider again the example of two mothers who ask the Virgin Mary to protect their newly-born babies. Tylor would say that this is an example of 'a blind belief in processes wholly irrelevant to their supposed results'.[31] What I am stressing is that such a description begs the question as to what is meant by 'belief', 'processes', 'relevance' and 'results' in this context. For Tylor, the supposed results would be the future material welfare of the child, and the irrelevant processes would be the bringing of the child to a statue of the Virgin Mary and the connections which might be thought to exist between this and the future fortunes of the child. How could the irrelevance be demonstrated? The answer seems to be simple. All one needs is a comparison of the material fortunes of babies for whom the blessing of the Virgin has been sought, and the material fortunes of those who have received no such blessing. The results will be statistically random. One is reminded of the suggestion that the efficacy of prayer could be shown by observing two patients suffering from the same ailment one of whom is treated medically and the other of whom is simply prayed for. The idea seems to be that prayer is a way of getting things done which competes with other ways of getting things done, and that the superiority of one way over the other could be settled experimentally. Now, of course, I am not denying that a mother who brings her baby to the Virgin Mary could have the kind of expectations which Tylor would attribute to *any* mother who asks the Virgin to protect her baby. And I agree that if these were her expectations, her act would be a superstitious one. What characterizes the superstitious act in this context? Firstly, there is the trust in non-existent quasi-causal connections; the belief that someone long dead called the Virgin Mary, can, if she so desires, determine the course of an individual's life, keep him from harm, make his ventures succeed, and so on. Secondly, the Virgin Mary is seen as a means to ends which are intelligible without reference to her: freedom from harm, successful ventures, etc. In other words, the act of homage to the Virgin Mary

[31] E. B. Tylor, *Primitive Culture* (London: John Murray, 1871), Vol. 1, p. 133.

has no importance in itself; she is reduced to the status of a lucky charm. What one *says* to the Virgin makes no difference. But someone may object to this. How can this be said? Surely, what is said to her makes all the difference in the world. If one worships before her one is blessed with good fortune, but if one blasphemes one is cursed with bad fortune. But this is precisely why I say that what one says to the Virgin makes no difference. *As it happens,* freedom from physical harm, fortune in one's ventures, is secured in this way, but the way is only important in so far as these things are secured. If they could be obtained more economically or more abundantly by pursuing some other way, that way would be adopted. What is said is only important as long as it leads to the desired end, *an end which can be understood independently of what is said.* On this view, the act of bringing one's child to the Virgin could be shown to be valid or invalid in terms of future consequences.

But why is it confused to understand *all* acts of homage to the Virgin in this way. The answer is because the religious character of the homage paid to the Virgin is completely ignored. Or, at least, it is assumed that its religious character is reducible to its efficacy *as one way among others* of securing certain ends. As I have said, bringing a child to a statue of the Virgin may be superstitious, but it may not. A mother may bring her new-born baby to the mother of Jesus in an act of veneration and thanksgiving: one mother greets another at the birth of a child. Connected with this act of greeting are a number of associated beliefs and attitudes: wonder and gratitude in face of new life, humility at being the means of bringing a child into the world, and, in this case, recognition of life as God's gift, the givenness of life. But what about the protection sought for the child? What is important to recognize is that the protection must be understood in terms of these beliefs and attitudes. These virtues and attitudes are all contained in the person of Mary, the mother of Jesus. For the believer, she is the paradigm of these virtues and attitudes. They constitute her holiness. Now when her protection is sought, the protection is the protection of her holiness: the mother wants the child's life to be orientated in these virtues. The first act in securing such an orientation is the bringing of the child to the Virgin. This orientation is what the believer would call the blessing of the Virgin Mary.

The difference between the two situations I want to contrast should now be clear. In the one case, the protection determines whether or not the act of bringing the child to the Virgin and the alleged holiness of the Virgin have been efficacious or not. In the other case, it is the holiness of the Virgin which determines the nature of the protection. In Tylor's

account there is no need to refer to the religious significance which the
Virgin Mary has for believers. But on the view I am urging, you cannot
understand the request for a blessing unless that is taken account of, or
think of the blessing as one way among many of producing the same
result.

The above remarks can be applied to one of Tylor's own examples.
Tylor believes that the soul is migrant, 'capable of leaving the body far
behind, to flash swiftly from place to place'.[32] He traces among various
peoples the belief in the soul as breath or a ghost:

> And if any should think such expression due to mere metaphor, they may
> judge the strength of the implied connexion between breath and spirit by
> cases of most unequivocal significance. Among the Seminoles of Florida,
> when a woman died in childbirth, the infant was held over her face to
> receive her parting spirit, and thus acquire strength and knowledge for its
> future use. These Indians could have well understood why at the death-bed
> of an ancient Roman, the nearest kinsman leant over to inhale the last breath
> of the departing.... Their state of mind is kept up to this day among
> Tyrolese peasants, who can still fancy a good man's soul to issue from his
> mouth at death like a little white cloud.[33]

Tylor thinks that the meaning of these examples is unequivocal:
power is being transferred from one being to another by means of the
transfer of a soul which he envisages as a non-material substance. Notice
the neglect of the situations in which these actions take place. All Tylor
sees is the alleged transfer of pseudo power by odd means. If we asked
Tylor why the mother's soul *should* be transferred to the baby rather than
to anyone else, or why the ancient Roman's soul *should* be transferred to
the nearest kinsman rather than to anyone else, I suppose he would
answer that such a transfer was laid down by social rules. He might
even say that such a transfer is natural. But the naturalness is not
brought out at all by Tylor's analysis. On his view, the power, via the
migrant soul, could have gone into *any* being, but, as it happened, it was
decreed or thought natural that it should go where it did.

We get a very different picture if we take note of the situations in
which these actions take place: the relationship between a dying mother
and her child, and the relationship between a dying man and his nearest
kinsman. In these cases, why should Tylor find the symbolic actions
odd? A mother has given her life in bringing her child into the world.
The breath of life, her mother's life, her mother's soul, is breathed into
the child. Surely, this is an act of great beauty. But one cannot under-

[32] Ibid., Vol. 1, ch. XI, p. 429.   [33] Ibid., p. 433.

stand it outside the relationship between a dying mother and her child. Similarly, it is in terms of the relationship between a dying man and his next of kin that the symbolic act of passing on authority and tradition is to be understood. It would not make sense to say that *anyone* could be the object of these acts. If the wrong child were held over the dying woman's face, what would be terrible is not, as Tylor thinks, that power has been transferred to the wrong person, but that this child hasn't the relationship to the woman that her own child has: it is not the child for whom she gave her life. The expression of love and sacrifice expressed in the mother's parting breath is violated if it is received by the wrong child.

In the examples we have considered, we have seen that the religious or ritualistic practices could not be what they are were it not for factors independent of them. The internal consistency of rules, something to which astrology could appeal, does not show that the rules have a point. To see this one must take account of the connection between the practices and other features of the lives people lead. It is such connections which enable us to see that astrology is superstitious and that many religious practices can be distinguished from superstition, while other so-called religious practices turn out to be superstitious.

But the main point I wish to stress is that it does not make sense to ask for a proof of the validity of religious beliefs, whatever that might mean. Consider finally the example of the mother who reacts to the birth of her baby by an act of devotion to the Virgin Mary. It is true that the act of devotion could not be what it is without the birth of the baby, which, after all, occasioned it. It is also true that the connection between the religious act and the baby's birth must not be fantastic.[34] It must be shown not to be superstition. But having made these points, it is also important to stress that birth is not evidence from which one can assess the religious reaction to it. People react to the birth of children in various ways. Some may say that the birth of a child is always a cause for rejoicing. Others may say that whether one rejoices at the birth of a child should be determined by the physical and mental health of the child, or by whether the family into which it is born can look after it properly. Others may say that one should always give thanks to God when a child is born. Others may condemn the folly of those responsible for bringing a child into a world such as this. All these reactions are reactions to the birth of a child, and could not mean what they do apart from the fact of the birth. But it does not follow that the various

[34] Of course, the matter may be further complicated by the fact that people may well disagree over whether a given connection is fantastic or not.

reactions can be inferred from the birth, or that they are conclusions for which the birth of the baby is the ground. All one can say is that people *do* respond in this way. Many who respond in one way will find the other responses shallow, trivial, fantastic, meaningless, or even evil. But the force of the responses cannot be justified in any external way; it can merely be shown. This is true of religious responses, the religious beliefs which have an absolute character and value. Philosophy may clarify certain misunderstandings about them. It may show the naivety of certain objections to religion, or that some so-called religious beliefs are superstitions. But philosophy is neither for nor against religious beliefs. After it has sought to clarify the grammar of such beliefs its work is over. As a result of such clarification, someone may see dimly that religious beliefs are not what he had taken them to be. He may stop objecting to them, even though he does not believe in them. Someone else may find that now he is able to believe. Another person may hate religion more than he did before the philosophical clarification. The results are unpredictable. In any case, they are not the business of philosophy.

VIII

BELIEF 'IN' AND BELIEF 'THAT'[1]

H. H. PRICE

PART I

Introduction

EPISTEMOLOGISTS have not usually had much to say about believing 'in', though ever since Plato's time they have been interested in believing 'that'. Students of religion, on the other hand, have been greatly concerned with belief 'in', and many of them, I think, would maintain that it is something quite different from belief 'that'. Surely belief 'in' is an attitude to a person, whether human or divine, while belief 'that' is just an attitude to a proposition? Could any difference be more obvious than this? And if we overlook it, shall we not be led into a quite mistaken analysis of religious belief, at any rate if it is religious belief of the theistic sort? On this view belief 'in' is not a propositional attitude at all.

On the face of it, this radical distinction between belief-in and belief-that[2] seems plausible to anyone who knows from the inside what religious experience of the theistic sort is like. But to many philosophers it seems to have hardly any plausibility. It seems obvious to them that belief-in is in one way or another reducible to belief-that. This reduction, they would say, is not really very difficult, certainly not difficult enough to be interesting; and that, presumably, is why epistemologists have seldom thought it necessary to discuss belief-in very seriously. Why make such a fuss about this distinction between 'in' and 'that', when it is little or nothing more than a difference of idiom?

I wish to suggest, however, that the distinction between belief-in and belief-that does at any rate deserve careful discussion. The question whether belief-in is or is not reducible to belief-that is by no means trivial, nor is it at all an easy question to answer.

From *Religious Studies*, 1 (1965), 1–27. Reprinted by permission of the author and Cambridge University Press.

[1] Much of Part I of this article is a reproduction of a lecture which was included in the writer's Gifford Lectures, delivered at the University of Aberdeen in 1959–60.

[2] From now on, I shall sometimes write 'belief-in' and 'belief-that' with hyphens.

It is not trivial. Religious belief, whether we like it or not, is quite an important phenomenon. Those who have no religious belief themselves should still try to understand what kind of an attitude it is, and they cannot hope to understand it unless they pay some attention to what is said by those who do have it. Moreover, as we shall see presently, religious belief-in is by no means the only sort. Nearly everyone believes 'in' someone or something, whether he believes in God or not.

.Nor is our question an easy one to decide. Quite a strong case can be made for each of the two views which have been mentioned, the 'irreducibility thesis' on the one hand, and the 'reducibility thesis' on the other. The decision between them is made more difficult (though also more interesting) because belief-in, or at least some instances of it, cuts across the boundary sometimes drawn between the cognitive side of human nature, concerned with what is true or false, and the evaluative side, concerned with what is good or evil. Either the boundary vanishes altogether, or we find ourselves on both sides of it at the same time.

There is also a preliminary inquiry, whose importance has not perhaps been fully appreciated by either party in this controversy. Neither perhaps has considered a large enough range of examples. The expression 'believe-in' is used in a good many different contexts. For all we can tell beforehand, there might be several different sorts of belief-in, and the reducibility thesis might be correct for some of them, but incorrect or highly questionable for others. Let us begin, then, by considering 'the varieties of believing-in'; and it may be as well to consider some examples of *dis*believing-in too.

The varieties of believing 'in'

First we will consider a number of examples which seem *prima facie* to support the irreducibility thesis. Whatever merits this thesis may have, it is certainly an over-simplification to say that belief-in is always an attitude to a person, human or divine.[3]

Surely it is perfectly possible to believe in a non-human animal. The blind man believes in his guide-dog. A medieval knight or a modern fox-hunter might easily believe in his horse. A falconer might believe

---

[3] We need not here consider in what sense God may be described as 'personal'. It is sufficient for our purpose that in theistic religion personal pronouns are held to be applicable to the Supreme Being: and not only the pronoun 'we', but also (and more important) the pronouns 'thou' or 'you'.

in this hawk and not believe, or believe less, in that one. And vegetable organisms, as well as animals, can be believed in. A keen gardener might believe in his chrysanthemums, but not in his strawberry plants.

Moreover, it is not only living things which can be believed in. One may believe in a machine. A motorist can believe in his car. Or, if he is more discriminating, he may believe in some parts of its mechanism but not in others, or not much. He may have great confidence in his brakes but less confidence in his battery.

It is even possible to believe in a non-living natural object. Let us consider a remark attributed to the seventeenth-century English statesman, Lord Halifax the Trimmer: 'The first article in an Englishman's creed is "I believe in the sea."' It is true that for many centuries Englishmen did believe in the sea, though nowadays they would be better advised to believe in the air. Nor need the belief in the sea be confined to inhabitants of islands. It could well be said that the Vikings of the ninth and tenth centuries believed in it too.

Again, one may believe in an event, as opposed to a person or thing. In a war, or at least in its early stages, many people believe in the victory of their country. In some religious beliefs, it is an event which is believed in, and it may be either a past event or a future one. Examples are the Christian belief in the Incarnation, and the Second Coming of Christ.

In all these cases, one is believing in an entity of some sort, whether personal or non-personal, whether a substance or an event. But one may also believe in an institution. An entry in *Who's Who* many years ago concluded with the words 'believes in the British Empire'. At the time when they were written, those words were perfectly intelligible, though if someone were to write or utter them now we should be puzzled, because there is no longer a British Empire to be believed in, or disbelieved in either. Again, most people believe in their own university or college or school, and have less belief, or none, in other universities, colleges or schools.

But, further, one can believe not only in an individual entity, but in a class of entities. The falconer may believe in goshawks, in goshawks in general, as a species, and not merely in this particular goshawk of his own. (Indeed, he need not own one himself.) Many people nowadays believe almost to excess in penicillin—not just in this dose of penicillin or that, but in penicillin as such. There are also many who believe almost to excess in computers. In such cases, what is believed in is something very different from an individual person. It belongs to a different logical type: though it is true that the class believed in may happen to be a class of persons ('I believe in men who have worked their way up to the top, not in those who were born with a silver spoon in their mouths.')

One may also believe in a class of institutions. Some people believe in private preparatory schools, though others disbelieve in them. In a letter to the London *Times* some years ago, the writer said, 'I believe in railways.'[4] more recently a spokesman for a well-known motor company was reported to have said 'we do not believe in waiting-lists'. The emphasis was on 'we'. Here we have the converse point. Most motor manufacturers do still believe in waiting-lists. This company's lack of belief in them, or, more probably, disbelief in them, was rather unusual. (Perhaps a waiting-list is not exactly an institution. But it is something like one. It could at any rate be described as 'a social device'.) Again, there are still some people who do not believe in banks and prefer to keep their money in a stocking or in a hole under the floorboards. They do not just disbelieve in this particular bank or that. They disbelieve in banks as such. But most people believe in 'the banking system' pretty firmly.

But what is believed in may be even more 'abstract' than this. One may believe in a procedure or method or policy. Indeed, this is a very common type of belief-in. At one time many Englishmen used to believe in taking a cold bath every morning, and probably some still do. Some people believe in classical education. Many nowadays do not. Instead, they believe in an education which fits one for life in the modern world. Some people believe in abstaining from alcohol when they have to drive a car or pilot an aircraft immediately afterwards. Most of us only go to our dentist when we have toothache. But there are some who believe in going to him regularly once a year, whether they have toothache or not. An interesting example of *lack* of belief in a method or procedure (or perhaps of disbelief in it) could be noticed in a recent statement by the President of a well-known educational body: 'Of course, we have never believed in measuring the effectiveness of what we do in terms of numbers alone.' There are many others who would say, more generally, that they have no belief in statistics. But there are some who seem almost to believe in nothing else.

Again, one may believe (or disbelieve) in equal pay for both sexes, in easier divorce, in the abolition of the House of Lords, in aid 'without strings' to under-developed countries, in settling all disputes by non-violent methods, and in all sorts of 'causes', good, bad, or indifferent.

[4] Sir Egbert Cadbury, *The Times*, 9 September 1959.

Indeed, it is not easy to set any limits at all to the types of 'objects' which may be believed in. (It will be obvious that many examples already given take us a very long way from belief in a person, either human or divine.) But since one must stop somewhere, I shall end my list with one more example, belief in a theory.

This is an instructive example, because at first sight belief in a theory might seem so obviously reducible to a set of beliefs *that*. What is a theory but a logically connected set of propositions? So when someone is said to believe in a theory, surely his attitude is just a rather complicated form of believing 'that'? He would believe *that p*, that *q*, that *r*, that *p* entails *q*, that *r* is highly probable in relation to *q*, etc. Now of course such beliefs-that are an essential part of belief-in a theory. But are they the whole of it? If this were a complete account of the believer's attitude, it would be more appropriate to say, 'he accepts the theory', or, 'he believes that it is correct', and not, 'he believes *in* it'. Belief *in* a theory has some resemblance to belief in penicillin, or belief in an instrument such as the electron microscope. The theory, when you have understood it, gives you power: a power of satisfying intellectual curiosity, of finding things out which were previously unknown, of making verifiable predictions which could not otherwise be made, and of reducing an apparently disconnected mass of brute facts to some sort of intelligible order. When someone believes *in* a theory, it is this power-conferring aspect of it which he has in mind, and he esteems or values the theory accordingly. It is a fact about human nature that power of this kind is very highly esteemed by some people.

Moreover, a person may still believe in a theory though he is aware that it contains paradoxes which have not yet been resolved. In that case he cannot believe that it is entirely correct. But he may still esteem it highly, and believe in it as an intellectually powerful instrument. He may use it constantly in his own investigations and encourage others to do the same. He relies on the theory, we might even say he trusts it. But in the belief-that sense he does not altogether believe it. If I am not mistaken, this was the attitude which many scientists had to the Quantum Theory in the early days of its development.

Something rather similar applies to metaphysical theories too, or at least to metaphysical theories of the synoptic type, which attempt to provide us with a unified 'view of the world' or 'world-outlook'. Such theories, one may suggest, are believed *in* rather than just believed in the belief-that sense, and disbelieved *in* rather than just disbelieved. Indeed, it is doubtful whether words like 'true' or 'false', 'correct' or 'incorrect' are the appropriate ones to apply to them. 'Adequate', 'not

wholly adequate', 'relatively satisfactory' are expressions which fit the
case better. The adherents of a particular metaphysical world view,
Schopenhauer's for instance, believe *in* it somewhat as a plumber believes in his bagful of tools or a housewife in her cookery-book. And
like the plumber and the housewife, they may 'believe in it' with some
reservations. What such a synoptic metaphysician offers us is a systematically ordered set of conceptual instruments, which will enable us (so
he claims) to make sense of human experience, to unify apparently disconnected facts and reconcile apparently conflicting ones. To put it
negatively, he claims to deliver us from the predicament of having to
experience the world as 'just one thing after another': a predicament
which some human beings dislike intensely, though others do not mind
it.

Reducible 'beliefs in'

We have now considered a number of examples of belief-in which
suggest that it is quite a different attitude from belief-that. We have also
seen how very various they are, although belief in a person (human
or divine) may well be the most important type of belief-in. Still, despite
these differences, they do all support the irreducibility thesis; or at least
they seem *prima facie* to support it.

But it is not very difficult to find examples which point the other way.
An obvious one is belief in fairies. Believing in fairies amounts to no
more than believing that fairies exist. Again, if someone believes in the
Loch Ness monster, he just believes that there is a very large aquatic
creature which inhabits Loch Ness. We often hear people say they 'do
not believe in the supernatural'. What they do not believe is *that* supernatural events occur or that supernatural beings exist.

The same applies sometimes even when one expresses belief in a
person. If someone says he believes in King Arthur, he just expresses
his belief *that* there was such a person, or at least a person who had
some of the characteristics attributed to Arthur in the earlier versions
of the Arthurian legend. For instance, he may believe that in the late
fifth and early sixth centuries there was a Romano-British *dux bellorum*
called something like Artorius, who commanded a troop of heavily
armed cavalry and defeated the Saxons at Mons Badonicus about the
year A.D. 500. This belief-in is very different indeed from the belief in
Artorius which one of his own heavily-armed cavalrymen ('knights')
may have had. There is nothing in it of esteem or trust or loyalty. It
is just a case of believing an existential proposition, believing that there
was a person to whom a certain complex description applied. It is much

the same when a classical scholar believes 'in' Homer. He believes *that* there was one poet and only one who wrote at least the greater part of the *Iliad* and the *Odyssey*, and that 'Homer' was his name.

Similarly, if someone disbelieves in Arthur or in Homer or in fairies, he just disbelieves an existential proposition. We may contrast this with the disbelief which British Tories had in Mr. Gladstone. It was an attitude of disesteem or distrust. We notice, however, that they could not have disbelieved in him unless they believed *that* there was such a person. To disbelieve in him in one sense they had to believe in him in another. Nor could they disbelieve in his foreign policy unless they believed *that* he had one.

There does seem to be an attitude which might be called minimal or merely factual belief-in. One might be tempted to call it existential belief-in, since what is believed here is an existential proposition. That indeed is what it is, in the logician's sense of the word 'existential', so far as these examples are concerned.[5] But existentialist philosophers have introduced a new and entirely different sense of the word 'existential'; and in *their* sense the word would apply to the kind of belief-in illustrated by our previous set of examples, where belief-in seems, on the face of it, to be irreducible to belief-that. It is perhaps one of their merits that they have paid more attention than most other philosophers to beliefs-in of this apparently 'irreducible' sort.

Be that as it may, there certainly is a minimal or merely factual sense of 'believe in'. This is a very common and familiar use of the expression 'believe in'; and 'believing in' in this sense certainly *is* reducible to 'belief that'. It is even possible that when a person says 'I believe in God' he is expressing no more than a minimal or factual belief 'in'. He may just believe *that* there is a God, or *that* God exists. When a religious person says it, he is almost certainly expressing something more; and this perhaps is the point of Pascal's distinction between *Dieu d'Abraham, Dieu d'Isaac, Dieu de Jacob*, and *Le Dieu des philosophes et des savants.* It is perfectly possible to believe that God exists without being a religious person at all; and certainly the ordinary use of language allows us to speak of this 'belief-that' as a 'belief-in'.

Similarly, in 1492 when Columbus set sail, there may well have been geographers who could say, sincerely, that they too believed 'in' a westerly sea-route from Europe to the Indies. Nevertheless, their belief-in differed very considerably from his. They just accepted an existential proposition, the proposition 'that there is' such a sea-route. Columbus

[5] We shall see presently that there are other examples where the propositions believed belong to other logical types (p. 150, below).

accepted it too. But he was prepared to risk his life on it. He 'put his trust in' this westerly sea-route which he believed to exist, and they did not.

Other examples of 'reducible' belief-in

There are also examples of a rather different kind where belief-in does seem to be reducible to belief-that. The proposition which the 'reduction' yields need not necessarily be an existential proposition. If I believe in the combustibility of nylon and the incombustibility of asbestos, I believe that nylon is combustible and asbestos is not. If I believe in the infrequency of lunar rainbows, I believe that lunar rainbows are infrequent. Again, if a philosopher says he believes in free will, the obvious rendering of this is 'he believes that all men (or all rational beings) have the power of free choice'. To say instead 'he believes that free will exists' or 'that there is such a thing as free will' is less explicit, and does not bring out the full force of the belief-in expression which we are trying to analyse.

Sometimes, no doubt, it does not matter very much whether the reduction takes an existential form or not. (One *can* say, 'he believes that there is such a theory as the longevity of tortoises'.) But there are other cases where it does matter. For instance, someone says, 'I have never quite believed in her blond hair'. If this is to be interpreted in a 'belief-that' sense, what exactly was the belief-that which the speaker could never quite hold? It certainly was not the belief that the blond hair existed. He never doubted its existence. But he did doubt whether it was the lady's own. He surmised that she wore a skilfully-made wig; or he surmised that though it was her own hair, its original colour had been very different. And now one or other of these surmises has turned out to be correct.

Finally, it is worth while to notice that the converse rendering of belief-that sentences into belief-in sentences is also possible, at least sometimes; and this gives some support to the doctrine mentioned earlier that the difference between the two is 'merely one of idiom'. Believing that all whales are mammals could equally be described as believing in the mammality of all whales. Believing that no Englishman plays ice hockey as well as some Canadians does not seem to differ from believing in the inferiority of all Englishmen to some Canadians as ice-hockey players. Believing that the Sahara would be habitable if it were irrigated does not seem to differ from believing in [the habitability of the Sahara on condition of its being irrigated]. But here we have to insert brackets to avoid an ambiguity. 'If the Sahara were

irrigated, then I should believe that it is habitable' and 'I believe that
if the Sahara were irrigated, it would be habitable' are two different
statements. We have to put in the brackets to show that our belief-in
statement is the equivalent of the second, not of the first.

Sometimes the change-over from 'that' to 'in' is not easy to make with
our existing terminological resources. The 'belief-in' rendering of a
'belief-that' sentence may be clumsy, long-winded, and inelegant: for
example, 'I believe in his either coming this morning after breakfast
or putting off his visit until lunch-time on the second Sunday of next
month.' But certainly there are a good many cases where the difference
between 'in' and 'that' can quite fairly be called a mere difference of
idiom, and there are more of them than we might have supposed.

The relevance of this to our main question 'Is belief-in reducible to
belief-that?' can now be seen. Equivalence is a symmetrical relation.
If A is equivalent to B, it follows logically that B is equivalent to A. So
if we are willing to use the syntactical expedients which have been
illustrated, the number of 'belief-in' sentences which have 'belief-that'
equivalents turns out to be much larger than we thought. Nor does it
matter if some of these 'belief-in' sentences have an exceedingly artificial
air, so that no one would in practice be likely to utter them. They are
intelligible, however complicated, long-winded, and inelegant they may
be.

Two different senses of 'belief-in'

It is only too obvious by now that the question 'Is belief-in reducible
to belief-that?' is a complicated and difficult one. There is much to be
said on both sides. We began by considering a number of examples
which suggest rather strongly that no such reduction is possible. Instead,
they suggest that belief-in is an attitude quite different from belief-that.
We have now considered a number of other examples, which suggest
equally strongly that belief-in *is* reducible to belief-that. What conclusion are we to draw when we consider both sets of examples together?

The obvious conclusion is this: there are two different senses of
'believe in'. On the one hand, there is an evaluative sense. This is illustrated by believing in one's doctor, or believing in railways, or believing
in a procedure such as taking a cold bath every morning. Something
like esteeming or trusting is an essential part of belief-in in this sense.
(The other part of it would be conceiving or having in mind whatever it
is that is esteemed or trusted.) As we have seen, the 'objects' of belief-in,
in this sense, are enormously various. It is a mistake to suppose that
its 'object' must always be a person. There is a corresponding sense of

'disbelief in', where our attitude is something like disesteem or distrust. This is quite commonly expressed by saying 'I do not believe in ...', much as dislike is quite commonly expressed by saying 'I do not like ...' It is illustrated by 'we do not believe in waiting-lists', or by the disbelief in Mr. Gladstone which most contemporary British Tories had. In this sense of 'believe in', believing-in does seem to be a quite different attitude from belief-that and irreducible to it. The same applies to the corresponding sense of 'disbelieve in'.

On the other hand, there is also a factual sense of 'believe in'. The most obvious examples of it are the belief in fairies or the belief in King Arthur. Belief-in, in this sense, certainly *is* reducible to belief-that. In these examples one believes an existentialist proposition. One believes *that* there is something to which such and such a description applies. But as we have seen, there are other examples of 'reducible' belief-in where the proposition believed is not an existential one. There is also a corresponding and equally reducible sense of 'disbelieve in'. If someone disbelieves in fairies, he just disbelieves that there are such creatures, or rejects the proposition that there are. And if he disbelieves (in this sense) in free will, he disbelieves or rejects the proposition that human beings have the power of making free choices.

Moreover, just because these two senses of 'belief-in' are different, the attitude denoted by the one can be combined with the attitude denoted by the other. One may *both* believe that there is such and such a thing *and* have esteem for it or trust in it. The writer to *The Times* who believed in railways is an example. So is Lord Halifax's Englishman, who believes in the sea. Again, one may both believe that there is such a thing and have disesteem for it or distrust in it, like those who say 'we do not believe in waiting-lists'. Here disbelief-in, in the evaluative sense, is combined with belief-in, in the factual sense: and there is no inconsistency in this combination. In St. James's Epistle a similar combination of attitudes is attributed to the devils who 'believe and tremble'. They believe that God exists, and we may suppose they believe it with full conviction too. At the same time they have an attitude of distrust towards him.

Connections between the two senses

Let us assume that there are these two different senses of 'believe in', the evaluative sense and the factual sense. If there are, there is also a close connection between them, when the 'object' of evaluative belief-in is an *entity* of any kind. I cannot trust my doctor unless I at least believe that there is a person to whom the description 'being my doctor' applies.

But the phrase 'at least' is important, as Norman Malcolm has pointed out. A person who is believed in, in the evaluative sense, may be known to the believer by personal acquaintance. Malcolm's example is a wife who says of her husband, 'I believe in Tom.' It would not be false to say of her, 'she believes that there is such a person', but it would be saying too little. Similarly, if you believe in your doctor you probably know him by personal acquaintance (in some degree at any rate) though you do of course believe that he is your doctor, and probably hold other beliefs-that about him as well, for instance that he is about forty years old, and that he lives at No. 50A Tankerville Avenue. Again, the blind man who believes in his guide-dog knows the dog by acquaintance almost as one knows a human friend.

On the other hand, personal acquaintance is certainly not a necessary condition for evaluative belief-in. On the contrary, when one comes to be personally acquainted with a person whom one believes in, one's belief in him may decrease or even vanish altogether. (Fortunately this also applies to disbelief in a person, which quite often decreases or vanishes when one meets him.) To take an example of quite a different kind: the Managing Director may believe in waiting-lists so long as he has no personal experience of being put on a waiting-list himself; but at last this experience befalls him, when he is trying to get his mowing-machine repaired, and then his belief in waiting-lists is considerably shaken and may even be replaced by a disbelief in them. The opposite 'conversion', from disbelief in a method or procedure to belief in it, may occur in a similar way. Many disbelieve in air travel so long as they have not actually tried it. But when they are compelled to try it, because there is no other way of getting to their destination in time, the result of this personal experience is that their disbelief in air travel vanishes and is replaced by a firm belief in it. These examples do, however, show that Professor Malcolm's point about acquaintance is relevant not only to belief in another person, but to other cases of evaluative belief-in as well.

Is factual belief-in a presupposition of evaluation belief-in?

Shall we say, then, that anyone who believes in X in the evaluative sense must also believe in X in the factual sense—this at least, though he may know X by acquaintance too? This is an attractive suggestion. It offers us a neat and tidy way of formulating the relation between the two senses of 'belief in'; factual belief-in would just be a necessary condition for evaluative belief-in, or a presupposition of it. But unfortunately this is too neat and tidy to be true, if 'believing in X in the factual sense' is taken to mean 'believing that X exists', which is the natural way to take it. So interpreted, the formula proposed would fit some of the many varieties of evaluative belief-in, but not all of them.

For instance, does it fit belief in a procedure such as taking a cold bath every morning? At first we may be inclined to think it does. For surely anyone who holds this belief-in does also believe 'that there is' such a procedure? Some people still take a cold bath every morning and many people did so fifty years ago. Perhaps it will also be said that anyone who believes in taking a cold bath every morning must himself take one every morning (or most mornings); for if he did not, he could not be sincere when he claims to believe in doing so. In that case he not only believes but knows that there is such a procedure, and moreover he has acquired this knowledge-that by personal experience of instances of the procedure.

But these two arguments are inconclusive. A man might believe sincerely and very firmly in taking a cold bath every morning, even though he had been a bed-ridden invalid all his life and had never been able to take a bath at all. Or he might be a Bedouin who lives in the Mesopotamian desert and never has enough water to take a bath. It is conceivable too that neither of these persons has ever heard of anyone else who took daily cold baths. Either of them might be an original thinker, who has managed to think of this curious procedure for himself; and having thought of it, he values it highly, without ever being able to put it into practice.

The same applies to belief in equal pay for both sexes. This is a policy which a man could believe in (and some presumably did) at a time when it had not been put into practice anywhere. Nor is it true that if such a man was sincere, he must have put it into practice himself, by paying his male butler and his female housemaid equally. He need not have had any employees himself; and if he had, they may all have been of the same sex.

In what sense, then, did he believe 'that there is such a thing as' paying the two sexes equally? Only in a pretty tenuous sense of 'there is'. It did not amount to much more than believing that the concept of paying the two sexes equally for the same work is not self-contradictory, or believing that the proposition 'the two sexes are paid equally for the same work', though false at that time, is not necessarily false.

Nevertheless, there was another and not quite so tenuous belief-that which he did have to hold, if he was sincere in believing in this policy. He had to believe that the policy was practicable, or in principle practicable, whatever obstacles might have to be overcome before it was put into practice. And if we like, we can describe this as a belief 'in its being practicable', and then we are using 'belief-in' in its factual sense. Similarly any sincere believer in taking daily cold baths must believe that this procedure is in principle practicable, even if he can never practise it himself and has never heard of anyone else who did.

But what shall we say of belief in an 'ideal', such as the ideal of complete unselfishness? A man who believes in this ideal does have to believe that complete unselfishness is logically possible, not self-contradictory as some have alleged that it is. But does he have to believe that it is practicable? Surely a man may sincerely believe in an ideal while admitting that it is quite 'unrealizable'? Indeed, it might be said that unrealizability is one of the distinguishing features of an ideal (as opposed e.g. to a policy). Still, there *is* a belief-that concerning practicability or realizability which a sincere believer in an ideal has to hold. Whatever his ideal is, he has to believe that approximations to it are practicable, and approximations closer, or much closer, than those which exist at present. It may not be practicable for any human being, still less for most, to be completely unselfish in all his actions, utterances, thoughts desires, and feelings. But it is practicable for almost anyone to be a good deal more unselfish than he has been hitherto. At any rate a person must believe that it is, if he sincerely believes in the ideal of complete unselfishness. And if we like, we can formulate this belief-that in 'reducible' or merely factual belief-in terminology. Such a believer may be said to believe in its being empirically possible for these approximations to occur.

'Belief in' and 'confidence in'

It does seem to be true that factual belief-in is a necessary condition for evaluative belief-in, or a presupposition of it. But we must be careful to add that this factual belief-in may take many different forms, corresponding to the many different varieties of evaluative belief-in. It need not always take the form of believing an existential proposition, believing that X exists or that 'there is such a thing as X', when X is what is evaluatively believed in.

Nevertheless, the cases where it does take this form are of considerable importance. They make it very clear that we must distinguish between two different senses of 'believe in', an evaluative sense and a factual sense; otherwise we are led into absurd misunderstandings.

For instance, little Belinda says she does not believe in Santa Claus any more. The Christmas presents he brings her now are not nearly so nice as they used to be, and there are not so many of them either. Shall we say, 'Naughty child! Little liar! You certainly do believe in him if you make these complaints about the way he has treated you'? Yet these comments would be justified if the factual sense of 'believe in' were the only one.

We may notice, however, that such misunderstandings do not arise if we use the phrase 'confidence in' instead of 'belief in'. 'Confidence in' does not have these two different senses, evaluative and factual; and the distinction between 'confidence in' and 'confidence that' is a pretty clear-cut one. If I say I have confidence in someone, it is pretty plain that I am expressing an evaluative attitude; and if I have lost confidence in him, because of something he has done or failed to do, what I have lost is pretty clearly an evaluative attitude. Of course, if I do lose confidence in him I must still retain my confidence *that* he exists. But no one is ever tempted to accuse me of inconsistency on that account.

Perhaps Belinda would have been wiser to say, 'I have no confidence in Santa Claus now.' Or she might have said, 'I have no faith in him now', or 'I don't trust him any longer.' Then we should have had no temptation to call her a naughty child or a little liar.

PART II

Another version of the 'reducibility' thesis

So far it has been argued that there are two senses of 'believe in'. First there is a factual sense. Here belief-in is clearly reducibile to belief-that. It is just the acceptance of a proposition; and the proposition accepted is often, though not always, an existential one. Secondly, there is an evaluative sense of 'believe in'. Here believing-in amounts to something like esteeming or trusting; and in this second sense, believing-in seems to be quite a different attitude from believing-that.

The conclusion one is inclined to draw is that the reducibility thesis ('belief-in is reducible to belief-that') is correct for one of the two senses of 'believe in' but incorrect for the other. Unfortunately the question cannot be settled quite so easily. Perhaps it has only been shown that the reduction has to take two different forms, one form for factual belief-in and another for evaluative belief-in.

A reductionist might quite well admit that there are these two different senses of 'believe in'. Yet he might still claim that evaluative belief-in can itself be reduced to belief-that, if we go the right way about it. All we have to do, he might say, is to introduce suitable value-concepts into the proposition believed. Once we have done this, the difference between factual and evaluative belief-in will turn out to be just a difference in the content of the proposition believed, a difference in the 'object' and not in the mental attitude of the believer; and believing *that* will turn out to be the only sort of believing, a conclusion very welcome to all sensible men.

In this revised version, the reducibility thesis is much more plausible; and whether correct or not, it draws our attention to certain important characteristics of evaluative belief-in which might easily be overlooked. But anyone who wishes to maintain it must indeed be careful to 'go the right way about it'. He must be careful to choose the appropriate value-concepts, if the proposed reduction is to be plausible. For instance, believing in one's doctor certainly cannot be reduced to believing that he is a morally good man. The value-concept which we must apply to him is not 'morally good' but 'good at ...' Nor will it suffice to believe that he is good at water-colour painting. Of course I may also believe this, and it may be true. But the kind of 'goodness at ...' is irrelevant if I believe in him *as my doctor*. I must believe that he is good at curing diseases, or perhaps at curing the diseases to which I myself am particularly liable.

This brings out an important point about evaluative belief-in. When someone expresses a belief in another person, it is always appropriate to ask, 'As what is he believed in by you?' or 'What is there about him, in respect of which you believe in him?' Again, if the falconer believes in goshawks, we may ask, 'What is there about goshawks, in respect of which he believes in them?' Presumably he believes that hawks of this species are good at catching geese and other large birds in flight. It is true that the phrase 'good at' is only appropriate to persons and animals. It hardly makes sense to say that railways are 'good at' or 'bad at' anything. But other terms closely related to 'good at ...' may be used, such as 'efficient', 'effective', 'good way of ...' The believer in railways believes that railways are an efficient or the most efficient way of transporting large numbers of persons and commodities over long distances by land. The believer in taking daily cold baths believes that this is an effective way of maintaining one's bodily health.

But we need to introduce another value-concept as well. Someone might believe very firmly that railways are a highly efficient way of transporting persons and commodities. But if he were very old-fashioned and eccentric, he might think that this was a reason for *not* believing in them. He might reject the view, held by nearly everyone else, that mobility is something good for its own sake. He might think it would be better if persons and commodities usually stayed where they are.

Again, we might believe that so-and-so is exceedingly good at extract-

ing information from others by means of torture. But this would be a
good reason for not believing *in* him, or *in* the policy of employing him
in the service of the government or the police. We disapprove of that
kind of efficiency, and the greater it is, the worse it is.

We see now what the other value-concept is, which has to be introduced into the proposition believed if this type of reductive analysis is
to be plausible. It is colloquially expressed by the phrase 'good thing
that ...' We do not believe it is a good thing that a man is good at
extracting information by means of torture. But we do ordinarily
believe it is a good thing that our doctor is good at curing diseases. Or
the proposition which we believe (according to this analysis) could be
formulated thus: 'My doctor is good at curing diseases, and a good
thing too!' Similarly, the falconer believes it is a good thing that
goshawks are good at catching large birds in flight. Some would not
agree with him in believing that this is a good thing, even though they
do agree that goshawks are good at doing it. Then they do not believe
in goshawks, or only in the factual sense of believing that there is such
a species of hawks.

Let us now consider Lord Halifax's Englishman who believed in the
sea. If this belief-in is to be reduced to belief-that, in the way suggested,
what is the proposition which the Englishman believed? It must have
been a rather complex one, something like this: 'It is a good thing that
my country, Great Britain, is completely surrounded by sea, since navies
are a more efficient and less expensive means of defence than armies.'
(Perhaps he also believed that navies are a more efficient and less expensive means of aggression and conquest.)

The same kind of analysis can be applied to the rather difficult example
of 'believing in oneself'. Most commonly we use this phrase in a negative
form. The trouble with Tom is that he does not believe in himself: he
will never make a success of his life. What is this belief-in which he
lacks? Certainly it is not just a factual belief-in. He does not lack the
belief that he exists. He still does not lack it, even if he is a philosopher
who accepts a very radical Humean or Buddhist theory of personal
identity. According to the analysis we are considering, the proposition
which he does not believe would be something like this: 'I am good at
performing most of the tasks I undertake, and a good thing too!' A man
who does believe such a proposition has a *general* belief in himself, as
we might call it. But belief in oneself can be of a more limited or
departmental kind. The question 'As what is so and so believed in by
you?' is still relevant, even when 'so and so' is yourself. Thus an under-
graduate might believe that he is good at understanding lectures, writing

essays, and passing examinations, and that this is a good thing. Then he believes in himself as a student. But he need not believe that he is good at other activities in which he engages, such as football or mending punctures in the tyres of his bicycle.

It seems then that the proposed reduction of evaluative belief-in to belief-that must introduce *two* value-concepts into the proposition believed: not only 'good at ...' ('efficient', 'effective'), but also 'good thing that ...' As we have seen, it need not be at all a good thing that someone should be 'good at his job' nor that something is an effective means or method of producing a certain result. And unless we do believe it is a good thing, we shall not believe *in* him or *in* it.

The prospective character of belief-in

One merit of this analysis is to draw our attention to the relation between evaluative belief-in and time. If we just say, 'I believe in Mr. So-and-so' or 'in such and such a policy or procedure', no temporal predicate is attached to the object of our belief-in. But when we substitute a that-clause for the noun or name-phrase we must use a verb, and verbs have tenses.

We then notice an interesting feature of evaluative belief-in. In all the examples so far given it has a reference to the future, though not necessarily to the future only. It has a prospective character. This is not true of factual belief-in, which can be concerned entirely with the past. Belief in King Arthur is an example. On the other hand, if I believe in my doctor, I believe not only that it is and has been a good thing that he is good at curing my diseases, but that it will continue to be a good thing and that he will continue to be good at curing them.

But does evaluative belief-in always have a prospective character? Surely there can be an evaluative belief in a past event? For instance, Christians believe in the Incarnation. This is not only a belief that it happened, that there was such an event more than nineteen centuries ago. It is an evaluative belief-in as well as a factual one. According to the analysis we are considering, they do of course believe that it *was* a good thing that this event happened, that the results of it *have* been highly beneficial to the human race, and that there *was* no other effective means of producing them. But this is not all they believe. They believe that these results will continue to be beneficial and that there never will be any other effective means of producing them, at least so long as the present world-order continues. This is the sense in which they 'put their trust in' the Incarnation; and it is clear that their trust does have a prospective character. To put it another way, there is a connection between evaluative belief-in and hope.

Similarly one may believe in a person who is no longer alive, without having to believe that he is still alive in another world. A student of the Roman Empire may believe in Tacitus and disbelieve in Suetonius, or believe in him much less. (In the factual sense, of course, he believes equally in both of them. He believes that both of them existed and that both were Roman historians.) Is there anything prospective about this belief-in? There is. Some of the writings of both these historians still exist and can still be read. It could be said of each of them that 'being dead, he yet speaketh'. So the question 'Do we trust him?' or 'How much do we trust him?' still arises. And there is something prospective about this question. Beliefs about the future are relevant to it. For instance, I believe that archaeological evidence will continue to confirm most of what Tacitus says, but will not confirm so much of what Suetonius says. Moreover, I believe that if the lost parts of Tacitus' writings are discovered some day, they too will be confirmed by archaeological evidence. Trusting Tacitus, then, is not altogether different from trusting one's doctor; and in both cases (according to the analysis we are considering) our trust consists at least partly in a belief-that of a prospective kind.

Again, Englishmen have ceased to believe in the sea, though in Lord Halifax's time they did, and so did their successors until about a generation ago. Why is this? The sea is still there and still surrounds our country. But we can no longer rely on it to continue to 'deliver the goods' (security, power, etc.) which it did deliver formerly. It never will deliver them again unless there is a complete breakdown in our present technological civilization. If Englishmen still have a creed of this geopolitical kind, the first article in it is certainly not 'I believe in the sea' but 'I believe in the air' or perhaps 'I believe in inter-continental ballistic missiles.' In that case, according to the analysis we are discussing, we believe not only that aircraft or ballistic missiles have been and still are efficient means of defence, but also that they will continue to be so for some years to come.

Interested and disinterested belief-in

This analysis suggests another question which we ought to consider. If I believe that it is a good thing that such and such a state of affairs exists, does the word 'good' just mean 'good for me', the believer? (Of course, what I believe to be a good thing for me may not in fact be a good thing for me at all. But this is not relevant. We are only concerned to elucidate what it is that I believe.) If 'a good thing' does always have this sense, we shall have to say that evaluative belief-in is always an *interested* attitude, never a disinterested one.

This is a plausible suggestion, provided that we are willing to stretch the meaning of 'for me'. 'Good for *us*' would often be a more appropriate phrase. For instance, the doctor may be the family doctor or the doctor of all the inhabitants of the village in which I live. Then, if I believe in him, I am likely to believe that it is a good thing *for us* that *our* doctor is good at curing diseases. Still, in order to believe so, I must in some way 'identify myself' with a group (my family or the inhabitants of my village) as the use of the first person plural indicates. It is not enough that he is in fact the family doctor or the village doctor and that I believe him to be so. I must be in some way concerned about the health of the other members of my family or of my fellow-villagers. It must matter to me whether they are well or ill.

Again, I may believe in the Queen's doctor. Then I believe it is a good thing 'for us' that he holds this position and is very good at his job. And now 'us' has expanded so far that it includes the whole population of Great Britain or even of the entire British Commonwealth. It might even expand so far that it includes the whole of humanity. The believer in penicillin may well believe that it is a good thing for all mankind, for all of us everywhere, that this drug has been invented and is such an efficient means of saving lives and curing diseases. Nevertheless, it seems permissible to say that these beliefs-in are still interested ones, even though it is a matter of 'our' interest and not just the interest of 'me', the individual believer. There are collective interests as well as individual interests.

There is another question which has a bearing on this one. Indeed, it is perhaps another way of formulating the same question, if 'interested' has the wide sense just suggested. We may ask whether 'good' (in 'good thing that . . .') always has the sense of 'instrumentally good', 'good as a means'. Clearly this is the sense it has in many of the examples so far considered. It is not an intrinsically good thing that people should take cold baths. If anything, it is an intrinsically bad one, since it is often a painful experience to take them. But according to those who believe in this procedure, it is good as a means for maintaining one's health. Again, if someone believes in easier divorce, he certainly need not believe that it is a good thing for its own sake that married couples should be divorced more easily. But he does believe, rightly or wrongly, that if divorce were made easier, this would be an effective means of increasing human happiness or decreasing human misery.

Belief in a friend

But now let us consider belief in a friend; or rather, let us say belief in someone *as* a friend, since we might also believe in him 'as' something else, for example as a scholar or as a bee-keeper. The analysis of evaluative belief-in which we are discussing makes use of two value-concepts 'good thing that . . .' and 'good at . . .' We find, however, that we have to take a new look at both of them when we consider belief in a friend.

If I believe in someone as a friend, I do believe that it is a good thing for me, advantageous to me, that he is my friend. I believe that he is disposed to be kind to me and to give me what help he can when I need it. So far, my belief in him is an interested one; I believe that my friendship with him is good as a means, a means to my own welfare or happiness, and that it will continue to be so. But is this all I believe? Clearly it is not. I also believe that my friendship with him and his with me is something good in itself, and will continue to be so. It is something which I value for its own sake. In this respect, then, my belief in him is disinterested. More than that, I value *him* for his own sake. According to the type of analysis we are discussing, this would amount to believing that it is just a good thing that he exists, and still would be even if I 'got nothing out of it'. In this respect again, my belief in a friend is disinterested.

Let us now turn to the other value-concept 'good at'. Does it make sense to say, 'So and so is a friend of mine, but I do not believe in him at all'? Apparently it must, if 'good at . . .' is an essential part of the analysis of evaluative belief-in. For surely I might be quite convinced that he is 'no good at anything', a thoroughly inefficient person; and yet he might be my friend. It might be suggested that he *is* good at being friendly, and that this, after all, is a pretty important sort of 'goodness at . . .' Very likely he is, but he need not be. I might be his only friend, the only person he gets on well with. Can it be said, then, that at any rate he is good at being friendly with me, though he is no good at being friendly with others?

But there is something odd about this use of 'good at . . .' It is true that my doctor might be good at curing the particular diseases from which I personally suffer, and this might be the reason why I believe in him. It is true too that he need not be good at curing any other diseases. But he *would* have to be good at curing other people who suffer from the same ones. Similarly, my friend, if he is 'good at' being friendly with me, must also be good at being friendly with anyone else who resembles me in the relevant respects, whatever respects they are.

It comes to this: 'good at ...', in the ordinary sense of the phrase, has a certain generality about it. It refers to a class of some kind. The class in question might in fact have only one member. I might happen to be the only person who has the characteristics required, e.g. the only indolent and red-haired person, educated at Manchester Grammar School, who has sailed twice round Cape Horn. But if 'good at' is the appropriate phrase, my friend would have to be good at being friendly with *anyone* who has this combination of characteristics, even though in fact there is no one else who happens to have them.

Perhaps we can now see what the trouble is. There is a sense in which every person is a unique individual. He is of course a member of many different classes. All the same, there is something unclassifiable about him. There is a sense in which he is 'just himself'. And this is what matters in inter-personal relations such as friendship. A friend likes me just as being myself, and I like him just as being himself. That is why it is inappropriate to say he is 'good at' being friendly with me, or that I am 'good' at being friendly with him.

Trusting is an essential factor in all evaluative belief-in. But it follows from what has been said that the trust we have in a friend is different from the trust we have in an expert who is 'good at' a particular job. The trust we have in an expert has a limited or departmental character. We trust him in so far as he is an engine-driver or an instructor in water-colour painting. But we need not trust him just as a human being. For all we can tell, he may be quite untrustworthy in some of his other activities. Trust in a friend, on the contrary, is non-departmental. We do trust him as a human being. Moreover, we trust him as the individual, unique human being that he is.

It seems then that the proposed analysis in terms of 'good thing that ...' and 'good at ...' does not apply very well to belief in a friend. The concept of 'good at ...' is not relevant to this very important variety of evaluative belief-in. The concept of 'good thing that ...' is indeed relevant to it. If we believe in a friend we do believe that it is and will continue to be 'a good thing' that he exists and is the individual person that he is. But we believe it is a good thing not only as a means, but also for its own sake. Belief in a friend cannot be just an interested belief-in. This is a logical impossibility. If our belief in another person were wholly interested, it would be improper to describe him as our friend.

To make matters more difficult, the expert on whose skill or efficiency we rely, for instance our doctor or teacher, may become our friend as well; and then we believe in him and trust him in two ways at once. Friendship may creep in, unawares, into many of the relations between one person and another. Something like it may also creep in when there is a relation between a person and an animal, for instance between the blind man and his guide-dog, or the falconer and his goshawk. And there is a faint analogue of it when someone gives a proper name to a machine on which he relies (he may call his motor-car 'Jane'). After all, the capacity for love, in all its many degrees and forms, is quite an important part of human nature. Philosophical analysts have to put up with it, even though it makes their work more complicated.

The merits and defects of this reduction

We have now considered two different proposals for reducing belief 'in' to belief 'that'. Both are useful. We learn something from each of them when we try to apply it to the many different sorts of examples in which the expression 'belief in' is used.

From the first we learn that there are two senses of 'belief in'; on the one hand, a factual sense where 'belief in' *is* reducible to 'belief that', and often though not always consists in believing an existential proposition; on the other hand, an evaluative sense, where 'believing in' is equivalent to something like esteeming or trusting.

What do we learn from the second and much more plausible proposal? The aim of it is to show that even though there is an evaluative sense of 'belief in', this too can be reduced to 'belief that' if suitable value-concepts ('good thing that ...' and 'good at ...' or 'efficient' or 'effective') are introduced into the proposition believed.

This second type of analysis is instructive and illuminating. It brings out the prospective character of evaluative belief-in, an important one which we might not otherwise have noticed. It also helps to make clear just what the content of a particular belief-in is. When someone or something is believed in, it is always appropriate to ask 'as being what is he (or it) believed in?' The answer often is 'as being good at such and such an activity' or 'as being a good (efficient) way of achieving such and such a result'. Moreover, the person believing does have to value the activity which he thinks A is 'good at' or the state of affairs which he thinks B is an efficient means of achieving; and this is the point of the phrase 'good thing that ...' There are many beliefs-in whose content cannot be fully explicated unless these two concepts 'good thing that ...' and 'good at ...' (or 'efficient') are brought in somewhere. Finally, once they are brought in, we see that there are two types of evaluative belief-in, interested and disinterested, and also that some evaluative beliefs-in are both at once, when 'good' in good thing that . . .' includes both 'good as a means' and 'good for its own sake'. This again is an important point, which we might not have noticed otherwise.

But there are defects in this analysis too, however helpful and instructive it is. We shall do well to make all the use of it we can, but it will not take us all the way. As we have seen, it does not fit one very important type of example, belief in a friend. Here the concept 'good at . . .' plays no part, although good thing that . . .' does. Our friend's efficiency, or lack of it, is irrelevant to our belief in him, if we do believe in him *as* a friend.

But further, the proposed reduction does not completely fit any of the examples to which we have tried to apply it. In all of them, it leaves something out. At an earlier stage of the discussion it was suggested that 'esteeming or trusting' is an essential feature of evaluative belief-in. We now see, I think, that *both* esteeming *and* trusting are essential features of it. This reductive proposal does provide fairly well for the esteeming, by means of the concepts 'good thing that . . .' and 'good at . . .' (or 'efficient'). But does it provide for the trusting? Can this be done by insisting on the prospective character of evaluative belief-in?

Suppose I believe not only that my doctor has been and is good at curing my diseases, but also that he will continue to be so; and not only that it is and has been a good thing that he is good at this, but also that it will continue to be a good thing. But what if I do believe these two propositions as firmly as you please? Believing them may be a necessary condition for trusting him, but it is not the same as trusting him. Trusting is not a merely cognitive attitude.

To put the same point in another way, the proposed reduction leaves out the 'warmth' which is a characteristic feature of evaluative belief-in. Evaluative belief-in is a 'pro-attitude'. One is 'for' the person, thing, policy, etc. in whom or in which one believes. There is something more here than assenting or being disposed to assent to a proposition, no matter what concepts the proposition contains. That much-neglected aspect of human nature which used to be called 'the heart' enters into evaluative belief-in. Trusting is an affective attitude. We might say that it is in some degree an affectionate one.

The beliefs-that, to which this reductive analysis draws our attention, are indeed an essential part of our belief-in attitude. When we trust someone or something, these beliefs-that are the ones we must mention in order to answer the question 'In respect of what do you trust him (or it)?'. And this question is a perfectly proper one, and does require an answer. But when it has been answered, we still have not explained what trusting is, or what it is like to trust or 'put one's faith in' someone or something. Perhaps we can only know what it is like by actually being in the mental attitude which the word 'trusting' denotes. But fortunately there are few persons, if any, who have never trusted anyone or anything; and if it is disagreeable to be compelled to talk about 'the heart', the fact remains that most of us have one, as well as a head.

Application to belief in God

The most important of all the varieties of evaluative belief-in is belief in God. It is also the most difficult to discuss, if only because so many of us nowadays do not know what it is like to have it. Still, one may ask whether any light is thrown on it by the conclusions we have reached, even though most of the examples discussed have been of a non-religious kind.

Belief in God (in the evaluative sense) clearly does have the 'warmth' or 'heart-felt' character which we have noticed in other evaluative beliefs-in. It is certainly a pro-attitude, and both esteeming and trusting enter into it. But does the distinction between 'interested' and 'disinterested' belief-in apply to it, and does it have a prospective character, as non-religious belief-in has?

It looks as if evaluative belief in God were both interested and disinterested at the same time, interested in some respects and disinterested in others. If the phrase 'good thing that ...' may be used here, then surely it is a good thing for the believer himself (and for all of us) that God is loving, compassionate and merciful, that he answers prayers, that he gives his grace to us, that he is a refuge to us in times of trouble. Nothing could be more advantageous to us than the existence of God, if he is what theists believe him to be. The prospectiveness is there too. We believe not only that all this is and has been 'a very good thing' for each of us individually and all of us collectively, but also that it will continue to be so. God has been 'good to us' and we trust him to be good to us always, come what may, and even at times when he seems not to be ('Though he slay me, yet will I trust in him.')

But if we were to stop at that, our belief in God would be an interested belief-in. His existence would only be good as a means, however important and even indispensable that 'means' might be; and if we loved him, our love (so far) would only be a kind of 'cupboard love'. From this point of view he is regarded just as 'the giver of gifts'. We value his gifts; we are sure that we could not get on without him. But so far, we do not value *him* for his own sake.

But as soon as we start thanking God for his gifts, being grateful for them with a gratitude which is not just 'a lively sense of favours to come', our belief in him ceases to be wholly interested. We are beginning to value him for his own sake, and to believe that it is a good thing, intrinsically good, that he exists and is what he is; and not just 'a good thing', but the fundamental 'good thing' without which there would be no others.

At this stage, the nearest analogue in inter-human relationships would be belief in a friend, where there is a similar combination of interested and disinterested believing-in. It is perhaps significant that some theistic mystics have referred to God as 'The Friend'. But as the definite article indicates, they did not think of him as just one friend among others. Friendship of the ordinary kind is a relation between equals, and in this important respect the analogy breaks down.

After all, if once we make the distinction between interested and disinterested belief-in, it is almost obvious that belief in God is normally a combination of both. It might be perfectly sincere if it were wholly of the interested sort, but we should be inclined to think that there was something incomplete about it. Even so, it would still be quite different from the belief-that of Pascal's *philosophes et savants* who believe in God only in the factual sense. Even a wholly interested belief in God is still evaluative and not merely factual. It cannot be reduced to the mere acceptance of an existential proposition.

IX

FROM WORLD TO GOD

R. W. HEPBURN

IF one is pessimistic about metaphysics and still wishes to defend Christian belief against recent attacks, it is tempting and plausible to argue thus. (i) To have meaning is no more or less than to have a use in language. Christian discourse does have a use—rather, several inter-connected uses; therefore it is meaningful. What sort of use does it have? (*ia*) In parable-fashion it specifies, makes imaginatively vivid, a pattern of life: in Professor Braithwaite's language, the agapeistic way of life.[1] Doctrinal utterances about God are analysable, not in terms of a metaphysically mysterious inferred entity—'Other' and 'Beyond'—but as the commendation of attitudes and polices in the here-and-now. (*ib*) Religious language is evocative of 'ways of seeing the world'. As a painter may see in a landscape desolation or sublimity and express these in paint, so religious language expresses a vision of the world as the handiwork of a supremely wise and beneficient creator, and sees humanity in the light of the doctrines of Creation, Fall, and Redemption. Again, we are speaking only of observable phenomena, and of how we interpret, what we 'make of', those phenomena.

(ii) Another way of trying to be both a metaphysical sceptic and a Christian is by means of a thoroughgoing Christological theology, in which every statement about God is reduced to statements about Jesus. This would be carrying to an attractive extreme a strong tendency within contemporary Christian thought. Questions about the divine love become questions about Christ's suffering for men. Questions about the divine creation are reinterpreted in terms of the New Creation and the Second Adam—and not the other way round.

Each of these approaches is vulnerable to the same type of criticism. They succeed in salvaging parts of Christian discourse, but they are inadequate as complete analyses of traditional Christianity. Both (*ia*) and (*ib*) are objectionable in that they identify God with his manifesta-

From *Mind*, 72 (1963), 40–50. Reprinted by permission of the author and the Editor of *Mind*.
[1] [See ch. IV of this volume. Ed.]

tions in the world, although in complex and indirect ways. They both seem to imply, 'If no world, no God': a view that in fact makes non-sense of divine creation. The source of the trouble is that an essential element of Christianity has been eliminated in both cases, that element which speaks of God as the kind of being who may be encountered, who acts and sends his son, and who, because he is capable of doing such things, is therefore not identifiable with ways of seeing phenomena or with attitudes taken up to phenomena. One cannot both be true to traditional Christian teaching about God and at the same time conceive of him as a logical construction out of phenomena, or as a purely symbolic principle of collection, integrating our experiences of the sublime and the saintly into a single vision. The God of Christianity must be more than this: a God to whom prayer may be addressed, and who can raise men again after death. Within traditional Christian theology, therefore, questions about the divine existence cannot be deflected into the question, 'Does "God" play an intelligible role in the language-game?'

But it might be doubted whether anything I have said, or could say, would lead the (i*a*) or (i*b*) theorists to recognize their position as inade-quate. For the traditional Christian's counter-statements, like 'God is *really* transcendent': 'There is a *real* life after death', will themselves be analysed as policy-specifying, vision-evoking bits of discourse. One has to admit that no single theological or religious statement would neces-sarily produce disillusionment: but that, if disillusionment were to come, it would be only by the accumulation of difficulties, of awkward and artificial analyses, increasingly sensed as going against the grain of the evident meaning of the statements analysed. It might also come by some forms of first-hand religious experience, experience as of encounter with God, experience of the 'numinous', experiences in which, contrary to the trend of the analyses, God is apprehended as *intrusion*.

The difficulties in the radical Christological approach (ii), are no less formidable. For at some stage we have to move from talking about the temporal and finite Jesus of Nazareth to talk about an eternal and infinite God; and the claim that these are two Persons of the same deity does not exonerate us from making logical sense of the transition. This is not, of course, to deny the importance of Christological thought for Christianity, but to deny its complete logical adequacy in the absence of a metaphysical account of how the finite relates to the infinite. Appeal to revelation-in-history is not an alternative to appealing to reason, to a reason that plays a metaphysical role. We have to *link* the allegedly revealing events and persons with the transcendent deity which they allegedly reveal; to show *how* the first can be a revelation of the second.

Difficulties cannot be avoided by talking of sheer leaps of faith; since equally awkward philosophical questions can be asked about the language that describes in what direction you are leaping and where your leap is taking you.

What conclusion can be drawn from all this? That part at least of Christian discourse speaks of God as of some sort of *individual*—albeit a quite unique kind of individual. The current theological stress on 'encountering' God, valuably and dramatically illuminates this. God is one who may be met. It is surely also this strand in Christian thought that keeps back Rudolph Bultmann[2] from a complete 'de-kerygmatizing' of Christian theology, that prevents him reducing it as a whole to talk of moral policies and attitudes, *à la* Braithwaite. Again, T. R. Miles in *Religion and the Scientific Outlook* goes very far with Braithwaite, but adds to the parabolic analysis religious 'silence'. Although Miles would, I suspect, be uneasy over calling God an individual, and although the role of 'silence' in his account is rather enigmatic, at least it bears witness once more to the inadequacy of merely reductive programmes.

If God is to retain the status of individual which some parts of Christian discourse undoubtedly accord him, we need not only a role-in-the-language for 'God', like a set of rules for the King in chess, but also an intelligible procedure for *referring* to God, a set of criteria for *identifying* him. And this is a demand of logic: one has either to accept it or eliminate that strand in Christian discourse that makes it a demand. I am not saying that without this we cannot give *meaning* to Christian discourse: use takes care of that. Thus I disagree with a writer like John Hick (*Faith and Knowledge*) who depends upon eschatological events to give meaning retrospectively to that discourse.

If 'singling out', 'identifying' God is a logically necessary task, it is also one that can easily be represented as blasphemous. It may be taken to imply that God belongs among finite, limited entities. For if he can be singled out, God can hardly be infinite in every possible way. There must exist that from which he is being singled out—over-against him, as it were. Two comments may be ventured on this antinomy.

(1) Whatever our final judgement, the theologian certainly deserves the utmost logical tolerance in trying to make his case. Because of the nature of the being with whom he claims to be concerned, we have no right to demand close parallels between (*a*) identifying or singling out

---

[2] [In *Kerygma and Myth* (London: S.P.C.K., 1953).]

a thing-in-the-world from other things-in-the-world, and (b) making the required identificatory gesture from world to God.

The minimal requirement for being able to carry through the identifying of God is that sense can be made of the 'cosmological relation', the relation between world and God, that relation on which the Cosmological Argument turns. This involves not only the recognizing of the various relational characteristics possessed by the world according to the different versions of the Argument—hints of derivativeness, incompleteness, fragmentariness: but also showing what sort of movement of the mind carries one from these to a transcendent God. I want, in fact, to suggest that the Cosmological Argument—or some transformation of it—is not just one approach to apologetics among others, one to be distinguished altogether from apologetics based on historical relation. It is an indispensable part of any Christian apologetics whatever, including those that centre on revelation. For, as we have seen, at some point appeal must be made away from the finite and historical locus of revelation to the infinite and eternal God to whom these allegedly testify.

It is clear that if one wishes to affirm the chief tenets of traditional Christianity, there are severe limits set upon metaphysical scepticism.

(2) Part of Christian discourse, I suggested, demands a God who is in some sense an individual entity. But other parts seem equally surely to demand a God who emphatically is not an individual entity. A God who is 'beyond being' or is 'being-itself' can hardly be an individual, nor could a God who is thought of in idealist style as the completion and consummation of cosmic process; as by Errol Harris, recently, in *Revelation through Reason*. If God—in order to *be* God—has to be infinite in the sense that involves comprehensiveness, being excluded by nothing, then his nature is again incompatible with any identificatory moves at all. In each of these cases, and many more could be cited, one reaches a notion of God that, for all its nobility, fails altogether to do justice to the *first-mentioned* part of Christian discourse, that which demands a God who acts, hears prayer, resurrects the dead.

Now these are tensions and strains occurring *within* the Christian conception of a religiously adequate deity. They may remind us how, in his renowned paper on God's non-existence, J. N. Findlay argued that the dialectic of the worship-worthy carries one on to a God of such a nature as (logically) could not exist.[3] The present point, though related, is different. The progressive stepping-up of the criteria of worship-

[3] *New Essays In Philosophical Theology*, ed. Antony Flew and Alasdair MacIntyre (London: S.C.M., 1955), pp. 47 ff.

worthiness, culminating in the conception of God as infinite, beyond being, etc., leads to judgements about God that clash violently with that other, equally basic strand in Christian doctrine, the strand that thinks of God as an individual. In the latter capacity, God is a being who stands in need of identification-procedures: but with the former notions of God it makes no sense whatever to ask for such. One is forced to wonder whether Christians are in fact making quite incompatible demands upon their object of worship—that he should possess characteristics belonging to subjects of radically different, and incompatible ontological status, while yet demanding that these two subjects should be really one God.

Let us assume for the time being, however, that theology *might* cope with these difficulties; and take up again the reflections of point (1) above. These concluded that the Cosmological argument was, in some form, crucial to the justification of Christian belief. But has not that argument been shown up as invalid? Does that, therefore, settle the case against theism? No. Those versions of the Argument are invalid, which (a) entail that God logically necessarily exists: that is, that existence is a predicate; or (b) claim that the world needs God as its cause—in the ordinary sense of 'cause'. But the world–God relation might be characterizable in terms other than these, and the motive-power of the Argument might be neither (a) a quest for logical necessity in the wrong place, nor (b) a zeal to halt and anchor the cause-effect regress. This is not an original reflection: several recent writers have been trying to reinterpret the Cosmological Argument so as to avoid the acknowledged inadequacies of its classical formulations. I intend now not to quote and expound individual new versions—they vary considerably among themselves—but to present briefly the most plausible revised version I can think up with their help. Then I shall raise some questions about its logical status and reliability, questions seldom considered by the rescuers of the Argument themselves.

If the cosmological relation is not a matter of *logical* dependence, it must be some sort of *factual* dependence. (Cf. T. Penelhum, *Mind*, Vol. 69 (1960), pp. 175 ff.[4]) Refusing to be pushed back towards equally invalid causal versions, let us put our whole emphasis on the utter uniqueness of the relation between God and the world. No examples of this relation can be reasonably demanded, for they would have to be drawn from the relations of finite, created thing with finite, created thing. At best we could see the whole cluster of dependence-relations, such as cause–effect, parent–child, etc., as preparing one to make a

[4] [Included as ch. X of this volume. Ed.]

final, and still sharp, transition in thought to the unconditional dependence of the cosmological relation itself. Because of this uniqueness,
the fate of the cosmological movement of thought cannot be tied to
the unhappy fate of arguments based on dependence-chains, such as
cause and effect, that *are* exemplifiable in the world of ordinary experience. The Cosmological Argument, so expressed, might be thought to
have a certain autonomy, and to be invulnerable to the usual criticisms.
If it is logically odd, strained, or broken, this is not a fatal defect: it is
only what one could have predicted *a priori*.

But this is not yet quite plausible enough. There might well be *no
such relation* as is held to be stammered at by these bits of logically
broken language. More positive confirmation can reasonably be demanded. It is worth asking seriously whether such confirmation might
be supplied, at least in part, by Rudolph Otto's account of the 'numinous'.[5] For, on that account, numinous experience is characterized by
a sense of out-and-out dependence, derivativeness, and creatureliness,
and by a peculiar haunting strangeness—an awesomeness or weirdness.
But all descriptions are held in the end to fail. The strangeness and awesomeness prevent the sense of dependence from being construed as
simply cause–effect dependence or as dependence of *any* other familiar,
intelligible type. We are in the sphere of the non-rational, the inexpressible: but it is just such an inexpressible and fundamental type of
dependence that our sophisticated versions of the Cosmological Argument are concerned with. Could numinous experience be taken as an
actual, privileged awareness of the world as related to God, of God as
related to the world?

Supposing it could. It is important to see exactly how far the old
Cosmological Argument would have been metamorphosed. It started
its career as a rational proof of God's existence. But it was unable to
prove God demonstratively. In shifting ground to the exploration of a
possible *factual* cosmological relation, experienced, however transitorily
and imperfectly, in numinous experience, we should be retaining some
essential ingredients in the old Argument, but thoroughly changing its
status. It would no longer move from premises intelligible to any
reasonable person to a conclusion, by way of a chain of inference open
to logical scrutiny. It would be taken now as a form of words that
evokes, or evokes the memory of, a special and elusive group of
experiences, not obtainable at will, nor perhaps *ever* actually obtained,
by every one. Yet, once again, the religious person is justified in saying

---

[5] [In *The Idea of the Holy* (London: Oxford University Press, 1950, and
Harmondsworth: Penguin, 1959).]

that this elusiveness does not necessarily invalidate the cosmological movement of thought—considering, as one must, the unique nature of its object.

Indeed, an increase in elusiveness seems in general a necessary price of making one's notion of God adequately worship-worthy. In most primitive religions there was no identification-problem for God. One could straightforwardly point at the divine stone, tree, the sky, at one's fetish or totem. But it is not possible to point at a God who is no longer exclusively *in* the tree or in the Temple, but 'beyond' or 'behind' all phenomena whatever. Yet I have been arguing that Christian theism cannot afford to renounce the identificatory gesture altogether.

The more religiously adequate the God on whose behalf one is arguing and whom one is seeking to single out, the less rationally and universally convincing one's apologetics are likely to become. And the more rationally transparent the apologetics, the less religiously adequate the God. In the work already mentioned, Errol Harris, rehabilitating an idealist type of rational theology, tries to leave a place for the numinous. Numinous experience is, to him, wonderment at a nature imperfectly understood, a nature whose consummation is deity. There is nothing of Otto's non-rational, surd-like quality in Harris's version, and therefore nothing of the thrill of mingled dread and strange exhilaration that pervades the Otto experience. The experiences are just not the same, despite the common label. The rational tidiness and integration of Harris's philosophy of religion are won only through the sacrifice of some fundamental elements of religious experience.

Yoked thus to numinous experience, the Cosmological Argument— in its formulations, dry, austere, and brief—may look singularly ill-equipped to play the evocative role for which it is now cast. True: but the reluctance of many religious people to abandon the Argument altogether, in face of logical criticism, might in part be attributed to a stiffening of numinous experience, whether developed or embryonic, that is the real though unrecognized source of its power over them. I agree with Professor H. D. Lewis (*Our Experience of God*), that the original cosmological movement of thought has been mishandled into the shape of a rational proof, whereas it has closer affinities with the poetry of a Vaughan or Traherne, with the Book of Job and some of the Psalms.

We cannot leave the matter there. It would be premature to speak of having in numinous experience an 'insight' *tout court* into the existence of a transcendent God. We may have bypassed the logical difficulties of the traditional Cosmological Argument, but that is not to say that the new interpretation has no difficulties of its own. We need seriously to ask, what are the risks of hoodwinking ourselves, of *mis*interpreting our experience when we make use of it?

This is a very hard question to answer: largely because numinous experience is itself notoriously difficult to analyse. It is not very helpful, either to sceptic or believer, to say numinous experience is an emotion. For emotions can be most complex affairs, involving not simply the having of feelings but the making of value judgements, the interpreting and appraising of situations in which we find or imagine ourselves. For example: to feel disdain for someone is to judge that one is superior to him, that to associate with him would injure one's dignity, and so on. Some emotions certainly carry with them a liability to thrills, shudders, or spine-tinglings, and numinous experience undoubtedly is one such. But having thrills and shudders cannot be the whole of what it is to have numinous experience: for again value-judgements and situation-interpretations are at least equally important features. Consider some of the concepts involved—concepts like creatureliness, self-abasement, reverence. Otto, of course, is correct, though also tantalizing, in insisting that numinous experience cannot be construed merely as the concurrence of shudderings, self-abasings and the like. The precise quality of the experience eludes all rational reconstruction. This elusiveness resembles the way in which I may recall on waking that a particular dream was emotionally impressive, and impressive in a quite distinctive way; but although I can recollect the sequence of dream-events even in some detail, yet I may be quite frustrated in reviving the precise emotive quality. That quality cannot be imaginatively reconstructed through reconsidering either events or my behavioural response to the events, i.e. what I did or said in my dream.

But our chief task was to say something to the question 'Are numinous experiences cognitive or non-cognitive?' Unhelpfully, I cannot see how to decide this issue, either way. It is not that uncertainties of the cognitive–non-cognitive type are unknown in other areas of experience. Thus we may be in doubt as to whether we are still hearing, or imagining that we are hearing, the sound of a distant train, whether we still perceive the ship's motion or imagine it even when the ship is in calm waters, whether the projector is still throwing a faint image on the screen, or is it I myself who have unwittingly become the projector? So with numinous experience—hovering on the frontier between cognitive and non-cognitive, between imagining and grasping, between fancy and insight, between feeling and perceiving. Only; the other cases mentioned admit of decision-procedures. 'You could not have been hearing the train,' we may be informed, 'it stopped one minute before you spoke.' 'The slide had been withdrawn from the projector ...' But nothing comparable helps us with the numinous.

In the midst of half-lights and inconclusiveness at least one negative point can confidently be made. It will not do for the religious person to present numinous experience simply as something that happens to him, an event suffered. If it were so presented, appeal to it could not possibly ease the theological predicament as we had hoped it might. For we should then need license to *take* that event as revelatory of God, license to move from the shudders, as finite occurrences, to God, as an infinite being. We should be back where we started, with the task of making sense of the move from world to God. But it was to make sense of that move that we originally appealed to experience of the numinous. Therefore, it is not possible to dodge the perhaps unsettleable issue 'cognitive or non-cognitive?' by exclaiming 'How indisputably real, how intense and impressive, are the thrills and shudders.' These by themselves are brute psychological events, and they cannot help the apologist where he needs help most.

There are quite a few points of close analogy between numinous experience and some sorts of aesthetic experience, types of sublimity, for instance. But the differences between them are all too easily ignored:

(i) Otto himself draws a parallel between musical experience and experience of the numinous. The main point of comparison is the qualitative elusiveness of both. It is often impossible to capture in words the exact emotional flavour of a piece of music; reference to ordinary human emotions, like nostalgia, melancholy, hopefulness, can be almost as misleading as helpful. Likewise, experience of the holy has its analogues in nameable human emotions but also defies analysis in terms of any of these. We do not make a mock of musical experience because it fits none of our conceptual pigeon-holes: how much less should we dismiss experience of the numinous on the same grounds.

But clearly the analogy is two-edged. It does nothing to help one over the decision-issue—cognitive or non-cognitive. To silence the sceptic, one would have to show not only that numinous experience is autonomous and wholly other, in the sense parallel to musical experience, but that it is the experience *of* a 'Wholly Other' being. And this has not been shown. The indescribability of some musical experience does not compel us to posit a mysterious other world of musical entities, to which music gives us access. One may ask: need the indescribability of *numinous* experience compel us any more to posit a transcendent Source?

(ii) There undoubtedly has been a historical development in the idea of the holy, a movement towards the unity and transcendence of the object of worship; from seeing holiness as in trees, wells or stones, ark of the Covenant or Temple to the final intense and splendid vision of holiness lodged in one deity, whom all phenomena veil. The main question is: how can one be sure that intensification of, and increase in the impressiveness of, the idea of the holy are correlated with an ever more adequate awareness of the one actual God? Of a composer's eighth or ninth symphony we might say: 'Here now is the full and glorious deployment of musical resources which were only hinted at in his first and second symphonies and developed gradually during numbers three to seven.' But in this case, it is not at all necessary or plausible to think of the development as the progressive *discovery* of something which from the start had existed in the world. Yet it is just this that the religious person is tempted to assume without much examination in the case of the development of numinous experience.

Neither felt uniqueness, degree of intensity, nor any other factor I can isolate in numinous experience guarantees that it is a veridical cognitive experience, that the experience is being correctly interpreted when taken as solving the identification-problem. The situation looks ambivalent in respect of theistic or naturalistic interpretations.

But it may be objected that if I am prepared to admit the occurrence of numinous experience, I am thereby committing myself to theistic belief. Definitionally, numinous experience is the experience of encountering deity. Strictly, I may have been misusing the expression 'numinous experience'—using it so as not to prejudge the question of whether it is *in fact* awareness of actual deity. I have retained a nuance of 'as if'; 'it is as *if* we were encountering ...' The judgement that the experience is veridical, that encounter is achieved, is not given in the experience itself. Because of this, my use of the expression seems to me a legitimately eccentric one. It is, further, because I am able to have the experiences and yet to challenge their theistic interpretation that I cannot accept H. D. Lewis's language of achieving, simply, 'an insight' into the existence of a transcendent being.

Not only can one have the experiences and reject the theistic interpretation, but one may oscillate in real and lasting doubt over which interpretation to adopt. The experiences have no claim to be called self-authenticating, immediate, unchallengable testimony to theism.

If the situation is ambivalent, this is a different sort of ambivalence from that acknowledged by some of the 'ways of life' and 'ways of seeing' approaches at which we looked at the start of this article. We might admit that many alternative ways of life can be conceived, and that there are many ways of seeing, many 'aspects' in the phenomena, one or other of which will dawn on us as we read various religious documents or participate in different religious cults. But the ambivalence that we are now considering is not a matter of rearranging the common, accepted furniture of the universe, but of whether these bits of furniture are related to what is not simply more furniture, more universe, but something radically different from them all.

One might be tempted to see in that ambivalence a vindication of atheism. For how could such an ambiguous universe be the work of perfect love and perfect power? Could this be a way to love and express love, to leave the loved one in bewildering uncertainty over the very existence of the allegedly loving God? Would we not have here a refined weapon of psychological torture? That is: if the situation is ambivalent, it is *not* ambivalent; since its ambivalence is a conclusive argument against the existence of the Christian God.

The Christian will protest, however. Ambivalence, he will say, is simply a tantalizing matter of fact to the sceptic, but to the believer it is a religious necessity. If the situation were not ambiguous, if God were incontrovertibly revealed, then our belief would be constrained, our allegiance forced, and no place would be left for free and responsible decision whether to walk in God's ways and to entrust oneself to him in faith. Divine elusiveness is a necessary condition of our being able to enter upon properly personal relations with God.

But, of course, I have not shown that the religio-sceptical situation is ambivalent, all along the line, in its totality: only that it seems to be so at one very crucial point indeed. It might, however, be the case that some problem, say the problem of evil, is overwhelmingly intractable to the Christian: so much that one might legitimately refuse to allow the ambivalence of numinous experience to hold the total issue in balance any longer. Or, the balance might conceivably be tipped the other way, because of incoherences in the sceptical opinion.

At any rate, if this analysis is correct in its main features, there can be no short-cut in the philosophy of religion past the painstaking examination and re-examination of problems in the entire field of apologetics. No single, decisive verification-test, no solemn Declaration of Meaninglessness, can relieve us of the labour.

X

DIVINE NECESSITY

TERENCE PENELHUM

THIS paper is a discussion of certain limited aspects of traditional theological doctrines of the necessity of the divine existence and attributes. In spite of being greatly indebted to a number of recent treatments of these themes, I still feel that something worthwhile remains to be said about them, and that certain important morals can be drawn from them regarding the relation of theistic belief to metaphysics and philosophical analysis. The traditional doctrines seem to me to be a paradigm case of the impossibility of presenting basic religious assertions as answers to metaphysical demands for explanation; but when the demonstrative trappings are carefully stripped away, what remains is seen to be of the very essence of theism, and any difficulties inherent in it are distinct from those associated with traditional attempts to *demonstrate* theism.

I shall be concerned throughout with general and not historical considerations; but those illustrative references I shall make will all be taken from the Thomistic system, since this is the most enduring and meticulous example of the doctrines I discuss, and is in one way or another normative for a great many religious thinkers. It is also considered by many to be the most modest in its metaphysical claims, but I hope to indicate that its relative agnosticism does not make it less open to the criticisms to which all forms of demonstrative theism are subject.

I

Apart from the Ontological Proof, demonstrations of God's existence have taken the form of insisting that there is some fact about the world which requires explanation, and that no explanation short of a deity will do. The fact chosen will vary from thinker to thinker or chapter to chapter, but there is one clear division among those facts said to be puzzling in the way required: on the one hand there is the bare fact

From *Mind*, 69 (1960), 175–186. Reprinted by permission of the author and the Editor of *Mind*.

that there *is* a world at all, that anything exists whatever; and on the other there is the fact, or indefinitely large group of facts, that the world is as it is, that it contains the particular sorts of quality or relation that it does. Since Kant there has grown up a habit of thinking of all the demonstrations based on each of these as just one argument, and forgetting the great variety of arguments that have been offered of each sort; this may not be very harmful in the first case, but it certainly is in the second: the world is a very varied place, and its orderliness is not the only feature of it that has been picked out as requiring God to explain it, even though this is the feature emphasized in the traditional Argument from Design. To avoid any restrictions associated with long-standing titles, I shall talk of Existential and Qualitative arguments.

In both there are certain features of great importance:

(1) In each case the force of the argument depends upon undermining the tendency to explain the fact singled out by means of more normal explanatory procedures, e.g. scientific ones. The most effective method is to render these *irrelevant* by making the puzzle too *general* for ordinary procedures to solve it. In the Existential case, temptations to explain the existence of a given object in terms of the causal action of another are circumvented by showing that such explanations are congenitally incomplete because they leave unanswered the general question of why anything exists at all. In the Qualitative case, if a certain natural feature were scientifically explained it could be said that the natural regularity of which it was thereby shown to be an example, or at least some all-embracing one of which it in turn was an example, required explanation; the fact of order itself might be picked on for this; or one could just ask why it was that we had the sort of world which, however naturally, gave rise to this or that feature.

(2) Although less perceptive theists have often not seen this, especially in the Qualitative case, the demands for extra-scientific explanation should logically force its users to be discontented with the mere reference to a higher being. If it is puzzling that *anything* exists, it should seem puzzling that *God* does; if a certain feature's presence in the universe is puzzling, then it should seem puzzling that it, or that which gives rise to it, should be present in God. In neither case is the explanation *complete*. To complete it more has to be built in: the being referred to has to be one whose existence, or whose possession of the relevant attributes, is self-explanatory. The potentially endless series of 'Why?'-questions has to end in an answer that covers not only the last 'Why?' but the next one too. So we have the doctrines of a being who

necessarily *is*, or necessarily is *what* he is. It is very important to see that exactly the same theoretical move is involved whether it is said that the divine existence or nature is self-explanatory to us or merely in itself; what is essential is that the explanation should be said to lie in the divine being, even if we do not know it.

(3) As Kant saw in part, and Aquinas saw very clearly, the Qualitative question presupposes the Existential. One cannot finally answer the question of why the world is as it is without explaining why it exists, for nothing can have features unless it exists; though this is naturally only a part of the answer, since showing why anything exists is not enough to show why this sort of thing rather than that does. A theist who saw this would naturally begin by asking the Existential question, and then try to show that the being needed to answer it is implicitly enough to answer the Qualitative. This is in part the procedure Aquinas adopts: the Existential query is clearly basic in the Five Ways, but the Qualitative is answered by implication in the discussion of the Divine Attributes, and is, I think, operative also in the Five Ways themselves.

A word here about these famous arguments. They are regularly treated, since Kant, as though they are in effect *one* argument, called the Cosmological Proof, which turns out when stated to be identical with the Third Way, or argument 'from possibility and necessity'. This is not confined to non-Thomists anxious to refute the arguments, E. L. Mascall, for example, says

> As I see it, the ultimate function of the Five Ways is to make it plain, by calling attention to five outstanding features of finite being, what the fundamental characteristic of finite being is. And that fundamental characteristic is its radical inability to account for its own existence.[1]

In other words, there is at bottom only one argument: since all the beings we know are such that their existence cannot be explained by reference to them, they must derive it from outside, and ultimately from a being whose existence does not require outside explanation, and who accounts for the existence of anything whatever. This certainly fits the Second and Third Ways well enough, and perhaps the First also; and it can be made to seem a reasonable reading of the Fourth and Fifth, which involve it. But it is surely over-simple to emphasize it to the exclusion of the Qualitative query. Aquinas is surely concerned not only with the contingency of the being of finite things, but also

---

[1] E. L. Mascall, *Existence and Analogy* (New York: Longmans, Green. and Co., 1949), p. 71.

with that of their manner of being; in the Fourth and Fifth Ways he begins with the degrees of perfection things have and the order they exhibit, and not with their mere existence, which is more immediately his theme in the Second and Third. To borrow his language, just as the essence of finite things does not account for their existence, so the fact of their existence does not account for their essence. The ultimate answer required here is a being whose possession of the attributes necessary to cause those of finite things is self-explanatory, i.e. to be accounted for in terms of him. This explanation, however, would seem to have to be in terms of his existence. What else in him could his essence be explained by? So the two questions coalesce, the second vanishing into the first, perhaps, and we conclude with a being who must, by the sort of being he is, exist, and also must, by the mere fact that he exists, be the sort of being he is: one in whom essence and existence are identical. While granting Aquinas the credit for seeing that the two questions merge, and that the Existential is primary, I think it is mistaken to stress it to the extent of ignoring the presence of the Qualitative dimension from the very beginning.

II

Whether this historical excursus is sound or not, we have two archetypal questions, which seem to have clear requirements for answers, and which tend to merge.

Those who ask for them recognize that the required explanations are of quite a different order from scientific ones. We have to step out of such mundane explanatory processes and enter upon another, for they are inevitably never complete—this is the import of St. Thomas's troublesome remarks about infinite regresses. The psychological mechanism of this transition is easy to share in, but its rationality is dubious from the start, just because the kind of process we step into is of such a different order from the one we step out of. For this same reason it cannot be regarded as the completion of the ordinary explanatory processes. This is easy to see when we reflect that the only reasons for stepping out of them into it, say, six finite causes back in the series rather than sixteen or six hundred are impatience or fatigue. Philosophers, contrary to common opinion, are prone to both, but they should not found arguments upon them. In the sense in which a Necessary Being explains, contingent causes do not explain incompletely, but are not attempts to explain at all. Sceptics might say that since the concept of explanation is formed by reference to contingent causes, the demands for explanation made in our questions are spurious; a question does not become intelligible merely because of the co-presence of a curiosity-feeling.

To this the metaphysical theist might reply that it is the spuriousness, and not the genuineness, of a question that need demonstrating, and that in the present case it is possible to explain quite clearly what sort of answer would satisfy the questioner. I would be the first to agree that when both sides insist that they are dealing with a unique case, considerations based upon this fact cannot be more than persuasive. But we do not need to rest content with these; nor do we need to consider the perplexing problem of whether there can be a question to which, in fact, there just is not any answer;[2] we need merely to assert that there can be no genuine question where the only possible answer to the purported one is demonstrably absurd. And both the Existential and the Qualitative questions are like this.

III (a)

'Why does anything exist?' is a total question. There can be nothing not mentioned in the question to bring in to explain what is mentioned in the question. There are therefore three possible ways of answering it. We could say that every individual thing is self-explanatory; we could say that the totality of things is self-explanatory, and individuals explicable by reference to it; or we could say that one part of what exists is self-explanatory, and the rest explicable by reference to that part. Of these three only the last is of interest, since all three make use of the same crucial concept of a self-explanatory being, and the first two have extra problems of their own beside this. The objection to this form of argument centres on the self-explanatory being. Kant held that the argument from contingent to necessary being in the Cosmological Proof reduced that argument to the Ontological Proof, and in spite of the fact that he located this reduction in the wrong place,[3] his claim is correct.

First, what is wrong with the Ontological Proof? It amounts to the claim that 'God exists' is an analytic proposition. The standard, and correct, objection to this is that which Kant raised, viz. that to assert the existence of something is quite different from asserting what *sort* of thing it is, and to know that either assertion is true is not to know

[2] R. L. Franklin, 'Necessary Being', *The Australasian Journal of Philosophy*, Vol. 35 (1957).

[3] J. J. C. Smart, 'The Existence of God', *New Essays in Philosophical Theology*, ed. Antony Flew and Alasdair MacIntyre (London: S.C.M., 1955).

the other is. If someone came in unannounced and said, 'It's blue!' we should not have much idea what he was talking about, but we would automatically know it was a visible physical object and not a philosophical theory or an Act of Parliament. But if he had come in and said, 'It exists!' we should know *nothing* about what sort of thing it was. Existence cannot vary in quantity or intensity, belong to some members of a class and not others, or be interrupted and then resumed.[4] Moore has brought out some of the pecularities of the word 'exist' in a very well-known paper.[5] From all this it follows that existence cannot be held to be a quality which a perfect being would have to have, since it is not a quality at all. So it further follows that no existential assertion *can* be analytic.

So much for the Ontological Proof. It is important to see that what refutes it is not a discovery about the structure of things, which might in a given case be different, but a logical discovery about the concept of existence, which sets it apart from other concepts; that no tautology can be existential is a consequence of this. Another consequence is the refutation of our Existential argument. For the distinctive character of the concept of existence precludes our saying there can be a being whose existence follows from his essence; and also precludes the even stronger logical move of *identifying* the existence of anything with its essence. These are the Anselmian error all over again. The only other way of explaining God's existence by his essence would be by asserting a causal relationship between them, but this would run us into absurdities like saying that God would have to pre-exist himself, or that his essence would have to have something almost, but not quite, amounting to existence in order subsequently to express itself in being.

So there is no way in which the existence of *any* being could be held to be a fact explicable by reference to that being itself. Before passing to the Qualitative argument, there are two important side-issues to discuss. One is the argument of G. E. Hughes[6] that 'God exists', though not analytic, might still be necessary, i.e. synthetically necessary; the other is the important historical claim that the Thomistic position is further removed from the Ontological Proof than any

---

[4] *Analysis*, Vol. 17, Competition No. 11 (June 1957).
[5] G. E. Moore, 'Is Existence a Predicate?', *Logic and Language*, Second Series, ed. Antony Flew (Oxford: Blackwell, 1953).
[6] J. N. Findlay, G. E. Hughes, and A. C. A. Rainer, 'Can God's Existence be Disproved?', *New Essays in Philosophical Theology*, ed. Flew and MacIntyre.

position I have considered, and is therefore unaffected by what I have said.

(i) To say that 'God exists' is synthetically necessary is to run counter to fashionable views about necessity in propositions, but, as Hughes insists, one can be out of fashion and right. The difficulty for our present purpose is the notorious one for believers in synthetic necessity, of *explaining* the necessary character of the examples offered. If all necessary propositions are tautologies, this explains *why* we cannot deny them; failing an equivalent explanation, purported cases of synthetic necessity seem to have a merely subjective certainty. I do not see what sort of explanation could be had in the present case: certainly a Kantian type of explanation is unsuitable.

(ii) Since Aquinas differs from Anselm in holding that God's existence has to be inferred from his effects and not from the mere concept of God, he is traditionally credited with having seen what was wrong with the Ontological Proof. He did see it was wrong, but not *why* it was, for he commits the same error himself. He says that we do not have the requisite knowledge of the divine nature to deduce God's existence from it; but his own argument leads us from finite beings to a being whose existence does follow from his nature, and this entails that *if* we knew God's nature we *could* deduce his existence from it— and *this* is the mistake. To say that although God's existence is self-evident in itself it is not to us, is to say that it *is* self-evident in itself, and the error lies here. It is not our ignorance that is the obstacle to explaining God's existence by his nature, but the logical character of the concept of existence.

In order to introduce the morals I wish to draw from this, I shall discuss briefly a recently expressed view of Necessary Being put forward as the basis of discussion by R. L. Franklin.[7] This is that a Necessary Being is just a being in whom the question 'Why?' stops, a being about whom it makes no sense to ask it. This looks to claim less than the Thomistic position, and Franklin claims that it offers an intelligible answer to the question of why anything exists, but not a demonstrable one. It is instructive to see why this is unsatisfactory: if we cannot ask why a given being exists there must be a reason why we cannot; if there were no reason, then we *could* ask this question—such at least is the assumption made in the initial stages of any version of the Existential argument. There are two possible reasons. The first is that the being in question is self-explanatory, which I have already tried to show to be an absurd reason. The second is that although the being

[7] Franklin, op. cit.

in question is the cause of all other beings, there is no other being to be found which is the cause of *it*. In this case there would be one unexplained being, by hypothesis, and it would not answer the question of why *anything* existed. Franklin says that 'Why does anything exist?' may not have an answer, but that if it does a Necessary Being (in his sense) would provide it. But a Necessary Being in his sense would not provide it, unless we went on to make it a self-explanatory being and thus reduced it to absurdity. It is not that something could provide an answer to the Existential question but maybe nothing does, but that nothing *could*.

Now for the morals:

(i) It is absurd to ask why anything exists, because the only possible answers are in terms of the logically *im*possible notion of a self-explanatory being. This is still logically impossible when it is softened by its user's saying that we personally do not know the explanation.

(ii) This in itself does not prevent us from saying that the existence of everything in the universe *except one* is due to that one (though we would presumably believe in that one for reasons not related to our present argument). But it does prevent us from going on to ask why that one exists, for *in this context* that would be *equivalent* to asking why *anything* does.

(iii) But unless you assume independently that a given being has no cause, you can always ask why it exists, i.e. what caused it. If you do assume it has no cause, you *ipso facto* make it impossible to ask why it is there.

(iv) So there *may* be a being who is the cause of everything else, but if there is he cannot explain the baffling fact of existence. For it is logically impossible to explain *everything*. The Principle of Sufficient Reason is demonstrably false.

(v) So the fact that things exist cannot entail the existence of God; it could only do so if God were self-explanatory. Failing this, the 'Why?' questions would only come to a halt if we had independent reasons for holding that the being we had reached was uncaused. And it would be these independent reasons that would bring us to theism. And it would not be a theism that *explained*. Theism cannot explain any more than atheism can.

III (b)

We turn now more briefly to our Qualitative question. The search for the complete explanation of the presence in the universe of any property is bound to lead to the claim that there is a being who has it, or some higher cause or analogate of it,[8] self-explanatorily. The objections in this case are similar:

(1) Let us call the property P. Our doctrine could mean that God has P because of some other properties he has, the relationship being causal. This clearly only pushes the problem back to those other properties themselves.

(2) The doctrine could mean 'God has P' is a necessary proposition. I will assume this to mean 'analytically necessary', since, as before, its being synthetically necessary might give it certitude, but not explanatory power. Now to say that 'God has P' is analytic does not solve our problem, which is that of accounting for the occurrence, in the whole realm of being, of P. If it is analytic that God has P, this just tells us that having P is part of what is meant by the word 'God', i.e. that no being would be accorded the title who lacked P. But this merely means that there is a connection between the *concepts* of divinity and P-hood. not why either the first or the second has instances (or even *whether* either has). To know that 'Birds have wings' is analytic is to know something important about the words 'bird' and 'wing', but nothing at all about why winged creatures came to be.

The analyticity of statements about God has been thought to raise more problems than it does. C. B. Martin[9] has claimed that since 'God is good' is analytic, God cannot be identified with the man Jesus, for 'Jesus is good' is synthetic. This can be resolved by using Martin's own distinction between 'God' as a proper name, and 'God' as a *concept*.[10] 'God(concept) is good' is analytic; but 'God(proper name) is good' is synthetic, and learned, if at all, by experience. In our present case the problem posed by the Qualitative query is that of explaining the fact reported by 'God(proper name) has P.' This is not explained by showing that 'God(concept) has P' is analytic, even though it is.

(3) Only one recourse remains. Since the divine possession of P cannot be explained by reference to the divine nature, it can only be explained by reference to the divine existence. Let us say, then, that God's having P is a deducible consequence of the fact of his existence. This would only explain his having P if his existence were previously said to be necessary, but let us ignore this. What is said of P would apply, by parity of reasoning, to all the divine attributes; so we come once

---

[8] This qualifying phrase will be assumed, but not stated, in what follows.

[9] C. B. Martin, 'The Perfect Good', *New Essays in Philosophical Theology*, ed. Flew and MacIntyre.

[10] Alan Donagan, Review of *New Essays in Philosophical Theology*, in *Philosophical Review*, Vol. 66 (1957).

more to the identity of the divine essence and existence, with some kind of priority being accorded to the divine existence. The connection between the Existential and Qualitative arguments is closer than Kant recognized.

The objections are not hard to find:

(i) Quite apart from the difficulties involved in saying God necessarily exists, we have gone in a circle if we fall back on this here. For we began by explaining his existence in terms of his essence, and we now find ourselves explaining his essence in terms of his existence.

(ii) The logical character of the concept of existence is not only enough to render it inadmissible to infer God's existence from his essence, but also renders it inadmissible to infer his essence from his existence—or, again, to identify them.

The morals to be drawn are the same:

(i) It is absurd to ask why anything has P, for the only possible answers are in terms of the logically *im*possible notion of a being in whom the presence of P is self-explanatory, etc.

(ii) This in itself does not prevent us from saying that the presence of P in any being in the universe *except one* is due to its presence in that one, etc. But it does prevent us from going on to ask why that being has P, for *in this context* that would be *equivalent* to asking why *anything* does.

(iii) But unless you assume independently that a given being has P without cause, you can always ask why it has P, etc.

(iv) So there *may* be a being who is the cause of all *other* beings having P who have it, but he cannot explain the baffling fact of P itself, etc.

(v) So the fact that P can be found cannot entail that there is a God who has P; it could only do so if God's having P were self-explanatory. Failing this, the 'Why P?'-questions would only come to a halt if we had independent reasons for holding that the being we had reached had P without cause, etc.

IV

There can, then, be no metaphysical compulsion to believe in God; for the sort of metaphysical questions which would necessitate theism are spurious. This does not refute theism, however. It would only refute it if the sort of explanatory demand we have been considering were inevitably involved in belief in God. This has been argued by J. N. Findlay;[11] he says that the attitude of worship entails God's complete

[11] Findlay, Hughes and Rainer, op. cit.

independence of all other beings, both in his existence and his possession of his excellences, and entails that he possesses these in the highest conceivable degree; if this is accepted, and it seems it must be, he claims we have to go on to say that God exists and has his excellences in some necessary manner; given the absurdity of this, God's non-existence follows.

Theism can be rescued from his argument. One can agree with Aquinas that it is no limitation on God that he cannot perform logical absurdities; and one can adapt this and say it is no limitation on him that he cannot *be* a logical absurdity; and that is what a Necessary Being, *in the sense we have examined*, is. I think the readiness of Findlay's disputants to agree that God's existence and excellence are necessary is due to a dangerous and crucial ambiguity in the terms 'necessary' and 'contingent' (an ambiguity almost, but not quite, recognized by Rainer). It is pedantic of philosophers to insist that these words only apply to propositions and not to things; but our previous discussion should show that they will mean something different in each case. We do not need to say precisely here what propositional necessity is: let us say that, roughly, a proposition is necessary if its truth can be known without reference to anything other than a clear understanding of what is said or implied in it; contingency in propositions is the absence of necessity (and of its contrary, viz. necessary falsehood or, if this is the same, self-contradiction). As applied to things or events, 'contingent' will mean 'dependent' or 'caused', one thing or event being contingent *upon* another; 'necessary' will mean 'not dependent on any other', and, in addition, 'having others dependent on it'. A thing is necessary if it is indispensable. For want of a better phrase I shall call necessity in this sense 'factual necessity'. To be a theist is to believe that there is a being, God, who is factually necessary, all other beings being dependent, contingent, upon him. But the *assertion* of this will be a contingent assertion, in the propositional sense (and not in the Thomistic sense that Rainer adopts, viz. contingent to us but necessary for God). God's existence and nature are unique in the universe in being free of factual contingency, but the assertions of them share in propositional contingency with all other assertions of fact.

Theists believe that God exists, that he is supremely great and good, that no other beings would exist if he did not, and that all their multitudinous features have their source in him. I have denied none of this. It merely means that God is factually necessary, indispensable. I have denied he can be necessary in any other sense, that he explains either his own existence or nature, or, ultimately, that of other things.

Since this ideal is bogus, God is not denigrated if he is not held to realize it. If there is a factually necessary being then, this fact, though the most important fact there is, could not be proved.

'Why, then, be a Theist?' Well, theism is older than the Cosmological Proof, and can survive it. Some have tried to present it as an ordinary empirical hypothesis, but this has seldom impressed. If theism is to be seen to be true at all, it looks as though this will have to happen through individual confrontation with what purports to be God's self-revelation. A person who accepts this and then proclaims it to others is not free from philosophical criticism just because he does not proclaim his belief as metaphysically necessary; for he still makes statements which do not always appear to others to have the relationship to evidence which all statements (they say) have to have; and if 'metaphysics' is defined in the required way, what he says will be metaphysical to them still. But the objections thus raised against theism when it is expressed in undemonstrated assertions by such a person, however strong they are, are distinct from those much stronger ones that can be brought against offering theism as the answer to the sort of confused question we have examined above; and the sort of 'metaphysics' that may be contained in them or spun around them is likely to be immune to the objections we have stressed, whatever its other defects may be. Philosophical analysis will not progress much in understanding religious assertions, especially their relationship to metaphysical speculation, unless these distinctions are carefully borne in mind

NOTES ON THE CONTRIBUTORS

ANTONY FLEW is Professor of Philosophy at the University of Keele. He is the author of *Hume's Philosophy of Belief* (1961) and *Evolutionary Ethics* (1967, editor of *Logic and Language*, First and Second Series (1951 and 1953), *Essays in Conceptual Analysis* (1956), and *Body, Mind, and Death* (1964), and co-editor with Alasdair MacIntyre of *New Essays in Philosophical Theology* (1955).

R. M. HARE in White's Professor of Moral Philosophy at Oxford. He is the author of *The Language of Morals* (1952), and *Freedom and Reason* (1963).

BASIL MITCHELL, the editor of this volume, is Nolloth Professor of the Philosophy of Christian Religion at Oxford. He is also the editor of *Faith and Logic* (1958), and the author of *Law, Morality and Religion in a Secular Society* (1967).

I. M. CROMBIE is a Fellow of Wadham College, Oxford. He is the author of *An Examination of Plato's Doctrines* (1962 and 1963).

JOHN HICK is Professor of Theology at the University of Birmingham, and was formerly Lecturer in the Philosophy of Religion at Cambridge. He is the author of *Faith and Knowledge* (1957), *Philosophy of Religion* (1963), *Evil and the God of Love* (1966), and editor of *The Existence of God* (1964), and *Faith and the Philosophers* (1964).

R. B. BRAITHWAITE was Knightbridge Professor of Moral Philosophy at Cambridge from 1953 to 1967. He is the author of *Scientific Explanation* (1953), and of many articles.

J. L. MACKIE is a Fellow of University College, Oxford. He has written articles on ethics and the philosophy of science as well as on the philosophy of religion.

ALVIN PLANTINGA is Professor of Philosophy at Calvin College in Michigan. He is the author of *Faith and Philosophy* (1964), and *God and Other Minds* (1967).

D. Z. PHILLIPS is Senior Lecturer in Philosophy at the University College of Swansea. He is the author of *The Concept of Prayer* (1965) and *Moral Practices* (1969) and General Editor of the series *Studies in Ethics and the Philosophy of Religion*.

H. H. PRICE was Wykeham Professor of Logic at Oxford from 1935 to 1959. His writings include *Perception* (1932), *Hume's theory of the External World* (1940), and *Thinking and Experience* (1935). His book *Belief* (1969) is an expanded version of his Gifford Lectures delivered in 1960.

R. W. HEPBURN is Professor of Philosophy at Edinburgh. He is the author of *Christianity and Paradox* (1958) and, with S. E. Toulmin and Alasdair MacIntyre, of *Metaphysical Beliefs* (1957).

TERENCE PENELHUM is Professor of Philosophy at the University of Calgary. He is the author of *Survival and Disembodied Existence* (1970), and co-editor, with J. J. MacIntosh, of *The First Critique* (1969).

BIBLIOGRAPHY[1]

The following books and articles deal with the issues raised in this volume, and are arranged according to the subject-matter of the text.

I: GENERAL

ALSTON, W. (ed.), *Religious Belief and Philosophical Thought* (New York: Harcourt, Brace and World, 1963).

AYER, A. J., *Language, Truth and Logic* (London: Gollancz, 1946) (esp. ch. VI).

BAMBROUGH, RENFORD, *Reason, Truth and God* (London: Methuen, 1969).

BRITTON, KARL, *Philosophy and the Meaning of Life* (Cambridge: Cambridge University Press, 1969).

CAMPBELL, C. A., *On Selfhood and Godhood* (London: Allen and Unwin, 1957).

CHRISTIAN, W., *Meaning and Truth in Religion* (Princeton, N.J.: Princeton University Press, 1964).

FERRÉ, F., *Language, Logic and God* (New York: Harper and Row, 1961).

FLEW, ANTONY, *God and Philosophy* (London: Hutchinson, 1966).

FLEW, ANTONY, and MACINTYRE, ALASDAIR, *New Essays in Philosophical Theology* (London: S.C.M., 1955). (See reviews by T. Penelhum in *Canadian Journal of Theology*, Vol. 4, 1958—'Logic and Theology'; and by H. D. Lewis, 'Contemporary Empiricism and the Philosophy of Religion', *Philosophy*, Vol. 32, 1957.)

GEACH, P. T., *God and the Soul* (London: Routledge and Kegan Paul, 1969).

HEPBURN, R. W., *Christianity and Paradox* (London: C. A. Watts, 1958).

HICK, JOHN (ed.), *Faith and the Philosophers* (London: Macmillan, 1964).

HICK, JOHN, *Philosophy of Religion* (London: Prentice-Hall, 1963).

HODGES, H. A., 'What is to Become of Philosophical Theology?', *Contemporary British Philosophy*, ed. H. D. Lewis (London: Allen and Unwin, 1956).

HOOK, S. (ed.), *Religious Experience and Truth* (New York: New York University Press, 1961).

LEWIS, H. D., *Our Experience of God* (London: Allen and Unwin, 1959).

MACINTYRE, ALASDAIR, *Difficulties in Christian Belief* (London: S.C.M., 1959).

MARTIN, C. B., *Religious Belief* (New York: Cornell, 1959).

MCPHERSON, T., *Philosophy of Religion* (London: Van Nostrand, 1965).

MITCHELL, BASIL (ed.), *Faith and Logic* (London: Allen and Unwin, 1957).

PASSMORE, J., 'Christianity and Positivism', *The Australasian Journal of Philosophy*, Vol. 35 (1957).

PLANTINGA, ALVIN (ed.), *Faith and Philosophy* (Grand Rapids, Mich.: Eerdmans, 1964).

[1] The Editor is indebted to C. C. Conti for help with this bibliography.

SMART, R. N., *Reasons and Faiths* (London: S.C.M., 1959).
TAYLOR, A. E., 'Theism', *Encyclopedia of Religion and Ethics*, ed. James Hastings, (New York: Scribners, 1928, T. and T. Clark, Edinburgh, 1910). (A useful historical survey of the entire subject of rational arguments concerning the existence of God.)
WISDOM, J., 'The Modes of Thought and the Logic of God', *The Existence of God*, ed. John Hick (London: Macmillan, 1964).

II: RELIGIOUS LANGUAGE
(Relevant to chs. I–IV in this volume.)

ALSTON, W. P., 'Ineffability', *Philosophical Review*, Vol. 65 (1956).
CROMBIE, I. M., 'Theology and Falsification' (arising from the symposium), *New Essays in Philosophical Theology*, eds. Flew and MacIntyre (*q.v.*).
EWING, A. C., 'Religious Assertions in the Light of Contemporary Philosophy', *Philosophy*, Vol. 32 (1957).
FERRÉ, F., 'Mapping the Logic of Models in Science and Theology', *The Christian Scholar*, Vol. 46 (1963), reprinted in *New Essays on Religious Language*, ed. High, *q.v.*).
HAYNER, P., 'Analogical Predication', *Journal of Philosophy*, Vol. 55 (1958).
HEPBURN, R. W., 'Poetry and Religious Belief', *Metaphysical Beliefs*, ed. Alasdair MacIntyre (London: S.C.M., 1957).
HIGH, D. M. (ed.), *New Essays on Religious Language* (Oxford: Clarendon Press, 1969).
HOLLAND, R. F., 'Religious Discourse and Theological Discourse', *The Australasian Journal of Philosophy*, Vol. 34 (1956).
HODGES, H. A., *Languages, Standpoints and Attitudes* (Oxford: Clarendon Press, 1953).
McPHERSON, T., 'Assertion and Analogy', *Proceedings of the Aristotelian Society*, Vol. 60 (1959–60). (Reprinted in *New Essays on Religious Language*, ed. High, *q.v.*).
NIELSEN, KAI, 'On Fixing the Reference Range of "God"', *Religious Studies*, Vol. 2 (1966).
PRICE, H. H., 'Religious Belief and Empiricist Philosophy', Lecture 10 in H. H. Price *Belief* (*q.v.*) (esp. the section on Braithwaite, pp. 479–87, and Hick, pp. 469–73).
RAMSEY, I. T., *Religious Language: an Empirical Placing of Theological Phrases* (London: S.C.M., 1957).
VESEY, G. N. A. (ed.), *Royal Institute of Philosophy Lectures, Talk of God*, Vol. 2 (1967–8) (London: Macmillan, 1969).
WISDOM, J., 'Gods', *Proceedings of the Aristotelian Society*, Vol. 45 (1944–5). (Cf. D. Z. Phillips, 'Wisdom's Gods', *The Philosophical Quarterly*, Vol. 19, 1969.)

III: THE PROBLEM OF EVIL
(Relevant to chs. V–VI in this volume.)

FARRER, AUSTIN, *Love Almighty and Ills Unlimited* (London: Fontana, 1961).

FLEW, ANTONY, 'Divine Omnipotence and Human Freedom', *New Essays in Philosophical Theology*, eds. Flew and MacIntyre (*q.v.*), pp. 144–69.

HICK. JOHN, *Evil and the God of Love* (London: Macmillan, 1966).

MACKIE, J. L., 'Theism and Utopia', *Philosophy*, Vol. 37 (1962) (Reprinted in *God and Evil*, ed. Pike, *q.v.*)

McCLOSKEY, H. J., 'God and Evil', *The Philosophical Quarterly*, Vol. 10 (1960). (Reprinted in *God and Evil*, ed. Pike, *q.v.*)

PIKE, N. (ed.), *God and Evil: Readings on the Theological Problem of Evil* (London: Prentice-Hall, 1964). (A very useful volume of introductory readings with selected bibliography.)

SMART, R. N., 'Omnipotence, Evil and Supermen', *Philosophy*, Vol. 36 (1961). (Reprinted in *God and Evil*, ed. Pike, *q.v.*)

WISDOM, J., 'God and Evil', *Mind*, Vol. 44 (1935).

IV: FIDEISM
(Relevant to ch. VII in this volume.)

DUFF-FORBES, D. R., 'Faith, Evidence, Coercion', *Australasian Journal of Philosophy* (1969).

EDWARDS, P., 'Is Fideistic Theology Irrefutable?', *The Rationalist Annual* (1966).

HICK, JOHN, 'Theology's Central Problem', an Inaugural Lecture (University of Birmingham, 1967).

HUDSON, W. D., 'Some Remarks on Wittgenstein's Account of Religious Belief', *Royal Institute of Philosophy Lectures, Talk of God*, Vol. 2 1967–8) ed. Vesey (*q.v.*).

MITCHELL, BASIL, 'The Justification of Religious Belief', *Philosophical Quarterly*, Vol. 11 (1961). (Reprinted in *New Essays on Religious Language*, ed. High, *q.v.*)

NIELSEN, KAI, 'Wittgensteinian Fideism', *Philosophy*, Vol. 42 (1967).

PHILLIPS, D. Z., *The Concept of Prayer* (London: Routledge and Kegan Paul, 1965).

V: RELIGIOUS EPISTEMOLOGY
(Relevant to chs. VIII–IX in this volume.)

GLASGOW, W. D., 'Knowledge of God', *Philosophy*, Vol. 32 (1957).

HICK, JOHN, *Faith and Knowledge* (Itraca, N.Y.: Cornell, 1967).

HICK, JOHN, 'Religious Faith as Experiencing-as', *Royal Institute of Philosophy Lectures, Talk of God*, Vol. 2 (1967–8), ed. Vesey (*q.v.*). (See Terence Penelhum's response, 'Is Religious Epistemology Possible?' in *Royal Institute of Philosophy Lectures, Knowledge and Necessity*, Vol. 3 (1968–9), ed. G. N. A. Vesey (London: Macmillan, 1970).)

LEWIS, H. D., and WHITELEY, C. H., 'The Cognitive Factor in Religious Experience', *Proceedings of the Aristotelian Society*, Supplementary Vol. 29 (1955).

MALCOLM, N., 'Is it a Religious Belief that "God Exists"?' *Faith and the Philosophers*, ed. Hick (*q.v.*).

MacINTYRE, ALASDAIR, 'The Logical Status of Religious Belief', *Metaphysical Beliefs*, ed. Alasdair MacIntyre (London: S.C.M., 1957). (Cf.

Mitchell's reply, 'The Justification of Religious Belief' in *New Essays on Religious Language*, ed. High, *q.v.*)

PHILLIPS, D. Z., 'Faith, Scepticism and Religious Understanding', in *Religion and Understanding*, ed. Phillips (Oxford: Blackwell, 1967).

PRICE, H. H., *Belief* (London: Allen and Unwin, 1969).

PRICE, H. H., 'Faith and Belief', *Faith and the Philosophers*, ed. Hick (*q.v.*). (See the resulting discussion involving Hartshorne. Aldrich, Gunderson, and Clarke.)

SCHMIDT, P. F., *Religious Knowledge* (New York: Free Press, 1961).

See *Theology*, Vol. 71 (1968) for Symposium on 'Belief and Understanding', articles by W. D. Hudson, John Hick, H. Palmer, and D. Z. Phillips. Also Symposium in the *Journal of Philosophy*, Vol. 51 (1954), 'Are Religious Dogmas Cognitive?'

VI: NATURAL THEOLOGY
(Relevant to ch. IX in this volume.)

BOYCE, GIBSON, 'Two Strands in Natural Theology', *The Monist*, Vol. 47 (1963).

EDWARDS, P., 'The Cosmological Argument', *The Rationalist Annual* (1959).

FARRER, AUSTIN, *Faith and Speculation* (London: A. and C. Black, 1967).

FARRER, AUSTIN, *Finite and Infinite* (London: Dacre Press, 1943).

FINDLAY, J. N., 'Can God's Existence be Disproved?', *New Essays in Philosophical Theology*, eds. Flew and MacIntyre (*q.v.*). (See John Hick, 'God as Necessary Being', *q.v.*)

GEACH, P., 'Causality and Creation', *Sophia*, Vol. 1 (1962), Nos. 1 and 3.

HARTSHORNE, C., *Natural Theology for our Time* (La Salle, Ill.: Open Court, 1950).

HICK, JOHN, 'God as Necessary Being', *Journal of Philosophy*, Vol. 57 (1960).

KENNY, A., 'Necessary Being', *Sophia*, Vol. 1 (1962), No. 3.

KENNY, A., *The Five Ways* (London: Routledge and Kegan Paul, 1969).

MALCOLM, N., 'Anselm's Ontological Arguments', *Philosophical Review*, Vol. 69 (1960). (Reprinted in *The Many-Faced Argument*, eds. John Hick and A. McGill (London: Collier-Macmillan, 1968).

MASCALL, E. L., *Existence and Analogy* (London: Longmans, 1949).

MASCALL, E. L., *He Who Is, a Study in Traditional Theism* (London: Longmans, 1943).

MATTHEWS, G. B., 'Theology and Natural Theology', *Journal of Philosophy*, Vol. 61 (1964).

MCPHERSON, T., 'The Argument from Design', *Philosophy*, Vol. 32, (1957).

PLANTINGA, ALVIN, *God and Other Minds: A Study of the Rational Justification of Belief in God* (New York: Cornell, 1967).

SMITH, J. E. and HUTCHINSON, J., 'Symposium on Natural Theology', *Journal of Philosophy*, Vol. 55 (1958).

For a select bibliography on the Ontological Argument see *The Many-Faced Argument*, eds. John Hick and A. McGill (London: Collier-Macmillan, 1968), pp. 357–70; especially Section VII.

VII: METAPHYSICS
(Relevant to ch. X in this volume.)

BAELZ, P. R., *Christian Theology and Metaphysics* (Philadelphia, Pa.: Fortress, 1968, London: Epworth, 1968).

EMMET, D. M., *The Nature of Metaphysical Thinking* (London: Macmillan, 1945).

FRANKLIN, R. L., 'Necessary Being', *The Australasian Journal of Philosophy*, Vol. 35 (1957).

HARTSHORNE, C., 'Necessity', *Review of Metaphysics*, Vol. 21 (1967).

MACINTYRE, ALASDAIR (ed.), *Metaphysical Beliefs* (London: S.C.M., 1957).

NIELSEN, KAI, 'On Fixing the Reference Range of "God"', *Religious Studies*, Vol. 2 (1966).

PLANTINGA, ALVIN, 'Necessary Being', *Faith and Philosophy*, ed. Plantinga (*q.v.*).

SHAFFER, J., 'Existence, Predication and the Ontological Argument', *Mind*, Vol. 71 (1962).

SMART, R. N., 'Myth and Transcendence', *The Monist*, Vol. 50 (1966).

WALSH, W. H., *Metaphysics* (London: Hutchinson, 1963).

Also, *The Many-Faced Argument*, eds. John Hick and A. McGill (London: Collier-Macmillan, 1968), bibliography Section VIII, 'The Logic of "Exists"', pp. 369–70; and Section IX, 'The Concept of Necessary Being'.

VIII: RELIGIOUS EXPERIENCE

COPLESTON, F. C., 'Hegel and the Rationalisation of Mysticism', *Royal Institute of Philosophy Lectures, Talk of God*, Vol. 2, ed. Vesey (*q.v.*).

FARMER, H. H., *Revelation and Religion* (London: Nisbet, 1954) (esp. chs. 1 and 10).

HOOK, S. (ed), *Religious Experience and Truth* (New York: New York University Press, 1961).

HORSBURGH, H. J. N., 'The Claims of Religious Experience', *The Australasian Journal of Philosophy*, Vol. 35 (1957).

LEWIS, H. D. and WHITELEY, C. H., 'The Cognitive Factor in Religious Experience', *Proceedings of the Aristotelian Society*, Suppl. Vol. 29 (1955).

MITCHELL, BASIL, 'The Grace of God', *Faith and Logic* (London: Allen and Unwin, 1957).

NIELSEN, KAI, '"Christian Positivism" and the Appeal to Religious Experience', *Journal of Religion*, Vol. 42 (1962).

OTTO, R., *The Idea of the Holy*, transl. J. W. Harvey (London: Oxford University Press, 1950, and Harmondsworth: Penguin, 1959) (esp. chs. 3 and 4).

SMART, R. N., 'Interpretation and Mystical Experience', *Religious Studies*, Vol. 1 (1965).

STACE, W. T., *Mysticism and Philosophy* (Philadelphia, Pa.: Lippincott, 1960, and London: Macmillan, 1961).

WEBB, C. C. J., *Religious Experience* (Pound Ridge, N.Y.: Milford, 1945, London: O.U.P., 1945).

ZAEHNER, R. C., *Mysticism, Sacred and Profane* (Oxford: Clarendon Press, 1957).

INDEX OF NAMES

(not including authors mentioned only in the Bibliography)